ILLUSTRATIONS OF
GREEK DRAMA

PHAIDON

Menander: *Theophoroumene*. Above: Mosaic from Pompeii, signed by Dioskourides of Samos, 100 B.C. Naples, Museo Nazionale (V, 3). Below: Mosaic in Mytilene, A.D. 300 (V, 4).

ILLUSTRATIONS OF
GREEK DRAMA

BY A. D. TRENDALL AND T. B. L. WEBSTER

PHAIDON

PHAIDON PRESS LIMITED, 5 CROMWELL PLACE, LONDON SW7

PUBLISHED IN THE UNITED STATES OF AMERICA BY PHAIDON PUBLISHERS, INC.
AND DISTRIBUTED BY PRAEGER PUBLISHERS, INC.
III FOURTH AVENUE, NEW YORK, N.Y.10003

FIRST PUBLISHED 1971
© 1971 BY PHAIDON PRESS LIMITED, LONDON
ALL RIGHTS RESERVED

ISBN O 7148 1492 X
LIBRARY OF CONGRESS CATALOG CARD NUMBER: 78-158099

PRINTED IN GREAT BRITAIN BY R. & R. CLARK LIMITED, EDINBURGH
AND COLOUR PLATES PRINTED BY CAVENDISH PRESS, LEICESTER

CONTENTS

TO

GISELA RICHTER

PREFACE

THE present work is in no wise intended as a corpus or as a replacement for Séchan's excellent *Études sur la tragédie grecque dans ses rapports avec la céramique*, but aims rather at presenting a series of illustrations representative of the history of Greek dramatic performances from the earliest times down to the third century B.C. The first two sections of the Introduction and the annotations of Attic monuments are the work of T. B. L. Webster, the third section and the annotations on Etruscan and South Italian are by A. D. Trendall, but both the preparation of the text and the choice of the illustrations were carried out in close consultation, the latter being conditioned to some extent by a preference for more recently discovered or less well-known monuments, when they were available. Most of the illustrations are taken from Greek and South Italian vase-paintings, but use has also been made of terracottas, sculpture, metalwork and mosaics – for the last notably those from the newly-excavated house in Mytilene with its detailed pictures of scenes from Menander's plays. For permission to publish these and for the use of the relevant colour-blocks we are particularly indebted to Mme Ghali-Kahil.

The history of the Greek theatre has been well studied and illustrated in several works, especially Margarete Bieber's *History of the Greek and Roman Theater*, and we have, as far as possible, confined our illustrations to those specifically dealing with dramatic performances. These have been divided into five sections – Pre-dramatic, Satyr-plays, Tragedy, Old and Middle Comedy, and New Comedy – each of which is provided with short descriptions of the monuments illustrated, together with a select bibliography, which will direct the reader to the most conveniently available sources of fuller information.

In the spelling of Greek proper names some inconsistencies are almost inevitable, but, in general, we have adopted the forms in common usage for the more familiar names (e.g. Aeschylus, Priam, Hecuba), and the Greek forms for those that are less well known (e.g. Chrysippos, Parthenopaios).

We should like to express our grateful thanks especially to Professor E. W. Handley, who read the proofs, and to the Institute of Classical Studies, London, for allowing the use of much illustrative material, in its collection; also to the following for photographs of objects in their collections or under their care, and for permission to reproduce them here: Drs. D. Adamesteanu, N. Alfieri, G. Belloni, L. Bernabò Brea, Ann Birchall, D. von Bothmer, F. Brommer, Marie-Louise Buhl, Prof. Alexander Cambitoglou, Drs. H. A. Cahn, H. W. Catling, Chr. Clairmont, A. De Franciscis, P. Devambez, G. Foti, A. Frova, Mme N. Gatalina, Dr. A. Greifenhagen, Mr. D. E. L. Haynes, Prof. J. M. Hemelrijk, Drs. Hedwig Kenner, F. G. Lo Porto, Mario Napoli, R. Noll, D. Ohly, P. Orlandini, V. Panebianco, Captain A. Ragusa, Mr. B. B. Shefton, Dr. Margot Schmidt, Mrs. G. Schneider-Herrmann, Dr. Axel Seeberg, Prof. Erika Simon, Dr. R. Stazio Pulinas, Miss M. K. Steven, Prof. Homer A. Thompson, Mrs. E. Touloupa, Drs. V. Tusa, Garofano Venosta, and C. C. Vermeule. We are also very grateful to Dr. I. Grafe of the Phaidon Press for his assistance in the preparation and layout of this volume.

Lastly we should like to offer our sincerest thanks to Miss Gisela Richter, from whom the idea for this book originally came and to whom we dedicate it as a token of our appreciation of her outstanding contribution to the study of Greek art.

A. D. Trendall
La Trobe University,
Australia

T. B. L. Webster
Stanford University,
California

January 1971

LIST OF ABBREVIATIONS

The following list gives the standard abbreviations used for periodicals, serial publications, and certain books or articles to which frequent references are made.

PERIODICALS AND SERIAL PUBLICATIONS

AA = Archäologischer Anzeiger

AE = Archaiologike Ephemeris

AJA = American Journal of Archaeology

AntK = Antike Kunst

AuA = Antike und Abendland

ArchCl = Archeologia Classica

ArchReps = Archaeological Reports

BaBesch = Bulletin van de Vereeniging tot Bevordering der Kennis van de antieke Beschaving te 's-Gravenhage

BCH = Bulletin de Correspondance Hellénique

BdA = Bollettino d'Arte

BICS = Bulletin of the Institute of Classical Studies, London

BMMA = Bulletin of the Metropolitan Museum of Art, New York

BMQ = British Museum Quarterly

BSR = Papers of the British School at Rome

BWPr = Berliner Winckelmannsprogramm

Class Phil = Classical Philology

CQ = Classical Quarterly

CR = Classical Review

CRAI = Comptes-rendus de l'Académie des Inscriptions et Belles-Lettres

CVA = Corpus Vasorum Antiquorum

EAA = Enciclopedia dell'Arte antica

FR = Furtwängler-Reichhold, *Griechische Vasenmalerei*

HSCP = Harvard Studies in Classical Philology

JdI = Jahrbuch des deutschen archäologischen Instituts

JHS = Journal of Hellenic Studies

JÖAI = Jahreshefte des Österreichischen Archäologischen Instituts

Mél Arch = Mélanges d'archéologie et d'histoire de l'École française de Rome

Mon Ant = Monumenti Antichi

Mon Piot = Monuments et Mémoires publiés par l'Académie des Inscriptions et Belles-Lettres, Fondation Piot

Mus Helv = Museum Helveticum

MWPr = Marburger Winckelmannsprogramm

NSc = Notizie degli Scavi di Antichità

RE = Pauly-Wissowa, *Real-Encyclopädie der klassischen Altertumswissenschaft*

Rend Pont Acc = Rendiconti della Pontificia Accademia Romana di Archeologia

Riv Ist Arch = Rivista dell'Istituto di Archeologia e Storia d'Arte

RM= Mitteilungen des deutschen archäologischen Instituts, Römische Abteilung
Rylands Bulletin= Bulletin of the John Rylands Library, Manchester

BOOKS AND ARTICLES

The following works, to which very frequent references are made, are cited only by their initials when no confusion
with the works of other writers is likely to arise.

By J. D. Beazley

ABV=*Attic Black-figure Vase-painters* (Oxford, 1956)
*ARV*²=*Attic Red-figure Vase-painters* (2nd ed.; Oxford, 1963)
EVP=*Etruscan Vase-painting* (Oxford, 1947)

By A. D. Trendall

FI= *Frühitaliotische Vasen* (Leipzig, 1938)
LCS= *The Red-figured Vases of Lucania, Campania and Sicily* (Oxford, 1967)
LCS Suppl I= First Supplement to the above (*BICS*, Suppl. 26, 1970)
PP=*Paestan Pottery* (*BSR*, 1936)
PPSupp='Paestan Pottery – a Revision and a Supplement', in *BSR* 20, 1952, 1–52
PAdd= 'Paestan Addenda', in *BSR*, 27, 1959, 1–37
*PhV*²=*Phlyax Vases* (2nd ed.; *BICS*, Suppl. 19, 1967)
SIVP= *South Italian Vase-Painting* (British Museum, 1966)

By A. D. Trendall and Alexander Cambitoglou:

APS=*Apulian Red-figured Vase-painters of the Plain Style* (Arch. Inst of America, 1961)

By T. B. L. Webster

GTP=*Greek Theatre Production* (Methuen, 2nd ed., 1970)
*MTSP*²=*Monuments illustrating Tragedy and Satyr-play* (2nd ed.; *BICS*, Suppl. 20, 1967)
*OMC*²=*Monuments illustrating Old and Middle Comedy* (2nd ed.; *BICS*, Suppl. 23, 1969)
*MNC*²=*Monuments illustrating New Comedy* (2nd ed.; *BICS*, Suppl. 24, 1969)

By other writers

Bieber, *History*²=M. Bieber, *The History of the Greek and Roman Theater* (2nd ed.; Princeton, 1961)
Gigante, *Teatro Greco*=M. Gigante, 'Teatro greco in Magna Grecia', in *Atti del VIº Convegno di Studi sulla Magna
                    Grecia, 1966* (Taranto, 1970)
Haspels, *ABL*=C. H. E. Haspels, *Attic Black-figured Lekythoi* (Paris, 1936)
Pickard-Cambridge, *Dithyramb*²= A. W. Pickard-Cambridge, *Dithyramb, Tragedy and Comedy* (2nd ed.; Oxford, 1962)
Pickard-Cambridge, *Festivals*²=——, *The Dramatic Festivals of Athens* (2nd ed.; Oxford, 1968)
Pickard-Cambridge, *Theatre*=——, *The Theatre of Dionysus in Athens* (Oxford, 1946)
Richter, *Furniture*², =G. M. A. Richter, *The Furniture of the Greeks, Etruscans and Romans* (2nd ed.; Phaidon, 1966)
Richter, *Perspective*, =——, *Perspective in Greek and Roman Art* (Phaidon, 1970)
Séchan=L. Séchan, *Études sur la tragédie grecque dans ses rapports avec la céramique* (Paris, 1926)

In the references to extant fragments of Greek drama, K=Kock, *Fragmenta Comicorum Atticorum*; N=Nauck,
Fragmenta Tragicorum Graecorum; P=Jebb and Pearson, *Fragments of Sophocles*.

INTRODUCTION

I. THEATRE ART AND ITS PATRONS

The objects illustrated in this book range in date from the end of the eighth century B.C. to the end of the third century A.D.; the majority of them represent situations from the tragedies of Aeschylus, Sophocles, and Euripides, which were first produced in the fifth century B.C. We know more about them than any other tragic poet, and of the comic poets only two have left us complete plays, Aristophanes, writing in the later fifth and early fourth centuries, and Menander a century later. Aristophanes is very slightly represented in this pictorial tradition; a few good examples of Menander illustrations are given below.

For the three great tragic poets a recent rough count of the total number of surviving illustrations gives some idea of the rise and fall of popularity. This survey gave 167 illustrations of Aeschylus, of which 89 can be dated in the fifth century, 58 in the fourth, and a handful later; 93 illustrations of Sophocles, of which 57 can be dated in the fifth century, 29 in the fourth and 7 later. Euripides makes quite a different showing: his total of 238 is made up of 29 illustrations in the fifth century, 111 in the fourth, 73 in the third and second centuries B.C., and 25 later. The illustrations are additional evidence that he was less popular than the other two in his lifetime but came right up in the fourth century and maintained his pre-eminence through the Hellenistic and Roman periods.

Of course we have to remember that some great plays such as the *Agamemnon* and *Oedipus Tyrannus* were scarcely illustrated. In fact our illustrations cover only 40 of the 82 plays of Aeschylus, 37 of the 123 plays of Sophocles, and 48 of the 87 plays of Euripides. In considering which plays were most popular we have also to remember that a particularly successful work of art may give rise to its own tradition, which has its own popularity and does not necessarily reflect the popularity of its subject as drama. (A good example quoted below is the *Prometheus Pyrkaeus* of Aeschylus.) But it would nevertheless probably be true to say that the most popular plays for illustration were Aeschylus' *Choephoroi, Eumenides, Phrygians*; Sophocles' *Andromeda, Dionysiskos, Nausicaa, Thamyras* (but in most cases this represents a comparatively short-lived early popularity); Euripides' *Aigeus, Alexandros, Andromeda, Hercules, Hippolytus, Iphigenia in Tauris, Kretes, Medea, Stheneboia, Telephos*.

We can get a more sensitive appreciation by noting the kinds of monument which carry illustration. We have to ask where each was found, where each was made, in what artistic tradition it stands, whether the artist is likely to have seen the play, whether whoever commissioned it or purchased it is likely to have seen the play. We probably cannot answer all these questions but it is well to keep them in mind.

The latest monuments reproduced in this book are the mosaics of Menander plays from a villa of about A.D. 300 in Mytilene. Its owner evidently had a passion for Menander, as he had his triclinium floor decorated with a portrait of the poet, the Muse of Comedy, a scene with Socrates and his friends, as in Plato's *Phaedo*, and scenes from seven Menander plays; further, four scenes were found in the corridor

and more may await the excavators. The mosaics each illustrate a particular scene, and those in the triclinium
have the names of the characters in addition to the name of the play and the number of the act. Costumes
and masks can be dated to the third century A.D., so that actual theatrical performances are not very far
behind the pictures. A possible explanation is that the owner or the artist possessed a fairly new illustrated
edition of Menander, from which the scenes for the mosaics were taken.

The paintings of scenes derived from tragedy and comedy on the walls of houses in Pompeii and
Herculaneum belong to the large general class of derivative Roman art, which includes, as well as
mosaics and sculpture, silverware and lamps. An Augustan silver cup (III. 1, 22) shows Hector's body
being weighed against Priam's gold; the theme probably came from Aeschylus' *Phrygians*, and the composition may have been in the silversmith's repertoire for four hundred years or more. Silverware, lamps,
and paintings all tell us that their owners were interested in these particular plays, but all belong also to
an artistic tradition which is older than the owner or the artist. This is as true of theatre-scenes in the
strict sense, which show masked actors, as of pictures which show a scene inspired by drama but executed
without any reference to stage production, like the pictures of Euripides' *Medea* and *Iphigenia in Tauris*.
In one case the transmission is fairly clear. A small painting from Stabiae of the first century A.D.[1] is a copy
of a small mosaic from Pompeii (V, 3), which, it now seems probable, illustrates Menander's *Theophoroumene*. The mosaic was made about 100 B.C. by Dioskourides of Samos, but is itself the copy of an earlier
picture in Asia Minor since two of its figures are repeated in terracotta statuettes of the second century
B.C. found at Myrina (V, 9 and 10). The terracotta statuettes of Myrina were often copied from contemporary or earlier paintings, and it is probable that the common original of the terracottas and the
Dioskourides mosaic was a picture of a Menander scene based on third-century theatre practice in the area
of the Ionian-Hellespontine Guild of Artists of Dionysos, who had a branch headquarters at Pergamon.

In view of the close connection between Rome and Pergamon, the Campanian theatre-pictures themselves, particularly those with late Hellenistic costume like the Amphiaraos and Hypsipyle,[2] may derive
from Pergamene originals. But for the theatre-pictures which go back to Early-Hellenistic or earlier
originals, like the picture of Euripides' Phaedra on marble,[3] we now have a parallel in a house of the
second century B.C. in Delos,[4] which is probably an illustration of the prologue of Sophocles' *Oedipus
Coloneus*. The absence of thick-soled kothornoi, which one would have expected in Delos at this date,
suggests that it is a copy of an earlier picture rather than an original, and presumably the same goes for
the picture of comedy[5] found in the same house and for the mask mosaic in the Maison des Masques
(IV, 8c). In Delos we know that there was a flourishing theatre,[6] and therefore interest in tragedy and
comedy. This general interest is enough to account for the pictures and the mask-mosaic. The mask-
mosaic decorated the floor of the men's dining-room; masks of Dionysos' drama are also appropriate
for the room in which Dionysos' wine was drunk.

We have always to remember three sides of Dionysos' godhead. He is the god of drama and dithyramb.
He is the god of the symposion, because he is the god of wine. He is the god of the mysteries, who
promises a better after-life to his initiates. But he is one Dionysos, and therefore illustrations of drama are
not only appropriate in the dining-room and on the mixing bowls, water-jugs, and cups used in the

---

[1] *MNC²*, NP 54.   [2] *MTSP²*, NP 9.   [3] *MTSP²*, NP 34.   [4] *MTSP²*, 119, DP 1.
          [5] *MNC²*, 295–6, DP 1–3.   [6] Cf. G. M. Sifakis, *Studies in Hellenistic Drama*, 7 ff.

symposion but also on offerings given to the dead. The terracotta statuettes of comic actors from Myrina which we have quoted were found in tombs, but there is no reason to suppose that they were made for tombs; they were put in tombs either because they were treasured possessions of the dead man or because they represented Dionysos and the hope of a blessed after-life. The two Early-Hellenistic terracotta masks from the Athenian Agora (V, 5–6) come from wells and are therefore likely to have been throw-outs from private houses. The mid-fourth-century comic actors in the Metropolitan Museum (IV, 9) are said to have been found in a tomb; but they belong to a large series, examples of which were exported all over the Greek world. They illustrate the widespread interest in Attic comedy in the fourth century B.C., and were probably bought by Athenians and foreigners who had seen performances of comedy at the City Dionysia.

So, too, vases with dramatic scenes are appropriate to the symposion but are also suitable offerings for the dead, because Dionysos is concerned both with the symposion and with the dead. (Dramatic scenes are very rare on perfume vases; one of the few is the pyxis by Aison with Nausikaa (III. 2, 7); but any woman could take pleasure in a picture of Nausikaa). In some cases we may say that a vase was painted for the party given to celebrate a particular performance. Generally the safer explanation is that the dramatic scene is relevant to the god of the symposion, and we must be content with the acquired knowledge that this dramatic scene was popular then.

One of the interests of South Italian vases is that they show the popularity of Greek tragedy and comedy in an area which was, or was later to be, in contact with the Romans. The main run of Campanian and Paestan dramatic vases was made in the second and third quarters of the fourth century B.C.; Campania became a Roman ally in 338 B.C. The earliest vases (380–360 B.C.) of the Dirce Painter and his colleagues may in fact have been made in Sicily and reflect the dramatic tastes of Dionysios I of Syracuse. Earlier still is the well-known Lucanian kalyx-krater (II, 11) with Odysseus' sailors preparing to blind Polyphemos while satyrs dance on the fringe; this attests knowledge, if not production, of Euripides' *Cyclops* in the West very soon after it was produced in Athens. But the most imposing series of vases is the Apulian series, which accounts for about a sixth of the total number of illustrations of the three classical tragedians. The series runs from 425 B.C. till late in the fourth century, and Gnathia vases (the best were certainly made at Tarentum) continue the use of tragic and comic masks as decoration into the first quarter of the third century B.C., a generation before Livius Andronicus took Greek drama from Tarentum to Rome.

In Attica in the fifth century B.C. sometimes the connection between vase and performers is demonstrably close. Just before the end of the century a special commission was evidently given to celebrate the performance of a comedy by a set of wine-jugs (*choes*) illustrating chorus and characters (IV, 5–6). The jugs are technically unusual in that the figures are painted in polychrome directly on the clay. This must have been a special order, and after the party four of them were thrown into a well in the Agora, and one found its way at last by whatever route into the British Museum.

The Pronomos vase (II, 1), painted about 400, has the cast and chorus of a satyr play, the poet, and the flute-player, with all the names (except those of the actors) painted against the figures. This too must have been a special order for a party after the play (perhaps primarily for the chorus as the actors are not named?). Then the vase via the second-hand market must have reached Ruvo, where the general relevance of Dionysos and drama made it a suitable piece of tomb furniture, unless we believe that some South Italian theatre-lover had been present at the party and managed to secure it. As on the Pronomos vase, it is the names on the Kleophon Painter's picture of a dithyrambic performance that prove it to have been painted specially for the party which succeeded the successful production (I, 17). The poet Phrynichos may have been the comic poet of the late-fifth century, and two of the singers' names are known from Attic inscriptions of the same date as the vase.

Attic vase-painters very often put a name on a vase accompanied by the word *kalos*. The word is a very general word of approval, and it is entirely wrong always to read erotic significance into it. If a name with *kalos* is written against a figure to whom it can apply, it may mean that the vase has been ordered by or is a present to that man or boy. If a *kalos* name is written on a vase without any obvious reference in the scene, the vase is still a special order in so far as, even if the scene is a stock-scene, the *kalos*-name must have been put on before the vase was fired. Two *kalos*-names are of some interest for our subject. A red-figure volute-krater of the mid-fifth century connected below with Sophocles' *Pandora* (II, 8) has the *kalos*-name Alkimachos. This Alkimachos appears on a contemporary pelike as a kitharode who had won victories at the Panathenaia, Nemea, Marathon, and the Isthmos.[1] It is tempting to suppose that he had some part in the production of Sophocles' *Pandora* and that this volute-krater was used at the party after the successful production.

The other *kalos*-name is that of Euaion, son of Aeschylus. The most interesting Sophoclean pictures are connected either with the great painter Polygnotos or with Euaion son of Aeschylus. Sophocles' *Thamyras* has two points of connection with Polygnotos; first, Sophocles was painted with a lyre in the Stoa Poikile because he had played the lyre in the *Thamyras* (*Vita*, 5), and Polygnotos was one of the artists of the Stoa Poikile, which was nearly finished in 460 B.C. Secondly, Sophocles' description of Thamyras' ruin (244P) agrees both with Pausanias' description of the blinded Thamyras as painted by Polygnotos in Delphi (X, xxx, 8) and with an Attic hydria of 440–420 B.C. found in Greece (III. 2, 10). The picture in the Stoa Poikile has been regarded as the source for an Attic volute-krater by Polion of 430–420 B.C.,[2] on which Apollo looks away while Thamyras stands to play his lyre and a woman raises both her arms (cf. Ovid, *Met.* 1, 767), at the altar of the Muses, not praying for victory but swearing that Thamyras will win. But there are two other vases, one from Nola, one from Vulci, painted by the Phiale Painter soon after 450 B.C. with Thamyras seated playing his lyre, two Muses on one side of him, and on the other an old woman preparing to crown him; above her head on one of the vases (III. 2, 9) is written the name Euaion *kalos*. We can, I think, accept that the *Thamyras* was produced before 460 B.C., that Sophocles played Thamyras, that the Muses formed the chorus, and that Thamyras' mother was a character in the play. Further, if we accept the connection of Polion's standing Thamyras with Polygnotos, the seated Thamyras of the Phiale Painter is a reminiscence of the theatre scene, *not* of Polygnotos. A nice additional point is that the Phiale Painter's Thamyras, who is playing his lyre, shows his right profile, but the blind Thamyras on the Oxford hydria (III. 2, 10) shows his left profile. We know from Pollux (iv, 141) that Thamyras had a special double-sided mask, presumably because he was struck blind on the stage.

Euaion's name is inscribed above Thamyras' mother on the Phiale Painter's hydria. On a wonderful

[1] Beazley, *ARV*², 1044, no. 9.   [2] *ARV*², 1171, no. 1.

white-ground kalyx-krater (III. 2, 1) by the same painter 'Euaion *kalos* son of Aeschylus' is written above Perseus, who is looking at Andromeda; Andromeda is wearing Oriental dress and is tied to a post. This Andromeda in Oriental dress appears on several other vases (e.g. III. 2, 2–3), either tied to posts or being supported while the posts are put in the ground, sometimes in the presence of Kepheus, once with Perseus looking on from a distance. The subject is new in Attic vase-painting. All the vases belong to the decade 450–440, and the conclusion seems inevitable that they reflect Sophocles' *Andromeda*.

The Phiale Painter painted another white-ground kalyx-krater, with Hermes giving the infant Dionysos to Papposilenos in the presence of the nymphs of Nysa.[1] (It was found at Vulci.) This was the subject of Sophocles' satyr-play *Dionysiskos*. The subject occurs slightly earlier on two vases[2] by the Villa Giulia Painter, which would push the date back before 450 B.C. Both the Phiale Painter's white-ground kalyx-kraters with Sophoclean scenes have Muses on the back, who have no obvious relation to scenes from drama. Dare we see in them an allusion to the Association (*thiasos*) of the Educated (actors whom he had trained?) which Sophocles founded to honour the Muses (*Vita*, 6), and is it too bold to guess that Euaion, son of Aeschylus, acted in early plays of Sophocles?

Euaion's name appears on another vase, a bell-krater by the Lykaon Painter of about 440 B.C. (III. 1, 28) found at Vico Equense; here the name without *kalos* is written above the figure of Aktaion, who is being torn to pieces by his hounds; to the left Zeus, to the right Artemis; and Lyssa (Madness, who, we know, was introduced on the stage by Aeschylus in the *Xantriai*) drives the hounds on. The same painter repeated the scene without Euaion's name on a kalyx-krater found at Gela.[3] This new conception of the Aktaion story must almost certainly be derived from Aeschylus' *Toxotides*, and Euaion may have acted Aktaion in his father's play. Was it a revival or a late memorial of the original? Aeschylus was revived during the fifth century (*Vita*, 12), but the same problem arises with the Euaion *Thamyras* vase, which must have been painted at least ten years after the original production, which was before 460 B.C. Revival in a *deme* theatre is perhaps a possibility, but another solution may be preferable.

We have a number of vases illustrating the *Thamyras*, *Andromeda*, *Dionysiskos*, *Toxotides*, all painted about the same time, and the *Thamyras* vases certainly painted ten or more years after the probable date of the play. It does not matter that all except one were found outside Greece, in Sicily, Campania, and Etruria, because they presumably came there by way of the second-hand or export market. Sophocles probably founded his Association in honour of the Muses about 450 B.C., if it was an association of actors, since that was the date when the actor's competition was started. May these vases not have been commissioned for the symposia of the association, commemorating past as well as present triumphs of its members? For the *Thamyras* we have three contemporary vases, for the *Andromeda* five, for the *Toxotides* two, but in each case only one has the name Euaion. These were then a special honour for him.

The *Toxotides* leads over into Aeschylus, and other vases with Aeschylean scenes may also have been painted for the Association. The many illustrations of the *Choephoroi* and *Eumenides*, which were produced in 458 B.C., provide some information about revivals at different times and places, but it is also interesting to note when they start. Both appear on Attic vases by about 440 B.C. On terracotta reliefs from the island of Melos (III. 1, 1) the type of Orestes and Pylades at Agamemnon's tomb is completely changed about 450 B.C.; earlier they are accompanied by their horses and an old man, and Elektra is

[1] *ARV²*, 1017, no. 54.   [2] *ARV²*, 618 no. 4, kalyx-krater; 619, no. 16, bell-krater.   [3] *ARV²*, 1046, no. 11.

followed by her nurse; now the three are alone, and this may well be due to Aeschylus; essentially this same scheme appears on an Attic skyphos by the Penelope Painter about 440 B.C. (III. 1, 2). Four Attic vases painted about the same time (e.g. III. 1, 12) illustrate the *Eumenides*; the presence of Athena on one of them shows that the painter had the Athenian sequel as well as the arrival at Delphi in mind. The long-nosed Furies with snakes in their hair recall theatre furies. The altar at Delphi on which Orestes takes refuge is a long platform composed of large stones, and the Attic *ekkyklema* may have been made to look like this.

A number of other Aeschylean illustrations are discussed in the text, and it is interesting that in most cases the earliest Attic illustrations seem to belong within or very near to the decade 450–440 B.C. Unfortunately, as with the vases illustrating the *Choephoroi* and *Eumenides*, they none of them have *kalos* names and so we cannot say that they were bespoke for a particular person. But when we see how few dramatic vases there are among the very large number of surviving red-figure vases, it is very tempting to suppose that they were special commissions either for the Association or for a party held after a revival. One of the illustrations of Aeschylus' *Phineus* (III. 1, 24) gives a small hint in this direction: not only is Phineus' mask clearly shown, but the Harpies are labelled *kalos*; the masculine form (quite apart from the inappropriateness of this adjective for a Harpy) shows that the painter means the men who played the Harpies (whether actors or chorus), and they may have ordered the vase.

We are in similar doubt about the Attic 'pre-dramatic' vases except for the two late fifth-century pictures of dithyramb (I, 16–17), which are shown by their inscriptions to be bespoke vases. The only one of the sixth-century Attic vases with a pre-firing inscription is the Oltos psykter (I, 15), on which the dolphin-riders each say 'On a dolphin'; this must then be a bespoke piece. All the other Attic pieces, tumblers, Knights, Titans and the rest, are so unusual that we believe they probably were specially ordered for the party after the performance. The only stock vase is the early krater with the padded dancers (I, 7); this is one of a large class of vases similarly decorated, and the point of the decoration is not to illustrate a unique performance of padded dancers but to show padded dancers because they are servants of Dionysos, who is also the god of the symposion. All except two of the Attic pre-dramatic vases discussed are symposion vases. Doubts arise only in the case of the two lekythoi, which are perfume pots (I, 14, 18). The fact that both were found in the West suggests that they came there by the second-hand market; but this does not rule out their having been placed on the steps of tombs in Athens and then after a decent interval cleared off and sold; this is the way in which funerary white lekythoi presumably reached the West. The connection of Dionysos with the dead, as has been said already, makes it possible that they were bought to place in the tomb, but it is equally possible and perhaps more likely that they held perfume which was used at the symposion.

As in Attica, so also in Corinth – and earlier than in Attica – padded dancers decorated symposion vases and perfume vases. The examples discussed here (I, 3–6) are all in one way or another unique and therefore are likely to have been special commissions: the skyphos and the krater (5–6) have painted inscriptions put on before firing. If the perfume pots were Attic and not Corinthian, one would say without hesitation that the alabastron (3) and the amphoriskos (4) were made for women. It is possible that the boundaries were not so clear in Corinth and that these shapes too could be used at a male symposion, for which the subjects are obviously suitable. But it has been argued[1] that in Corinth the padded dancers

---

[1] A. Seeberg, *JHS* 85, 1965, 108; *Wissenschaftliche Zeitschrift der Universität Rostock*, 16, 1967, 523.

performed at the Eukleia, which was a festival of Artemis; this would naturally make their performances suitable for vases made for women.

Our chief concern in what follows is to consider how the artists represented pre-dramatic and dramatic performances at different times between the eighth century B.C. and the fourth century A.D. and what information the vases give us about the plays both as pieces for the theatre and as literature. The purpose of this introduction has been to consider the point of view of the ancient purchaser: what did these illustrations mean to him and how often did he commission them rather than taking them from stock? The most interesting moments are the few occasions in Athens and South Italy when we can plausibly say that this vase was commissioned to celebrate this particular dramatic victory.

2. THEATRES, SCENERY, AND COSTUME

The vases, terracottas, and reliefs illustrated in this book constitute a primary source of information on production in the ancient Greek theatre, and the details are fully discussed in the commentary of each picture. Here it is necessary only to give a general historical survey.

Except for the three pictures of dithyramb sung in Athens by men and boys (I, 17, 19–20), which are included because dithyrambic contests of men and boys formed part of the City Dionysia, the festival at which tragedy and comedy were produced, the first section shows disguises which antedate the official introduction of tragedy and comedy in Athens. The Tiryns Gorgon (I, 2) stands by itself as a representation of ritual dances performed in ugly masks. We cannot say anything about the actual place of production of these early ritual dances, which are illustrated also from Miletos (I, 1), Corinth (I, 3–6), and Athens (I, 7–15).

For Athens two suggestions[1] have been made and both may be true – the Agora, and in front of the Old Temple of Dionysos under the south slope of the Acropolis. The references to drama in the Agora are mostly late, but Socrates speaks of buying a book at the Orchestra in the Agora, and it is a plausible suggestion that the name of the dancing floor survived in the Agora after the performances had been transferred to the theatre under the Acropolis.

We know that tragedy and comedy were performed in honour of Dionysos Eleuthereus, the god of the Old Temple under the Acropolis. What is very difficult at first sight to understand is why the theatre was built out of relation to the temple. The auditorium backs on to the Acropolis and partially embraces the circular dancing-floor of the chorus (*orchestra*), which has the stage-building on the other side; the temple is well below, over on the right, with its long side nearly parallel to the back of the stage-building. Yet the normal background of classical tragedy was a temple- or palace-front of about the same size as the front of the Old Temple. Ancient sources speak of a collapse of grandstands in the early fifth century, and the auditorium of the classical theatre was certainly remodelled and possibly actually made at about the same date. A possible explanation is that performances did take place originally in front of the Old Temple, using it as a background, and that because of the steep slope of the ground the southern side of

[1] See *Rylands Bulletin* 42, 1960, 495 ff.

the auditorium consisted of grandstands; the collapse of these was sufficiently disastrous to cause the construction of a new auditorium safely backed on the slope of the Acropolis although this meant dissociating the performance from the Old Temple.

The first theatre[1] probably lasted from the early fifth century to about 435 B.C. What remains is only a few stones, probably of the retaining wall of the orchestra on one side and of the edge of the orchestra on the other. We have to rely on the plays for our knowledge of the stage-building. It must have been possible for an actor to get off either by the wings or by the stage-building, change mask and costume, and come on again through wings or stage-building. No tragedy, and no comedy till the middle of the fourth century, needs more than a single practicable door into the stage-building. The appearance of the watchman at the beginning of Aeschylus' *Agamemnon* shows that the roof of the stage-building was viable and could also be used for the appearance of gods at the beginning or end of the play. The beginning of Aeschylus' *Eumenides* can only be staged with a roll-out platform (*ekkyklema*) to carry the sleeping Furies and Orestes into view of the audience when the priestess has opened the temple doors. This was the obvious way also for the chest containing Danae and Perseus to be brought ashore in Aeschylus' satyr-play *Diktyoulkoi* (II, 3). The other piece of stage machinery was the *mechane* or crane, which the lexicographer Pollux associates with Aeschylus. The essential use of the *mechane* was to bring someone from the sky to the ground or from the ground to the sky. (Appearances in the sky could, of course, be staged with the *mechane*, but for gods who spoke prologue and epilogue an appearance on the roof was often thought sufficient.) Two South Italian vases of the late fifth century illustrate the use of the *mechane*: to show Sleep and Death bringing Sarpedon's body to Europa in Aeschylus' *Carians* (III. 1, 17) and to take Medea away from Corinth in a snake-chariot (III. 3, 34).

The first theatre of which we have considerable remains is the remodelling which is generally assumed to have been made about 435 B.C. What remains are the foundations of a long wall stretching beyond the *orchestra* on each side and of a wide 'nose' sticking out from the long wall into the *orchestra*. The long wall backed on to a stoa, which at its west end filled the space between the theatre and the Old Temple. The floor of the Stoa was about 7 feet below the level of the orchestra, and there was no communication this way between the theatre and the Stoa. (A tooled stone in the Stoa wall behind the 'nose' has been regarded as evidence for a doorway but probably supported some object, relief, picture, or inscription, on the Stoa wall.) The long foundation is slotted to take beams, which formed the back wall of the stage building. They were presumably tied to corresponding beams which formed the front wall of the stage-building. The front wall was what the audience saw; the space between the two walls was the concealed passage from the 'nose' to the wings, housed the staircase to the roof and the machinery of the *mechane* and *ekkyklema*, and gave a place for the actor to change mask and costumes. The front wall is usually reconstructed with projecting wings at each end. There is no material evidence for or against these, but the vases which seem to come nearest to the actual appearance of the stage-building – particularly the Attic picture of Euripides' *Iphigenia in Tauris* (III. 3, 27) – emphasize the central door (on the 'nose') and give no hint of projecting wings.

If we accept that there were no wings, the audience saw a long wall with a central door and low stage projecting from it. The central block was about 25 feet wide, and the long wall, which extended about

------

[1] *GTP* 5 ff.

Menander: *Synaristosai*. Above: Mosaic from Pompeii, signed by Dioskourides of Samos, 100 B.C. Naples, Museo Nazionale (V, 1). Below: Mosaic in Mytilene, A.D. 300 (V, 2).

I, 12 (London). Flute-player and two chorusmen in bird-costume.

35 feet in each direction, was divided by the beams into four panels on each side. These held the scenery. The programme of three tragedies, a satyr play, and a comedy, performed during the hours of daylight of a single day, excluded any change of scenery except between plays. (The rare changes of scene within tragedy were chiefly indicated by the chorus leaving the orchestra and returning to say that they had arrived somewhere else.) The theory[1] which seems best to account for the evidence – mentions of great artists painting scenery, inscriptions recording dedications of scenery by rich citizens, descriptions of scenery deriving from the Hellenistic age, reflections on vases and later wall-paintings – is that at any given time the theatre had three sets, one for tragedy with pictures of buildings and colonnades in perspective (the Greek word for perspective is 'scene-painting', *skenographia*), one for satyr-play with caves, rocks, and vines, and one for comedy, which probably in the classical period represented the wall of a men's dining-room with symposion decoration, wreaths, jugs, cups, and the like. Probably for a tragedy set in the country (like Sophocles' *Philoktetes*) the set for satyr-play would be used instead of the set for tragedy.

The costume[2] of tragic actors and choruses frequently appears on vases, very often for isolated figures in the pictures, e.g. Iphigenia and Thoas but not Orestes and Pylades in the Attic picture of Euripides' *Iphigenia in Tauris* (III. 3, 27). The instances are discussed in the text and here only two negative points need to be made. First, there is no sign of the thickened soles which give extra height to the actors. The *kothornos* of classical tragedy is a boot which comes some way up the legs but has normal soles. Secondly, the masks have normal hair over the forehead; there is no sign yet of the triangular *onkos* of hair over the forehead of which Pollux speaks. The Pronomos vase (II, 1) shows that heroic characters in satyr-play wore the same costumes as heroic characters in tragedy. Papposilenos,[3] however, whose part is taken by an actor, wears tights flocked with wool and the mask of an old satyr wreathed with ivy. The chorus wear satyr-masks and shaggy loin-cloths, which support phallos and tail. In comedy[4] the actors wore tights, which in the case of male characters support the phallos, either rolled up or dangling. The tights are the characters' skin, and over this males often wear a short skin jerkin which leaves the phallos visible. They may also wear a small himation over one shoulder falling to the waist or a large himation which envelops them completely. Actors taking female characters probably wore white tights and over them chiton and himation.

The next major rebuilding of the Athenian theatre was about 330 B.C. under the statesman Lykourgos.[5] The façade was now in marble and was some 15 feet in front of the 'nose' of the classical theatre. The orchestra and the auditorium were pushed farther into the slope of the Acropolis so that the auditorium became steeper. The foundations show that the new façade had projecting wings enclosing a low stage 60 feet long. It is always assumed that the façade was pierced by three doors to give the three houses or the two houses and a shrine which are necessary for New Comedy. In fact, the remains show no trace of doors, but Menander's *Dyskolos* makes the necessity entirely clear. We cannot, of course, tell whether the plan of the Lykourgos theatre had been anticipated in wood: if the old façade was extended by one more panel at each end and the last two panels at each end were set forward, it would have been practically identical with the Lykourgos façade. What is clear is that in the new plan the width of the stage was

[1] *GTP* 13 ff.; *Rylands Bulletin* 45, 1962, 242 ff.; *MTSP*², 3 ff.
[2] *GTP* 35 ff.; *MTSP*², 5 ff.; Pickard-Cambridge, *Festivals*², 180 ff.   [3] *GTP* 31; *MTSP*², 5 ff.; Pickard-Cambridge, *Festivals*², 180 ff.
[4] *GTP* 55 ff.; *OMC*², 7 ff.; Pickard-Cambridge, *Festivals*², 218 ff.; Bieber, *History*², 36.   [5] *GTP* 20 ff.

more than doubled, and this was in the interests of comedy, not of tragedy, where the action was con-
centrated on the central door. In Aristophanic comedy confusion of place added to the fun; but when
comedies of identical twins were introduced, which seems to have been about 350 B.C., confusion of
place would have been intolerable and the long stage with three doors became a necessity.

The next step, which involved a further rebuilding, was to move the action on to a stage about 12 feet
above the ground. This was done by moving the wings and the upper storey of the façade back so as to
give acting space between the wings. This gave something like the modern picture-frame stage with the
bottom as well as the sides well defined; the entrances from off-stage were in the sides of the projecting
wings. The effect was to separate the actors vertically from the chorus. Again this change, which was
made by 290 B.C. in Athens, was in the interests of comedy;[1] in comedy from the time of Menander at
least there was no communication between the actors on the high stage and the chorus in the orchestra;
the chorus merely sang interludes between the acts. The same may have been true of tragedy in the
fourth century and the Hellenistic age, but it cannot have been convenient for the yearly revivals of
classical tragedy. We know that sometimes when communication was essential the high stage was connected with the orchestra by a ladder.

The archaeological evidence[2] suggests that the tower of hair over the forehead of the chief characters
was introduced with or soon after the building of the Lykourgos theatre. It made the heroic characters
more imposing and emphasized their emotions. They were made still more imposing by the thickened
soles, which on our evidence came in first in the area of the Ionian–Hellespontine Artists of Dionysos in
the second century B.C.

The New Comedy[3] of Menander, which was essentially social comedy, could not do with the gro-
tesquely padded and obscene actors of Aristophanes. Before the end of the fourth century all male characters wore chitons which reached at least halfway down their thighs, and only slaves were padded. A
number of new masks were introduced which made the young men and their fathers look like respectable Athenian citizens. Subsequent alterations were comparatively minor. Something like the tragic
onkos appears sometimes on young men's masks in the second century B.C., and the mouths of slave
masks became larger and larger to emphasize their greed and boastfulness. Finally in the third century
A.D. slaves were quite often given full-length chitons like their masters.

---

[1] Bieber, *History*², 108 ff.; G. M. Sifakis, *Studies in Hellenistic Drama*, 127 ff., 131.　　　　　　[2] *GTP* 43 ff.; *MTSP*², 8 ff.
[3] *GTP* 73 ff.; *MNC*², 5 ff.; Pickard-Cambridge, *Festivals*², 223 ff.; Bieber, *History*², 87 ff.

3. SOUTH ITALIAN VASES AND THE STAGE

Red-figured pottery of local manufacture makes its appearance in South Italy in the third quarter of the fifth century B.C., and almost from the start vase-painters show a remarkable interest in subjects associated with dramatic performances.[1] One of the earliest vases by the Pisticci Painter, the first of the colonial vase-painters, represents a scene from a satyr-play (II, 10) and some years later his pupil, the Cyclops Painter, decorated a vase with the blinding of Polyphemos (II, 11), the inspiration for which almost certainly came from the *Cyclops* of Euripides. During the fourth century scenes from Attic tragedies are frequently found, especially on the larger Apulian vases, which by their size were particularly well adapted to such representations. As the characters are often shown as wearing stage costumes, there can be little doubt that such vases are directly connected with theatrical performances and on two (III. 2, 8 and III. 6, 1) the actual stage is shown, as it is more frequently on vases with scenes from comedies or phlyax plays (see below, p. 12). On others the setting seems to be associated with the stage background (cf. III. 3, 26, 29, 46), on one occasion (III. 1, 17) possibly also combined with the use of the *mechane*. The pictures, however, are often not referable to a particular episode from a given play but rather aim at giving a compendium of the play as a whole, somewhat after the manner of a poster, which shows one or two highlights of the play, several of its principal characters, and often adds a selection of divinities, some of whom may have a direct connection with the drama as speakers of prologue or epilogue, but including others who are only very remotely concerned (cf. III. 1, 27; III. 2, 11; III. 3, 17 and 40; III. 4, 4; III. 5, 4).

The fondness for such dramatic representations, especially for the plays of Euripides, testifies to the continued popularity of the great Attic tragedians throughout the fourth century in Magna Graecia, where their plays must have been constantly revived, especially at Tarentum. A tomb found in 1963 at Policoro (anc. Herakleia) contained five vases with themes inspired by Euripidean tragedies (e.g. III. 3, 14, 20 and 34), all made locally about 400 B.C.; it may well have been that of an actor, or at least an admirer, of Euripides' plays, which were obviously known to the inhabitants of South Italy fairly soon after their production in Athens.

Further evidence for an early interest in the stage comes from the vases of the Tarporley Painter, who flourished round the turn of the fifth–fourth centuries B.C.; one (II, 2) shows us actors dressing to act in the chorus of a satyr-play, another (IV, 13) is one of the earliest representations of a phlyax play, and several (e.g. B.M. F 163; *SIVP*, pl. 6b) show actors, holding masks in their hands, in the company of Dionysos. By the second quarter of the fourth century the interest had still further increased, and the bulk of vases with dramatic themes may be placed between *c.* 370 and 330. Most of them are Apulian, but they are also to be found in all the other fabrics, although there are fewer in the west, probably because Paestum and the cities of Campania, being under Samnite domination from the later fifth century, had less opportunity for dramatic performances or recitals than places like Tarentum or Syracuse.

Among the liveliest products of South Italian vase-painting in the fourth century B.C. are the so-called *phlyax* vases,[2] which take their modern name from the representation upon them of *phlyakes*, a word

---

[1] See Marcello Gigante, 'Teatro greco in Magna Grecia', in *Atti del VI° Convegno di Studi sulla Magna Grecia*, 1967 (1970), 83–146.
[2] A complete catalogue of these vases up to 1967 will be found in Trendall, *Phlyax Vases*[2] (BICS, Suppl. no. 19), with full bibliographies.

which seems to have been used to designate both the actors in a certain type of rustic farce (Pollux ix, 149) as well as the performances themselves which, according to Sosibios (quoted by Athenaeus xiv, 621 f), were the South Italian equivalent of what the δεικηλισταί performed in Sparta. The word itself has been generally connected with *phlyarein* (= to talk nonsense), but it is more likely to have been derived from *phleō* (swell),[1] which would be highly appropriate as applied to the actors in their well-padded costumes, which recall those of the padded dancers on Corinthian vases (cf. I, 3–6).

Some 200 phlyax vases have survived and they testify to the popularity throughout Magna Graecia of this sort of farce. They are to be found in all five of the South Italian fabrics, although they are very rare in Lucanian and, so far, confined to its early phase, when it was still closely associated with Apulian, to which nearly two-thirds of the extant vases may be assigned. Of the remainder, some thirty vases are Paestan, mostly from the workshop of Asteas and Python, and about fifteen each come from the fabrics of Campania and Sicily.

The subjects depicted range from a simple mask to a quite elaborate comic scene, in which the characters may be identified by inscriptions (e.g. IV, 18, 21, 30–32, 35), and in one instance (IV, 13) with what appear to be actual quotations from the play. Many vases show us a phlyax actor, either alone or in the company of Dionysos (e.g. IV, 10–11), again laying stress on his association with dramatic performances. Others burlesque gods and heroes (IV, 19–25), parody well-known tragic themes (IV, 32–4) or deal in comic fashion with scenes from every-day life, especially the sorry lot of the slave (IV, 13, 15, 17–18). This sort of comedy reached its highest level in the work of the Tarentine poet Rhinthon, who flourished in the early third century B.C., at least a generation after the latest of the phlyax vases, and he must in consequence be regarded rather as having given literary form to an already existing type than as being its creator.[2] It is also most probable that many of the vases reflect Attic comedies of the fourth century (on IV, 13 and 18 the inscriptions use Attic forms, not Doric, as one would expect for a Tarentine production, and on IV, 22 Phrynis and Pyronides are also Attic), which were presumably performed locally in much the same way as Attic tragedies.

The various types of stage which appear on the phlyax vases point in many instances to an impromptu kind of performance, in which light, movable sets could be used to indicate the required background – temple, house, or street. On one vase (IV, 25) there is a mere suggestion of the stage in the form of a low platform, apparently built of logs; sometimes we are shown only the floor of the stage (IV, 22), more often it is supported by posts (e.g. IV, 27), occasionally with draperies hung between them (IV, 26). The posts can be replaced by columns, suggesting a more permanent structure (e.g. IV, 18), again sometimes with draperies (IV, 11), and on a few vases a much more elaborate stage setting is represented, with taller supports, cross-beams, and columns to represent the background (e.g. IV, 14, 24). Very often a single door (cf. IV, 14, 18, 26) is shown (see above, p. 8), sometimes with a porch or pediment (cf. IV, 13 and 35).

The uniformity in the treatment of both subjects and performers suggests that a fairly standard type of production obtained throughout the different areas of Magna Graecia. The typical phlyax costume is like that of comedy (see above p. 9) and consists of close-fitting tights, intended to simulate nudity, with

[1] Radermacher, *Zur Geschichte der gr. Komödie*, 3–10.
[2] Webster, *Hellenistic Poetry and Art*, 126; Pickard-Cambridge, *Dithyramb*[2], 138 f. ; Gigante, *op. cit.*, 85 ff.

padding in front and behind, and a large phallos. A cloak or tunic may be worn as required, and in Paestan and Sicilian these are often coloured red or white; characteristic of the former is the presence of a white seam running down the arms and legs of the tights (cf. IV, 10, 14, 17, 19). With the costume is worn a mask appropriate to the rôle being performed; for women, who wear normal dress, the masks can be painted white (cf. IV, 11).

The following list of comic masks is based on that given in *OMC²*, 7–12 (cf. also *PhV²*, 12–13), with accompanying illustrations on pls. 7–10.

MALE

A. Good head of hair (black or white), short wedge beard (e.g. IV, 7a, 8b – right)

AA. Variant on A, with fuller hair

B. Good head of hair (black or white), short beard, open (trumpet) mouth – one of the masks most frequently used for slaves on phlyax vases (e.g. IV, 11, 13, 16, 26–7)

C. Peaked hair, longish beard (e.g. IV, 20, 23)

D. Straggly hair, longish straggly beard, hooked nose (IV, 23)

E. Scanty white hair, short beard, short nose (e.g. IV, 13, 26, 35)

F. Bald, with tuft of hair, scrubby beard, turn-up nose (IV, 3)

G. Scanty white hair, considerable beard, hooked nose (e.g. IV, 19, 20, 25, 32)

H. Neat hair and beard (IV, 3, 22)

J. Herakles – staring eyes, raised brow; short, curly beard (e.g. IV, 2, 22–3)

K. Good head of hair, wide triangular beard (IV, 8a, 9e)

L. Good head of white hair, longish beard (e.g. IV, 11, 16, 20, 22, 29)

M. Good head of white hair, shortish square beard (IV, 8a, 31)

N. Fuzzy hair, triangular beard coming to small point (e.g. IV, 2, 8a)

O. Clean-shaven, longish hair (e.g. IV, 8a, 31)

P. Bald, short spade beard (e.g. IV, 18, 35)

PP. Tettix – balding, triangular beard

Q. Clean-shaven, fat face

QA. Parasite – bald, clean-shaven

QQ. Sexless – balding, large ears (IV, 6)

Z. Clean-shaven, shortish hair, raised brows (e.g. IV, 19, 27, 29)

ZA. Clean-shaven, longish hair (foreigner?) (IV, 13)

FEMALE

R. Mop of hair, straight nose (e.g. IV, 8a, 16)

RR. Wolfish woman, long nose (e.g. IV, 30, 32)

S. Kore – short, parted hair (e.g. IV, 8a, 11, 33)

SS. Kore – long, parted hair (e.g. IV, 14)

T. Black hair, snub nosed (e.g. IV, 2, 4, 18, 26, 27)

TT. Long hair each side of the face, short nose (bride or wife) (e.g. IV, 28)

U. White hair, snub nose, fine wrinkles (e.g. IV, 13, 30)

V. Bunch of hair in peak above forehead, long locks (e.g. IV, 9b, 24)

W. Hair tied in bow above forehead

X. Hetaira – elaborate hair-do

XA. Hetaira – kekryphalos and side hair

XB. Hetaira – kekryphalos without side hair (common in Gnathia) (e.g. IV, 11)

XC. Hetaira – lampadion (e.g. IV, 10)

XD. Melon hair (only in Gnathia)

Y. Fat old woman, with thick wrinkles (e.g. IV, 24)

I, 1 (Balat). Padded dancers

I, 2 (Nauplion). Gorgon mask

I. PRE-DRAMATIC MONUMENTS

Tragedy was introduced into the festival of Dionysos, the City Dionysia, by Thespis in 534 B.C. The essential change which created a new art form was the addition of prologue and speeches spoken by the masked poet-actor to the old established art-form, the choral dance. The use of the mask is attested in several Greek cities including Athens long before the introduction of tragedy. One example is given (2) from Tiryns, and the earliest use of the mask seems to have been for a priest or priestess to impersonate the god or goddess and their attendants. Thus the mask worn by the Athenian tragic actor can be derived from the mask worn by the Athenian priest when he impersonated Dionysos.

Aristotle's conjecture that the first tragedy was an improvisation by leaders of the dithyramb is the reason for including pictures of the dithyramb here (16–20) although all of them postdate the introduction of tragedy.

Comedy did not start at the City Dionysia until 486 B.C., and it is reasonable to suppose that the development of earlier comic choral dances into comedy was inspired by the existence of the flourishing art-form, tragedy. We have many more illustrations of early comic choruses than of early tragic choruses. Choruses wearing the padded costume of Attic comic choruses were illustrated in Miletos about 700 B.C. (1), Corinth in the early sixth century (3–6), Athens in the sixth century (7).

For Corinth we have the evidence that these dancers impersonated beings akin to satyrs (5) and that men representing hairy satyrs took part with them (4). In Athens from about 540 B.C. onwards we find evidence for dithyramb danced and sung in satyr costume (16, 18). This is part of the ancestry of the classical Athenian satyr-play, which was added to the festival early in the fifth century; from that time onwards each tragic poet produced three tragedies and one satyr-play every year that he was chosen to produce.

Just as the padded dancers represent beings akin to satyrs, the men dressed up as women who dance with them (7) represent beings akin to Nymphs or Maenads. Besides all these we have pictures of special choruses: Titans (10), tumblers and runners with sticks (13), Knights (9), dolphin-riders (11, 14–15), birds (12), most of which look forward to choruses in later comedy. These pictures not only illustrate the ancestry of costumes; they also show that the dance-steps known from pictures of classical tragedy, satyr-play, and comedy had a long ancestry behind them. Each dance-step represented is an instant of dance-rhythm frozen for ever. But if the steps persisted it is probable that the rhythms to which they belonged also persisted. These rhythms, which the chorus danced, were also the

metre to which the words sung by the chorus were set. Thus a demonstration that dance-steps persisted is also a demonstration that the metrical units which are built up into the new intricate patterns of Greek tragic, comic, and satyric choruses were themselves traditional.

I, 1

Balat.

East Greek vase-fragment from the Temple of Athena, Miletos; 700–675 B.C.

Actors and chorusmen taking male or female parts in Attic comedy were heavily padded in front or behind. This costume appears to derive from the much earlier padded dancers known from sixth-century monuments in various parts of Greece. Their frequency from an early date in Corinth has led to the claim that this and other elements of Attic comedy had a Dorian ancestor. The discovery of the fragment illustrated, however, places the earliest known padded dancers in Miletos, a city whose cults and rituals were strongly influenced by Athens.

Other choruses represented on vases of this and earlier date dance much more soberly without raising their knees, and they are normally in rows with linked hands. On this fragment the arms seem to cross without touching, and the posture of each dancer may be an early stylization of the posture of the dancer on the right of the Corinthian skyphos, I, 5 below.

P. Hommel, *Istanbuler Mitteilungen*, 9–10, 1959–60, pl. 60, 2; Pickard-Cambridge, *Dithyramb*², no. 109; R. Tölle, *Frühgriechische Reigentänze* (Hamburg, 1964), 53.

I, 2

Nauplion 4506–8.

Terracotta masks from sanctuary of Hera at Tiryns; c. 700 B.C.

The masks worn by actors and chorusmen in drama derive ultimately from the masks worn in cult when a god or goddess and his or her attendants were impersonated. The big bearded Gorgon mask and two slightly smaller beardless masks from Tiryns are the earliest surviving life-size examples and about a century older than the similarly hideous life-size masks from the sanctuary of Ortheia in Sparta, which appear to be stylized on Phoenician masks. Probably these large terracottas were the moulds on which the masks actually worn

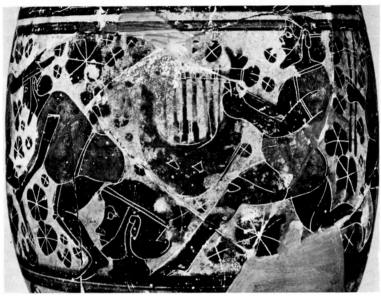

I, 3 (Paris).
Padded dancers

were made, and were subsequently dedicated to the goddess. Such dances are known from many parts of Greece; the goddess and her attendants are represented in this terrifying aspect not so much to frighten mortals as to frighten away evil spirits which might spoil her work of fructification.

R. Hampe, *Frühgriechische Sagenbilder*, 63, pl. 42; H. Kenner, *Theater*, 22; Webster, *Greek Art and Literature 700–530*, 65; G. Karo, *Personality in Archaic Greek Sculpture*, 32 ff.; Pickard-Cambridge, *Dithyramb*², 167, no. 69: R. Higgins, *Greek Terracottas*, 50; Karagiorga, *Γοργείη Κεφαλή*, pl. 14.

I, 3

Paris, Louvre S 1104.
Corinthian alabastron; 625–600 B.C.

This large scent bottle has two friezes: above, a boar-hunt; below, two men fighting a lioness, and five padded dancers. As often, there is no connection between the scenes. Here, instead of dancing about a phallos, the dancers dance about a bearded male head rising from the ground (presumably

Dionysos). Again, an Attic black-figure lekythos of the early fifth century provides a parallel (*BCH* 68–9, 1944–5, 298, pl. 25). Dionysos, or the phallos, rising from the earth is the new fertility of the spring. More commonly it is the earth goddess who rises revitalized: she appears once on a Corinthian padded-dancer vase (Payne, *Necrocorinthia*, no. 734a) and often on Attic vases (cf. below on Pandora, II, 7).

The padded men to the right of the head are musicians; the first runs forward holding a seven-stringed lyre; the second dances holding a double-flute. The three to the left of the head are dancers: the man on the right seizes the next man by the leg. This one, the man in the middle, has a misshapen foot bandaged (?) at the ankle. This is a feature of Hephaistos (cf. below 4) and has been connected with magical powers; here it belongs rather to the character whom the dancer represents than to the dancer himself.

CVA 9, pl. 33, 1–6; Payne, *Necrocorinthia*, no. 461; Seeberg, *Corinthian Komos Vases* (*BICS*, Suppl. 27), no. 216; Pickard-Cambridge, *Dithyramb*², 100, no. 35; Buschor, *Satyrtänze*, 19, fig. 9; Webster, *Rylands Bulletin*, 36, 1954, 581; *Greek Chorus*, 11; H. Metzger, *Recherches sur l'imagerie athénienne*, 49, pl. 25.

I, 4 (Athens, N.M.).
'Return of Hephaistos'

I, 4

Athens, N.M. 664.
Corinthian amphoriskos; 600–575 B.C.

A very popular version of the release of the earth-goddess in the spring was the Return of Hephaistos. The lame smith-god Hephaistos had presented his mother Hera with a magic chair which held her when she sat down in it. Hephaistos refused to return and release her. Finally Dionysos made him drunk and brought him back on a mule. The story is shown on four Corinthian vases, and takes place in the presence of padded dancers, so that it may be assumed that they sang the story. On the British Museum version (B42) the scheme is much the same: in front on the right two padded dancers, then the procession: a leader, bearded Hephaistos on the mule, Dionysos bearded, wearing long chiton and himation, two attendants – one with wineskin and jug. On the Athens vase the leader has moved back behind the mule, the first attendant carries a vinebranch with clusters, the second an amphora. Hephaistos is beardless, so is the figure corresponding to the British Museum Dionysos, who apparently wears a scale-

patterned shawl as well as a long chiton and himation. Interpretations have varied: either this is a beardless Dionysos (and the scaled shawl might allude to Dionysos Melanaigis, 'the black goatskin') or a woman – either one of the Nysai, the nurses of Dionysos who became the maenads, or Aphrodite, who was given to Hephaistos when he released Hera, or an unknown goddess involved in this version of the story. Ahead and separated from the mule by a tree, two phallic figures in padded-dancer costume (but without belts). The one on the right is in a dance posture welcoming the procession. The one on the left is also in a dance posture (cf. below no. I, 8): a large head with wild hair and beard (perhaps a mask), spotted chiton (the spots may represent hair), fruits in his hands. It is tempting to suppose, as Seeberg suggests, that these vases were based on a cult procession in Corinth (cf. the Attic and Klazomenian ship-car vases) in which the padded dancers took part.

Payne, *Necrocorinthia*, 142, no. 1073; Bieber, *History*², fig. 130; Webster, *Rylands Bulletin* 36, 580; *Greek Chorus*, 11; Pickard-Cambridge, *Dithyramb*², 171, no. 38; Seeberg, *op. cit.*, no. 227a; *JHS* 85, 1965, 103 ff.; *Symbolae Osloenses* 41, 1966.

I, 5 (Paris). Padded dancers

I, 5

Paris, Louvre CA 3004.
Corinthian skyphos; 600–575 B.C.

Five of the six padded dancers on this vase are named (the one under the handle on the extreme left is nameless): from left to right, Lordios (back-bender), Vhadesios (pleasure-seeker). Paichnios (plaything?), Komios (reveller), Loxios (side-bender). These are not the names of ordinary men – Lordon, with Kybdasos (forward-bending), is the name of a fertility spirit to be propitiated by lovers in an early fourth-century Athenian comedy (Plato, fr. 174K). Komos is an Attic satyr-name (cf. II, 4). The beings represented by the padded dancers are, therefore, closely akin to satyrs, and the names must have

been quoted in the song; it is noticeable that they would go easily into trochaic-cretic rhythm and this may be the rhythm associated with the three dance-postures, recognized by A. Seeberg, which recur again and again on padded-dancer vases: A, Paichnios, the middle of the five; B, Lordios, on the left, Loxios on the extreme right (cf. on I, 1 above); C, Vhadesios, left of centre, and probably Komios, right of centre. The other side of the vase has a picture of Herakles killing the hydra; conceivably this was the subject of the dancers' song, but it is more likely that the two scenes are unconnected.

P. Amandry, *Mon. Piot*, 41, 1944, 23 ; Seeberg, *op. cit.*, no. 202; Webster, *Rylands Bulletin* 36, 1954, 580; *Greek Chorus*, 11, no. 76, fig. 2; Pickard-Cambridge, *Dithyramb²*, 100, no. 40; R. Arena, 'Iscrizioni corinzie su vasi' (Memorie Lincei VIII. 13, 1967), 80, no. 23, pls. 5–7.

I,6 (Paris). Padded dancers with krater and mixing-bowls

I, 6

Paris, Louvre E 632.
Corinthian column-krater; 600–575 B.C.

Two padded dancers on the left, one playing the double flute, in posture A, one in posture C with large bearded head, probably correctly interpreted as a mask. They are detached from the rest of the scene like the padded dancers in the pictures of the Return of Hephaistos. The scene on the right, and possibly also the scene on the back of the vase, may be the subject of their song. On the right, three naked men: Eunos and Ophelandros carry a krater, and are followed by Omrikos with two sticks. On the back of the vase, stacked mixing-bowls on the left; a woman brings food to two clothed men in the stocks. Interpretations have differed widely. Omrikos could be either Rainy or Umbrian. If he is Rainy, this is a title of Dionysos in Halikarnassos, and he, Well-Disposed (*Eunos*) and Benefiting-man (*Ophelandros*) will be fertility-spirits. If he is Umbrian, he is a slave and the other names are possible slave-names. The names are not attached to the padded-dancers; if the padded-dancers are near-satyrs, they can sing either of other near-satyrs or of slaves. The action has been interpreted as stealing a mixing-bowl or as stealing wine. Against the first is the obvious weight of the bowl, which should be full rather than empty. The scene has therefore been interpreted as a theft of wine, and connected with the Spartan *deikelistai* who imitated men stealing fruit (the word could be used for 'wine'). Most recently A. Seeberg has noted that there is no evidence that the mixing-bowl of wine is being stolen; the pictures may represent preparations for a party and aftermath of a party, as described in a fragment attributed to the fifth-century Sicilian comic poet Epicharmos (fr. 148 Kaibel): 'after the feast drinking . . . After drinking abuse, after abuse swinishness, after swinishness litigation, after litigation condemnation, after condemnation fetters and stocks and fine'. This would be a suitable sequence for the padded dancers' song.

Payne, *Necrocorinthia*, 122, no. 1178; Bieber, *History*², fig. 132; Webster, *Rylands Bulletin* 36, 1954, 579; Pickard-Cambridge, *Dithyramb*², 171, no. 41; Bouzek, *Studies presented to G. Thomson*, 61; Seeberg, *BICS* 14, 1967, 25 ff.; *Wiss. Zeitschrift Rostock*, 16, 1967, 523; *op. cit.*, no. 226; R. Arena, *Parola del Passato*, 111, 1967, 478; and *op. cit.*, 84, no. 27, pl. 8.

I, 7

Berlin, Staatliche Museen, 1966.17.
Attic red-figured column-krater; 600–575 B.C.

In the early sixth century the Attic potters took over from Corinth the fashion of decorating pottery with padded dancers, and the group of vases to which this column-krater (attributed by Dr. A. Greifenhagen to the KY Painter) belongs, owes much to Corinthian painting. But on the earliest Attic pictures, like this one, the dancers dance with similarly padded and dressed women. In Corinthian pictures women do not appear quite as early as this, and when they do appear they are naked. The Attic painters (although the impulse to represent padded dancers came from Corinth) were painting Attic padded dancers (cf. above on I, 1); the women are probably boys representing women, and the women they represent are akin to Nymphs just as the men are akin to satyrs. On this vase from the left, two men in posture C dance with a woman in posture B; two men in posture A dance up to a mixing bowl; a woman in posture B dances with a man in posture C.

Unpublished. In general see Webster, *Rylands Bulletin*, 36, 1954, 582; *Greek Chorus*, 12, 70; Pickard-Cambridge, *Dithyramb*², 170.

I, 8

Amsterdam, Allard Pierson Museum 3356.
Attic black-figured kylix by the Heidelberg Painter; 560–540 B.C.

On each side of the cup six dancers divided by a flute-player in the middle: the right-hand trios on each side are identical. All the figures wear a chiton and over it a red garment with a long black stripe. The chitons of the flute-players and the trio on the left of B stop short of the knee; the chitons of the other nine dancers are long. All on A wear a headband with a descending cheek flap. All except the left-hand trio of A wear pointed caps; the left-hand trio of A have what are probably feathers in their headbands. The cheek flaps and neck flaps are sometimes worn by maenads; they are probably Eastern but are not tiaras, because they do not have the distinguishing peak of the tiara.

The artist thought of four trios: (1) on the left of A is a trio 'greeting', (2) the trio 'advancing' from the right of A, (3) on the left of B, a 'dancing' trio which looks back at the 'advancing' trio, which has passed them, (4) on the right of B, a second advancing trio.

The 'advancing' trios are closely paralleled on a contemporary hydria which has five bearded men with feathers in their headbands and long, coloured chitons advancing on a flute-player in a short striped chiton.

It has been suggested that the 'greeting' trio are *ithyphalloi*, who wore masks of drunkards and female clothing and escorted the phallos-pole into the theatre. But now that the Basel hydria shows that they wear feathers and not phalloi in their headbands, the explanation becomes less likely.

The dance of the 'greeting' trio is similar to the dance of a stage maenad in the early fifth century (*MTSP*², AV 10). The dancing trio have the same attitude as the stone-thrower on the Corinthian amphoriskos (I, 4). The members of the 'advancing' trios are not unlike a bearded figure in long chiton advancing with lyre on a black-figure psykter-amphora which Sir John Beazley has connected with pictures of Anakreon and his boon-companions dancing in female clothing. Anakreon described such dances as 'playing the maenad'. Perhaps our artist thought of a chorus of men dressed up as maenads and singing of maenads journeying through hazards (the dancing trio) to join their companions. Later comedies had titles like *Archilochoi*, Archilochos and his companions; on this analogy, the dance here may have been entitled 'Anakreontes'.

CVA, Scheurleer coll., III He, pl. 2, 4: *ABV* 66, no. 57; Webster, *Rylands Bulletin* 36, 1954, 574 and 584; *Greek Art and Literature, 700–530*, 60; *Greek Chorus*, 14, 70; Pickard-Cambridge, *Dithyramb*², 81, 141, no. 21; H. Brandenburg, *Studien zur Mitra*, 83.
Cf. hydria in Swedish private collection (Münzen und Medaillen, Basel, Auction 34, May 1967, pl. 31, no. 121); psykter-amphora in Rhodes (*CVA*, pl. 19, 1–2; *ABV* 115, no. 3).

I, 9

Berlin F 1697.
Attic black-figured amphora by the Painter of Berlin 1686; 550–540 B.C.

The panel illustrated shows a flute-player, in a long chiton and himation striped with red, playing for three beardless men mounted on the backs of three bearded men, who wear horse masks and horse tails. (The same position is held by a satyr riding on the shoulders of another satyr on an Attic kalyx-krater of about 460 B.C., *Dithyramb*², no. 100, reverse.) The riders wear helmets, each with a different type of crest, breastplates, short chitons decorated with spots; their left hands are raised. The 'mounts' have their hands on their knees. The horse masks leave most of their faces visible; they wear short red chitons, to which the tails are attached. On the second and third the chitons come just below the shoulder, on the third it appears to be belted. The inscription in front of the first horse is a jumbled collection of letters as often on black-figure vases. (The other side of the vase has satyrs and a maenad.)

The vase shows that the chorus of Aristophanes' *Knights*, produced 424 B.C., had an ancestor more than a century before. Comedy was first produced at the City Dionysia in 487/6, but may have been earlier at the Lenaia. It is, however, unlikely

I,7 (Berlin). Padded dancers

I,8 (Amsterdam). Dancers and flute-players

I,9 (Berlin). Flute-player and mounted dancers

I,10 (Christchurch, N.Z.). Chorus on stilts

that official comedy preceded the introduction of tragedy in 534 B.C. We must therefore reckon this chorus of Knights as one of the traditional elements which the later comic poets could reintroduce.

ABV 297, no. 17; Bieber, *History*[2], fig. 126; Pickard-Cambridge, *Dithyramb*[2], 153, no. 23; Webster, *Greek Chorus*, 20, 93; Koller, *Musik und Dichtung*, fig. 19.

I, 10

Christchurch (N.Z.), University of Canterbury, Logie Collection 41/57.
Attic black-figured amphora by the Swing Painter; *c.* 530 B.C.

The flute-player is absent, but five men advancing on stilts must be a chorus. They wear long-pointed caps, to which apparently their beards are attached, short red chitons, breastplates, one of leather, the rest of animal skins. The steps

of the stilts can be seen under their feet. The lexikon of Hesychios gives *Kadalion* and *Kolobathristes* for stilt-walker. (Kadalion was carried on Orion's shoulder.) Pollux speaks of the Lakonian *gypones*, who danced on stilts, but they were swathed in diaphanous Tarentine material. The stilts here may chiefly be used for height, and the chorus may represent Titans. The pointed caps are Scythian and would suit Titans if they were visiting Prometheus in the Caucasus as later in Aeschylus, *Prometheus Lyomenos*. If they are Titans, they, like the Knights (I, 9), anticipate a chorus of Attic comedy, Kratinos' *Ploutoi*. Lucian (*de Saltatione*, 79) also speaks of Ionian nobles 'dancing Titans' but we do not know how old the custom was. For other choruses which may have used stilts, see I, 11, 14, 15; IV, 5.

Fasti Archaeologici, 12, 1959, no. 251; Pickard-Cambridge, *Dithyramb*[2], 153, no. 24; Brommer, *AntK* 11, 1968, 50, pl. 15, 1; *AA* 1962, col. 755, fig. 8: Webster, *Greek Chorus*, 15, 70; Trendall, *Greek Vases in the Logie coll.* 59, no. 27, pls. 20a and 21a–c, and frontispiece.

I, 11 (Boston). Flute-player and *(a)* dolphin-riders, *(b)* ostrich-riders.

I, 13 (Thebes). Old men and flute-player. Tumblers and flute-player

I, 11

Boston 20.18.
Attic black-figured skyphos of the Heron Group; 500–490 B.C.

A. Six men in helmets and cloaks riding dolphins; flute-player in himation. See also I, 14 and 15.
B. Six young men with wreaths and military cloaks, carrying spears, ride ostriches. They are watched, or met, by a small Pan, wrapped in a cloak. At the end, a bearded flute-player playing. The small Pan recalls the stone-thrower on the Corinthian amphoriskos (I, 4) and the dancing trio on the Amsterdam cup (I, 8). It is impossible to say whether the little Pan only occurred in the song of the riders as one of the hazards of their journey, or whether he is our earliest picture of a comic actor, whether he welcomes the chorus like 'Demosthenes' in Aristophanes' *Knights* or objects to them like Dikaiopolis in the *Acharnians*.

ABV 617; Haspels, *ABL* 108, 144, 163; Bieber, *History*², fig. 125; Pickard-Cambridge, *Dithyramb*², 152, 159, no. 25; F. Brommer, *AA*, 1942, 67; E. Bielefeld, *AA*, 1946–7, 47; C. M. Bowra, *Mus. Helv.* 20, 1963, 121 ff.

I, 12 (Ill. opp. p. 9)

London, British Museum, B 509.
Attic black-figured oinochoe by the Gela Painter; 500–480 B.C.

Flute-player in long himation. Two men in bird-costume running. This is the entry of the chorus: the steps are repeated much later by the Cake-bearers in a late fifth-century comedy (cf. IV, 6). The men wear cockscombs on their heads, and have red beards. Wings are attached to their shoulders, and they appear to wear feathered tights (not unlike the tights with flocks of wool worn by Papposilenoi, cf. below I, 16), which support the combs on their knees; a small himation partly red is twisted round their waists with the ends hanging down. A very different pair of cocks is shown on a contemporary amphora in Berlin; they follow their flute-player muffled in large cloaks (like the youths of I, 19 below); this must have been an entry to a much statelier metre.

ABV 473; Haspels, *ABL*, 214, no. 187; Bieber, *History*², fig. 123; Pickard-Cambridge, *Dithyramb*², 152, no. 26; Koller, *Musik und Dichtung*, fig. 20.
Contrast the amphora Berlin F1830; Bieber, *op. cit.*, fig. 124; Pickard-Cambridge, *op. cit.*, 152, no. 27; Koller, *op. cit.*, fig. 18.

I, 14 (Palermo). Flute-player and dolphin-riders

I, 13

Thebes, B.E.64.342.
Attic black-figured skyphos; 530–510 B.C.

A. Old men running with long sticks towards flautist. Their heads, in comparison with the flautist, are very large and probably represent masks. Their white hair is bound with a red fillet; they wear large himatia with red stripes; their sticks have white heads. They advance rapidly with long strides like the cock-men on I, 12. Pollux (iv, 104) mentions a Laconian dance of *hypogypones*, old men with sticks, which may be in the same tradition.

B. Similar, or the identical, old men standing on their heads and waving their legs to the accompaniment of a bearded flute-player wearing a large striped himation. The dancers wear short, red chitons (belts are marked on the two nearest the flute-player). Tumblers leading dancers are already known to Homer, but he does not say that they stood on their heads. On a Corinthian padded-dancer vase of the early sixth century one of the dancers stands on his head. About the same time the Athenian Hippokleides lost his chance of marrying the daughter of the Sikyonian tyrant Kleisthenes (Herodotus iv, 129) by calling for a table and standing on his head and waving his legs. Much later we know of dancing dwarfs who stood on their heads.

Unpublished.
Corinthian vase: Athens 3444; Payne, *Necrocorinthia*, no. 1004; Seeberg, *op. cit.*, no. 210; *Greek Chorus*, 20, 93.
Dancing dwarf: Beazley, *JHS* 59, 1939, 11.

I, 14

Palermo, from Selinunte.
Attic black-figured lekythos by the Athena Painter; 490–480 B.C.

Bearded flute-player in long chiton. Two men riding dolphins. They wear helmets, breastplates, greaves, large himatia, and carry spears. Another lekythos from the same workshop in the Kerameikos Museum in Athens is identical except that the flute-player, who is beardless, is between the dolphin-riders and they converge on him. A contemporary cup in the Louvre CA 1924 'by the Theseus Painter or near him' (Beazley) has a similar flute-player and eight similarly armed dolphin-riders but they do not have cloaks. These three vases and the Boston skyphos (I, 11) are so nearly contemporary that they may represent the same performance: the painter of the Louvre cup omitted the cloaks and the painter of the Boston skyphos emphasized them.

The performance is more likely to have been a pre-comic chorus like the Titans, Knights, and Cocks already discussed than a dithyramb in which the chorus described dolphin-riders, as has been suggested. The known dolphin-riders, such as the lyric poet Arion and Phalanthos, the hero-founder of Taras, do not seem relevant. These may perhaps be Attic Knights who have taken to dolphins for a naval expedition. For fish-riders in later Attic comedy see on iv, 5, below.

Arch. Reports, 1966–7, 40, fig. 19.
Lekythos in Athens and kylix in Louvre: F. Brommer, *AA*, 1942, 70; Beazley, *ARV²*, 1622; Webster, *Greek Chorus*, 20, 93

I,15 (Cambridge, Mass., Schimmel coll.). Dolphin-riders

I,16 (New York). Flute-player and satyrs

these dolphin riders have shields which none of the others have. Probably then the vase celebrates an earlier performance; the later performance repeated the disguise but there is no reason to suppose that the chorus sang the same song.

*ARV*², 1622; H. Hoffmann, *Norbert Schimmel Collection*, 1964, no. 25; G. M. Sifakis, *BICS* 14, 1967, 36; Webster, *Greek Chorus*, 20, 93.

I, 15

Cambridge (Mass.), Norbert Schimmel coll.
Attic red-figured psykter by Oltos; 520–510 B.C.

Six dolphin riders wearing helmets, breastplates, and short chitons, carrying single spears. Each rider has the inscription ΕΠΙΔΕΛΦΙΝΟΣ (on a dolphin) coming from his mouth. Prof. G. M. Sifakis has brilliantly interpreted this as the words of their song. The words fit very well into anapaestic dimeters, which is one of the two obvious rhythms for a choral entry, a marching rhythm as distinct from running trochaics. The stem of the psykter, as Prof. Sifakis notes, sits in water so that the dolphins would appear to swim; the addition of the flute-player would have disturbed this illusion. More than ten years separate this vase from those already described, and

I, 16

New York 25.78.66.
Attic red-figured bell-krater by Polion; 425 B.C.

Three men, dressed and masked as old satyrs, playing kitharai (concert lyres) and singing, as they advance towards a flute-player, who wears an ivy-wreath and a long, sleeved chiton, and has lowered his flutes. Costume and masks are those of Papposilenos in the satyr-play (cf. II, 1). Both the walking

I, 17 (Copenhagen). Poet, flute-player and chorus

step of the first two satyrs and the prancing step of the third can be traced back on earlier vases of satyrs with lyres (cf. I, 18). The inscription calls them 'singers (victorious at) the Panathenaia'. A contest of dithyrambs was part of the Panathenaic festival, and satyr costume and ivy-wreath suggest Dionysos, in whose honour the dithyramb was sung.

In a song by Pratinas, which Wilamowitz believed to be a dithyramb, a satyr-chorus criticize their flute-player for trying to dominate their song, the primacy of which they reassert. W. Schmid thought our vase illustrated Pratinas' chorus. This was difficult to believe when some fifty years separated the poet from the vase, but Professor Lloyd-Jones has recently suggested that there was a later Pratinas, a lyric poet of the late fifth century, to whom the song is better ascribed. As has been suggested for the Dolphin-Riders and as can be proved for the Knights, a chorus wearing a traditional disguise may sing a new song.

Schmid-Stählin, *Geschichte der gr. Lit.*, I, 2, 179 n. 2; Bieber, *History*[2], fig. 17; *ARV*[2], 1172; Beazley, *Hesperia*, 24, 1955, 314; Pickard-Cambridge, *Dithyramb*[2], 20, 34, no. 1; Webster, *Greek Chorus*, 28, no. 244, fig. 9.
Pratinas: text, Pickard-Cambridge, *op. cit.*, 17, 292; H. Lloyd-Jones, *Fondación Pastor*, Madrid, no. 13, 18.

I, 17

Copenhagen 13817.
Attic red-figured bell-krater by the Kleophon Painter; *c.* 425 B.C.

Five men wearing long chitons and wrapped in large himatia sing to the accompaniment of a flute-player wearing sleeved chiton and himation; his flutes go into the *phorbeia*, which he wears round his cheeks. He stands beside a pole, which rises from a tripod base covered with ivy-leaves. All the men wear wreaths of ivy, and the two on the left carry sprigs of ivy. Their names are inscribed from left to right: Epinikos (?),

Pleistias, Phrynichos (frontal), Amphilochos (flute-player), Theomedes, Chremes. Pleistias and Theomedes are known from Attic inscriptions of similar date. Phrynichos is probably the comic poet of the late fifth century (comic poets did sometimes write dithyrambs). They are then poet, flute-player, and chorus, and the wealth of ivy suggests that they are singing a dithyramb. This dithyramb was clearly a stately song like the preserved dithyrambs of Pindar and Bacchylides, and essentially different in metre and dance from the supposed dithyramb of Pratinas discussed in I, 16. Costume and postures are closely paralleled on a fourth-century relief which celebrates a dithyrambic victory at the Panathenaia. Dithyrambs were produced at the City Dionysia in late March and at the Panathenaia in July; it has been argued that the ivy-pole here and the spring-flowers quoted in a Pindaric dithyramb (fr. 63 Bowra, 75 Snell) imply an earlier festival, the Anthesteria in late February, although the dithyramb is not recorded for it and the City Dionysia is connected with spring by Aristophanes (*Clouds*, 307 and *Peace*, 800).

K. Friis Johansen, *Arkaeol. Kunsthist. Medd. Dan. Vid. Selsk.* 4, no. 2, 1959; *CVA* 8, pls. 347–9; *ARV*[2], 1145, no. 35; Pickard-Cambridge, *Dithyramb*[2], 35, 37, 65 n. 1, no. 4 and *Festivals*[2], fig. 15; A. Rumpf, *Bonner Jahrbücher*, 161, 1961, 212; Webster, *Greek Chorus*, 29, 32, 133, 193, fig. 11.
Fourth-century relief: Athens, Acropolis Museum 1338.

I, 18

Taranto 6250, from Satyrion.
Attic black-figured lekythos by the Gela Painter; 490–480 B.C.

Choruses of satyrs with lyres can be traced back long before Polion (I, 16). On a lekythos of about 490 B.C. in the British Museum five shaggy old satyrs with small lyres walk round the vase; on a neck amphora of 530–520 B.C. three satyrs in the prime of life play concert-lyres (*kitharai*); the first prances, the other two walk. The lekythos illustrated here also has

I, 18 (Taranto). Satyrs with lyres

three satyrs in the prime of life, one walking, one prancing, one bringing his left foot down. Thus Polion's chorus, its lyres, and its steps are in a tradition which can be traced back for about a century. But on our slight evidence *old* satyrs seem to be an innovation about 490 B.C. The lekythos illustrated alone adds some scenery; the satyrs start from a Herm, pass a block, and approach a flaming altar. Herms were square pillars with a head of Hermes and genitals on them. The best known were in the Agora on the North side. This may give a location for this chorus. Xenophon, in the fourth century, recommends that the Knights should start from the Herms and ride round the Agora, doing honour to all the statues and shrines of the gods, before they return to the Herms; and he gives as a parallel the fact that at the Dionysia the choruses dance in honour of other gods and the Twelve. The Gela Painter may have indicated three points on the route of a processional chorus in the Agora: the Herms, the altar of the Twelve Gods (in the centre of the Agora), and the block may be the round altar of Hestia in the Council House. This is, of course, conjecture; but the Herm gives a fairly reliable pointer to the Agora.

F. G. Lo Porto, *NSc*, 1964, 269, fig. 86.
Lekythos in the British Museum, B 560: *ABV* 495, no. 158; Pickard-Cambridge, *Dithyramb*[2], 20, no. 2; Webster, *Greek Chorus*, 20, 93.
Neck-amphora: *ABV* 285, no. 1.
Xenophon, *Hipparchicus*, III, 2 = R. E. Wycherley, *The Athenian Agora*, iii, no. 203.

I, 19

New York 27.74.
Attic red-figured kylix by the Briseis Painter; 480–470 B.C.

On both sides, four boys wrapped in cloaks singing to a flute-player in front of a row of columns. The flute-players wear long, sleeved chitons. The boys in dress and posture recall the dithyramb-singers of the Copenhagen krater (I, 17). Some wear shoes, some have bare feet (the Copenhagen singers are all bare-footed). Inside the cup, a young man in similar clothes with a trainer or judge's wand, looking at a wooden framework with holes in the bars and chips on top of them, probably a device for checking on the number of the chorus present. Rehearsal for a tragedy or rehearsal of a chorus of

I, 19 (New York). Flute-player and chorus of Boys

Boys for the dithyramb has been suggested. If the painter wanted to suggest tragedy, he would surely have given the boys sleeved chitons and masks, and the small number of tragic choreuts (12 at this date) hardly needed such an elaborate control. But the two sides of the cup are perhaps best interpreted as two rival choruses of boys at the dithyrambic competition either at the Panathenaia or at the Dionysia. The row of columns suggests a Stoa, and the Stoa of the Herms in the Agora, the first Stoa in Athens, was erected in time to receive the Herms dedicated by Kimon after the victory at Eion in 476/475 B.C., so that it may have been very new when this cup was painted.

ARV², 407, no. 18; M. Bieber, *AJA* 45, 1941, 529; *History²*, 20, figs. 60–61; Webster, *MTSP²* 44, AV 5; *Greek Chorus*, 22, 93.
Stoa of the Herms: R. E. Wycherley, *The Athenian Agora*, iii, 104; the Stoa is now attested by an inscription published in *BCH* 86, 1962, 640.

I, 20

Oxford G 263 (305).
Attic red-figured kylix by the Painter of Louvre G 265; 480–470 B.C.

The painter belongs to the same group of late-archaic cup-painters as the Briseis Painter, who painted I, 19. Two boys, in clothing and posture like the boys on I, 19, with a bearded flute-player in long-sleeved chiton at an altar in front of a Herm. Above the herm hangs a votive tablet with the silhouette of a runner. This must be a similar chorus of Boys. The setting recalls the satyr chorus on I, 18, but this chorus has arrived back at the Herms. The votive tablet may be a dedication for success in the Panathenaic games, which at this time took place in the Agora.

ARV², 416, no. 3; *CVA*, Oxford 1, pl. 7, 1; Webster, *Greek Chorus*, 22, no. 192, fig. 7.

I, 20 (Oxford). Flute-player and chorus of Boys

II, 1 (Naples). Pronomos krater – cast of satyr-play

II, 2 (Sydney). Chorusmen of a satyr-play

II. SATYR-PLAYS

II, 1

Naples 3240 (inv. 81673), from Ruvo.
Attic red-figured volute-krater by the Pronomos Painter;
400 B.C.

In the centre Dionysos reclines in a bower represented by the vine with grape-clusters to the left. The scene is marked as the sanctuary of Dionysos by the two tripods at the sides. Ariadne sits beside Dionysos, and at the end of the couch, separated by the winged Himeros (desire), a woman in tragic costume holding a white female mask with long black hair and a Persian tiara. Beyond her, an actor who played Herakles: he wears metal breastplate, quiver, sleeved short chiton, high boots; he carries a club; the lionskin can be seen below his left arm; its head surmounts the yellow-white mask with shortish hair and beard which he carries in his right hand. Next to him an actor who played Papposilenos in flocked tights with bare feet (cf. I, 16); a panther skin hangs over his left shoulder, he holds a stick in his left hand and a wrinkled mask with white hair and beard and a wreath of ivy leaves. On the other side of Dionysos an actor in sleeved long chiton, himation, high boots, holding a yellow-white mask with tiara, black hair and beard. Satyr-play, like tragedy, was performed in honour of Dionysos, whose presence is thus explained. Three actors only took part, as in tragedy: the costume and mask of the girl are therefore given to the woman (a maenad?) sitting at the end of Dionysos' couch. The story of this satyr-play is probably, as the tiaras suggest, the rescue of Hesione, daughter of Laomedon, from the sea-monster by Herakles.

The actors are not named. Of the other fourteen human figures, poet, flute-player, lyre-player, and chorus, all except two are named (like the participants in the Copenhagen dithyramb, I, 17). The vase must have been painted for celebration of a victory in a satyr-play. When the tragic poet Agathon celebrated his first victory at the City Dionysia in 416 B.C., Plato describes it as 'when he and his chorusmen made a sacrifice' (*Symp.* 173a): the actors are not included. This must have been a similar occasion; we do not know how the vase found its way to Ruvo in S. Italy, not far from Taranto (Taras), which was a great theatrical centre. The flute-player Pronomos is known from inscriptions. The poet Demetrios may be the comic poet of that name (it would seem that sometimes the satyr-play was not written by the poet who wrote the tragedies, but by a separate author).

The flute-player in sleeved chiton and himation sits in the position of honour immediately below Dionysos. The lyre-player takes his leave because with the arrival of Pronomos the rehearsals are over and the performance is on. This is represented by the chorusman Nikoleos, who dances in his mask. The poet sits back and watches with his text rolled up in his left hand, and his lyre behind him. The other chorusmen stand or sit about, all except one holding a mask of the same kind as the dancing satyr, Nikoleos. The satyr masks are red and have dark hair. All the chorusmen wear a shaggy loin-cloth with phallos in front and tail behind, except Eunikos on the top at the left, whose loin-cloth is smooth and decorated with a rosette, and the one standing to the right of the tripod on the right. He wears short decorated chiton and himation: either he has not yet shed his ordinary clothes or this is the special costume of a leader.

Nikoleos alone dances, left leg and left arm raised, right hand on hip. The posture is repeated on a slightly earlier Attic vase (*MTSP²*, AV 29) and on several vases representing the Prometheus story (cf. on II, 4).

On the back of the Pronomos krater Dionysos holding a lyre is led by Ariadne holding a torch, while satyrs and maenads dance round them. The three satyrs are in dance attitudes, which recur on the Prometheus vases (II, 4) and on the Pandora vases (II, 7 etc.).

ARV², 1336; Bieber, *History²*, figs. 31–3; Pickard-Cambridge, *Dithyramb²*, no. 85, fig. 49; Webster, *GTP* 40, no. A 9; *MTSP²*, AV 25; *Greek Chorus*, 30; Brommer, *Satyrspiele²*, no. 4, and *AA*, 1964, 110; Arias-Hirmer, fig. 218; Metzger, *Imagerie*, pl. 34; Immerwahr, *Studies in Honor of B. L. Ullman* (1964), 35; *La Grèce classique*, figs. 314–15 (colour); Mingazzini, *Greek Pottery Painting*, fig. 57 (colour).

II, 2

Sydney 47.05.
Apulian bell-krater by the Tarporley Painter; 400–380 B.C.

Three chorusmen for a satyr-play. They wear decorated loin-cloths to support phallos and tail (cf. on II, 1). The two on the left hold their masks; the one on the right wears his mask and has adopted a dance position, which can be paralleled on the *Prometheus Pyrkaeus* vases (cf. on II, 4). A tambourine lies on the floor behind him.

Cambitoglou and Trendall, *APS* 32; Pickard-Cambridge, *Dithyramb²*, no. 89; Webster, *GTP*, A 27; *MTSP²*, TV 18; *Greek Chorus*, 31; Brommer, *Satyrspiele²*, 15, fig. 7; Koller, *Musik und Dichtung*, fig. 14.

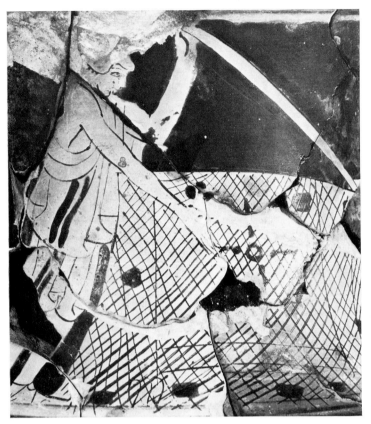

II, 3 (Princeton, Clairmont coll.). Aeschylus, *Diktyoulkoi*

II,4 (Oxford). Aeschylus, *Prometheus Pyrkaeus*

II, 3

Princeton (N.J.), C. Clairmont coll.
Attic red-figured pyxis by the Wedding Painter; *c.* 450 B.C.

There are two groups of three figures – A: three men in short chitons and furry hats round a chest covered by a fishing net: one still holds the rope, which has pulled it ashore, one raises a hand in astonishment, one lifts the lid; B: a young man in a short chiton, holding a furry hat in his left hand points the way to a woman and a small boy. Aeschylus' *Diktyoulkoi* told the story: Danae and the infant Perseus had been put to sea in a chest by her father Akrisios, King of Argos, who feared an oracle prophesying death at the hands of his grandson. The play opens with the fisherman Diktys and another sighting the chest washed up on the shores of Seriphos (the *ekkyklema* must have been used for this). They summon the inhabitants to help, and Papposilenos and the satyr-chorus arrive. The vase shows two moments – A: the chest is pulled ashore and Diktys opens the lid; B: Diktys leads Danae and Perseus off (perhaps this was the end of the play).

C. Clairmont, *AJA* 57, 1953, pls. 50–2; *ARV*², 924, no. 35; *MTSP*², 139.
Ekkyklema: *GTP* 18.
Text: H. Lloyd-Jones, Loeb Classical Library, Aeschylus, II², 531.

II, 4

Oxford 1937.983.
Attic red-figured kalyx-krater by the Dinos Painter; 425–420 B.C.

The upper picture is the labours of Theseus; the lower the satyrs lighting their torches from the fire stolen by Prometheus in a long fennel stalk. Aeschylus produced the *Prometheus Pyrkaeus* (fire-lighter) in 472 B.C. as the satyr-play to the trilogy which included the *Persians*. A papyrus fragment gives the satyr-chorus singing in gratitude for the gift of fire; it must come very soon after the scene depicted on the Oxford vase. A fragment, also in Oxford, of a red-figured bell-krater of about 440 B.C. ties the scene to the stage because the satyr wears a loin-cloth. About fifteen vases (including two Lucanian) are known with this scene; they start about 440 B.C. and most of them were painted in the next fifteen years or so. Perhaps we should suppose that Aeschylus' satyr-play was revived after his death.

The satyrs are named from left to right Komos, Sikinnis, Simos. Their postures are repeated on other Prometheus vases. The stage-satyr on the Oxford fragment has a fourth posture: legs like Nikoleos on the Pronomos vase but both arms raised. These four postures (and variations of them) must have been well known and easily recognized steps in satyr-dances because they recur again and again in pictures inspired by the satyr-play.

The following list gives the examples of each posture illustrated in this selection:

(1) Komos. No. 14, right; no. 13, left.
(2) Sikinnis. No. 7, middle of right trio; no. 14, second from left.
(3) Simos. No. 1, back, top left; no. 7, right of centre; no. 9, right hand pair.
(4) Oxford fragment: no. 1 (variant), no. 1 back, bottom pair; no. 7; left pair, and extreme right; no. 9, left; no. 11, variant: no. 14, left and second from right; no. 13, right (variant).

The Sydney satyr (2) is not so common but recurs on two of the Attic *Prometheus* vases, the lekanis in Berlin and the fragment in Syracuse.

*ARV*², 1153, no. 13; Beazley, *AJA* 43, 1939, 618 ff.; 44, 1940, 212; Brommer, *Satyrspiele*², nos. 9, 187–99; Webster, *MTSP*², AV 22, and p. 144; *Greek Chorus*, 28, 118 f.
Text: Loeb Classical Library, Aeschylus, II², 562.

II, 5 (Naples). Aeschylus, *Sphinx Satyrike* (?)   II, 6 (Boston). Sophocles, *Inachos* (?)

II, 5

Naples 2846 (inv. 81417).
Paestan bell-krater by Python; third quarter fourth century B.C.

The sphinx is shown perched upon an ornamental rock, decorated with black and white spots on a background of golden-brown wash to represent a volcanic breccia; she looks down calmly at the papposilen standing before her and holding up a bird in his right hand. He is an actor dressed for the rôle, wearing flocked tights over which is a dappled fawn-skin and a small piece of red drapery, patterned with white dots, in front of his thighs and over his left arm. In front of the rock a small snake rises up hissing, its forked tongue sticking out at the papposilen.

The scene is probably based upon some comic version of the Oedipus legend (for a caricature of it cf. the oenochoe Boston 01.8036, *PhV*², no. 200; and for a phlyax version the oenochoe in the Ragusa coll. IV, 32) and may possibly have been inspired by the *Sphinx Satyrike* of Aeschylus, the satyr-play which completed the Theban trilogy. On our vase the papposilen holds up a bird (cf. the Paestan bell-kraters, also by Python, in Mannheim and Dundee; *PP Supp*, nos. 153–4), which suggests an analogy with the fable of Aesop (no. 55) in which a man, desiring to confound Apollo, visited his oracle with a live bird concealed beneath his cloak and asked the god to declare whether the bird he held was alive or dead, intending to throttle it if Apollo gave the former answer, or leave it alive, if the latter. A similar episode relating to the Sphinx seems to be represented here; she perhaps failed, unlike Apollo, to perceive the trap, and if she gave a wrong answer, this could have provided a suitably comic ending.

Watzinger, FR iii, 373, pl. 180, 2; Robert, *Oidipus*, i, 259, fig. 45; Séchan, 583; Trendall, *PP* 68, pl. 21*a* and *PP Supp*. no. 155; Brommer, *Satyrspiele*², no. 178, fig. 47; Bieber, *History*², fig. 37; Webster, *GTP*, no. A 40; *MTSP*², 83, PV 4.

II, 6

Boston 00.366.
Lucanian oinochoe by the Pisticci Painter, 440–430 B.C.

Hermes with drawn sword moves to attack Argos, who is driving off Io in the guise of a cow with human head but horns. It is possible that this picture is inspired by the lost Sophoclean *Inachos* and therefore gives a bottom date for the play, which was probably a satyr-play. The play told of Zeus' love for Io, the daughter of Inachos, King of Argos. She was changed into a cow to avoid the jealousy of Hera, but Hera sent the many-eyed Argos to guard the cow. Argos was then killed by Hermes. The further wanderings of Io to Egypt fell outside the play. A papyrus gives a messenger-speech describing the transformation of Io with horns and hooves that beat on the loom-bench. Io must have been seen after this since we have another fragment in which Hermes in a cap of darkness beguiles Argos. In Aeschylus' *Prometheus Vinctus* Io appeared as a woman with cow's horns on her forhead (cf. the new skyphos from Pisticci, Metaponto 20150; *Arch Reps* 1969–70, 39, fig. 13). Sophocles' *Io* must have appeared more radically changed, as she does on the Boston vase (cf. Aristophanes, *Birds*, 100 f.).

LCS 16, no. 9; *MTSP*², 149.
Text: *P.Oxy.* 2369; D. L. Page, Loeb Classical Library, *Greek Literary Papyri*, I, no. 6; Webster, *Sophocles*², 16, 191.

II, 7

Ferrara T.579.
Attic red-figured volute-krater by the Painter of Bologna 279; 450 B.C.

Sophocles wrote a satyr-play called *Pandora or Hammerers*. Two interpretations are possible: (1) the Hammerers were craftsmen who made the robot Pandora; (2) the Hammerers hammered on the ground to release the earth-goddess Pandora. If the second interpretation is right, the following four vases may be relevant, but the tradition of hammerers releasing an earth-goddess goes back before the time of Sophocles and without an inscription it is impossible to say who the earth-goddess is.

The neck of the Ferrara krater is certainly inspired by a satyr-play, as is shown by the flute-player in formal robes on the left. The man in ordinary himation, who watches on the right, may be the choregos (the rich man who produced the play) or the poet. The little boy is perhaps his son, joining in the fun. The satyr-chorus dances excitedly (for the steps see on II, 4). In the centre the earth-goddess rises: she has an elaborate crown and holds a sceptre. The *ekkyklema* must have been used for this appearance (cf. II, 3). Behind her, a man wearing chiton and another garment over it; he has a laurel wreath in his hair and a long torch in each hand. Two sets of names have been given to the central figures: Persephone and the priest of Eleusis, or Pandora and Epimetheus. The first interpretation may well be right. The very elaborate crown might be a point in favour of Pandora: in Hesiod's account of her making she is given a very special wreath (*Theogony*, 578 ff.). Nothing distinguishes the man as Epimetheus, but the torches might mark him as Prometheus and his overgarment may be a smith's smock; his stern glance at the joyful satyrs would then be a glance of disapproval.

Beazley, *ARV²*, 612, no. 1, and *Hesperia*, 24, 1955, 311, pl. 46; Buschor, *Feldmäuse*, 19, fig. 7; Brommer, *Satyrspiele²*, no. 15, fig. 49; *CVA*, Ferrara 1, pls. 9–10; Webster, *MTSP²*, AV 18, and p. 150; *Greek Chorus*, 24 and 134.
On early hammerers see: Buschor, *op. cit.*, 10, fig. 5; Metzger, *Imagerie*, 12, pl. 3 (Athena Painter, *c*. 490–480 B.C.); *MTSP*, AV 3 (Eucharides Painter, *c*. 480 B.C.).
On the subject in general see: M. Guarducci, 'Pandora e i Martellatori', in *Mon Ant* 33, 1929, 5–38.

II, 8

Oxford G 275 (V525).
Attic red-figured volute-krater; *c*. 450 B.C.

Here the inscriptions – Zeus, Hermes, Epimetheus, Pandora – fix the identity of the figures. Pandora rises from the ground; like the goddess on II, 7, she has her himation over the back of her head and an elaborate crown (but of different design). Epimetheus, wearing a wreath rendered in red-paint (perhaps a laurel-wreath like the figure behind the goddess on II, 7), has released her from the ground with his hammer. If, therefore, this vase is connected with Sophocles' *Pandora or Hammerers*, he must have been in some sense the leader of the hammering satyrs: he may have summoned them to help him, as in Aeschylus' *Diktyoulkoi* the satyrs arrived to Diktys' summons (see on II, 3). Zeus sends Hermes to Pandora with a flower; Eros flies to Epimetheus carrying a fillet. This implies that Epimetheus will marry Pandora (in spite of the warnings of Prometheus).

CVA, Oxford 1, pls. 21–2; *ARV²*, 1562; *MTSP²*, 150.

II, 9

Stockholm, National Museum 6.
Attic red-figured bell-krater, Group of Polygnotos; *c*. 450–440 B.C.

Three satyrs dancing, two with hammers (on their postures, see on II, 4). A goddess rises from the ground in front of a tree. She does not wear a crown, and her drapery and gestures show no connection with II, 7 and 8. The tree also is new. The extremely wintry look of the tree suggests that in this story there was great emphasis on the barrenness of the land, possibly then the rising of Persephone, but this is quite uncertain as the tree recurs again on II, 10 and there the goddess wears a crown like Pandora.

ARV², 1053, no. 40 (recalls the Peleus Painter); Buschor, *Feldmäuse*, 27; Brommer, *Satyrspiele²*, no. 16; Langlotz, *Die Antike* 6, 1930, p. 7, fig. 6.

II, 10

Matera 9975.
Early Lucanian bell-krater by the Pisticci Painter; *c*. 440 B.C.

The scene on this vase resembles that on the Stockholm krater (II, 9), but shows only a single satyr who grasps a large hammer firmly with both hands, in an attitude clearly indicating that he has been using it to beat the ground. In the centre is a wintry tree, and to right a goddess, wearing a crown as in II, 7 and 8, and almost completely emerged from the earth. She extends both arms towards the satyr, in a gesture as if to entreat him to cease his hammering. There can be little doubt that this vase, like II, 7 and 9, is connected with a satyr-play, and it is interesting to note such an association with the stage on one of the first red-figured vases to be made by a Greek in South Italy. The resemblance between the crown here and that on the Oxford krater (II, 8) points in favour of the

II, 7 (Ferrara). Sophocles, *Pandora*

II, 8 (Oxford). Sophocles, *Pandora* (?)

II, 9 (Stockholm). Sophocles, *Pandora* (?)

II, 10 (Matera). Sophocles, *Pandora* (?)

II, 11 (London). Euripides, *Cyclops*

identification of the goddess as Pandora and a connection between this vase and the satyr-play by Sophocles.

BdA 28, 1934, 436, fig. 1; Brommer, *Satyrspiele*[2] no. 17; Trendall, *LCS* 14, no. 1, pl. 1, 1; Webster, *MTSP*[2], 151.

II, 11

British Museum 1947. 7–14. 8.
Early Lucanian kalyx-krater by the Cyclops Painter; *c.* 415–410 B.C.

This vase is of particular interest since it seems to have been directly inspired by the *Cyclops* of Euripides. It is unfortunate that this play cannot be precisely dated; it has been placed variously between 438 and 408 B.C. and, on linguistic grounds, a comparatively late date appears most likely. In that case there can have been only a very short interval between the production of the play and the appearance of the vase, which can hardly be dated later than, if indeed as late as, 410 B.C.
In the centre lies the drunken Polyphemus, in the typical attitude of the sleeper with one arm flung around his head; beside him stands the cup, and next to it, suspended from a lopped branch of a small tree, the almost empty wine-skin (cf. III. 6, 2), the contents of which have reduced him to his present state. Above, three followers of Odysseus, under the direction of the hero himself, bring up the sharpened tree-trunk, heated in the fire, with which they intend to bore out the single eye of the sleeping Cyclops. To the left are two more of his companions, and to right two satyrs, who connect the scene with the play. One clasps his hands together, and draws up his left leg in a pose reminiscent of a satyr-dance, the other runs up with outstretched arms, both obviously in eager expectation of the event about to take place, in which, however, they are reluctant to play a more active rôle than giving encouragement to the followers of Odysseus in an excited little song (*Cyclops*, 647 ff.).
The grouping of the figures shows the painter's interest in the rendering of spatial depth.

Trendall, *LCS* 27, no. 85 (with bibliography), pl. 8, 1; D. E. Strong, *The Classical World*, p. 89, colour-plate 59; Brommer, *Satyrspiele*[2],
19–21, figs, 11–12, no. 98; Webster, *MTSP*[2], 157; Touchefeu-Meynier, *Thèmes odysséens dans l'art antique*, 20, no. 13, pl. 4, 1; W. Jobst, *Die Höhle im griechischen Theater*, fig. 16.
On the dating of the *Cyclops* see in particular: J. Duchemin, *Le Cyclope*, pp. vii ff.; E. Delabecque, *Euripide et la guerre du Péloponnèse*, 165 ff.; A. M. Dale, *Wiener Studien*, 69, 1956, 106 (= *Collected Papers*, 129); Webster, *Greek Chorus*, 179–80.

II, 12

Parma, National Museum of Antiquities, C 100.
Etruscan red-figured kalyx-krater by the Sommavilla Painter; early fourth century B.C.

In the centre of the main scene is the radiate disk of the sun, on which, against a black background, appears the bust of Helios, seen as a youth with profile head and frontal chest. Around are five young satyrs in attitudes expressive of fear or amazement. Beazley (*EVP* 38) has plausibly associated the picture with a lost Attic satyr-play, which might have had the title *Helios* and been based either upon an eclipse of the sun or upon Helios as 'the all-seeing detector of wrong-doers'. The black background on the sun's disk favours the first interpretation, in which case the satyrs are expressing their amazement and shading their eyes from the dazzling rays of the restored sun; if the latter is correct, then they may be expressing guilt or fear, and trying to shield themselves from the sun-god's penetrating gaze. The reverse shows the Sphinx, also with a nimbus, between two youths, one fleeing in alarm, the other, probably Oedipus, looking quietly on.
There is a companion vase to this (Parma C 101), the reverse of which shows a sphinx in the company of two satyrs, one holding lyre and plectrum, the other dancing, and which is perhaps to be related to a satyr-play dealing with the sphinx (cf. II, 5); it certainly indicates that the Etruscan artist had an unusual interest in this type of dramatic performance.
The two vases, both from Sommavilla Sabina, are based on Attic originals of about 420 B.C. and are probably to be dated early in the fourth century.

Schauenburg, *Helios*, 11 ff. (with full bibliography on p. 48, note 11); Albizzati, *Mél. Arch.* 37, 1918–19, 168, fig. 24; Beazley, *EVP* 37–9; Brommer, *Satyrspiele*[2], no. 172; Bloch, *Etruscan Art*, pl. 70 (colour); *MTSP*[2], 169; *CVA* 2, IV B, pls. 1–3.

II, 12 (Parma). (*a*) Lost satyr-play (*Helios*?), (*b*) Oedipus and the Sphinx.

II,13 (Milan, Moretti coll.). Lost satyr-play (*Atlas*?)

II,14 (Taranto). Lost satyr-play (*Perseus*?)

II, 13

Milan, Moretti coll.
Apulian bell-krater; *c.* 380 B.C.

Atlas has gone to fetch the golden apples of the Hesperides for Herakles, who meantime has agreed to support the world in his place. He is shown in the centre of the picture, standing on rocky-ground, his lion-skin knotted in front of his chest and hanging down his back, with both hands upraised to support his globe. While he is thus occupied two satyrs have crept up, one has taken his bow and quiver, and the other his club; the latter dances off with a mocking gesture of farewell to Herakles, whose anguish at being unable to prevent the theft of his equipment is clearly expressed in his face.

The scene is probably taken from a lost satyr-play, perhaps entitled *Atlas*. The vase is of particular interest, since the other side (IV, 18) shows a scene from a phlyax play.

*PhV*², 38, no. 45, pl. 2b; *MTSP*², 169; Bieber, *History*², fig. 14.

II, 14

Taranto 124007.
Fragment of an early Apulian kalyx-krater; *c.* 380–370 B.C.

The theme of Perseus terrifying the satyrs with the head of the
Gorgon is not uncommon in South Italian vase-painting in
the first half of the fourth century B.C. and must look back to
a now lost satyr-play. In its simplest form we are shown
Perseus holding up the gorgoneion, while a satyr hides his
face from it (e.g. Bonn 79; Schauenburg, *Perseus*, pl. 34, 1);
in another version Athena reflects the gorgoneion in a pool
or well for Perseus, and the satyr averts his gaze (e.g. Leipzig
T 83, Brommer, *Satyrspiele*[2], fig. 24; Basel, H. A. Cahn coll.
203). Our vase, like the reverses of the Karneia krater (Taranto

8263; *LCS* 55, no. 280, where bibliography, pl. 24, 1–2) and
of the Bonn nestoris (*LCS* 113, no. 584, where bibliography,
pl. 59, 2), shows a fuller version of the scene with Perseus
holding up the gorgon's head with one hand and the satchel
in the other, with three or more satyrs in various attitudes of
surprise or terror grouped around, and here and on the Bonn
vase with Athena as well. The general similarity of treatment
suggests that all three look back to a common original, probably of the late fifth century, since the Karneia krater must be
dated *c.* 400 B.C. The Taranto fragment is a generation later
and is near in style to the Painter of Naples 3231.

Arch Reps, 1967, 42, fig. 12.
On Perseus and satyrs see Brommer, *Satyrspiele*[2], 32 ff., nos. 37–43;
Schauenburg, *Perseus*, 97 ff.; *MTSP*[2], 169–70.

Detail from II, 8

III.1, 1 (Berlin). Aeschylus, *Choephoroi*

III. TRAGEDY

1. Aeschylus

Choephoroi

III. 1, 1

Berlin, Staatliche Museen, Terr. Inv. 6803.
Terracotta relief from Melos; 450–440 B.C.

These terracotta reliefs from the island of Melos are flat plaques, probably meant for decorating wooden boxes and chests (or for hanging on walls). They were originally painted. Most of them have mythological scenes (cf. III. 1, 20). Here Orestes and Pylades wearing travelling hats (*pilos*) sit beside Agamemnon's tomb. Elektra stands on the step with her left hand to her head in lamentation; a hydria stands beside her. On earlier Melian reliefs the scheme is different; Elektra has her nurse beside her, Orestes and Pylades are attended by a servant, who holds their horses. The new scheme was probably inspired by the *Choephoroi*, the second play of the *Oresteia*, which Aeschylus produced in 458 B.C. The play opens with Orestes (with Pylades) praying to Hermes as he offers two locks of his hair on the tomb of Agamemnon. He sees women in black bringing libations (the hydria). They are the chorus and Elektra, who enter as the young men stand aside. The chorus instruct Elektra to pray for vengeance on the murderers of Agamemnon as she pours the libations sent by Clytemnestra. As she makes her prayer she sees the hair offered by Orestes and his footprints. The recognition of brother and sister follows. The artist here has carefully dis-

sociated Orestes and Pylades from Elektra, who is making her prayer.

P. Jacobsthal, *Die melischen Reliefs*, 1931, nos. 104–5. Contrast nos. 1, 2, 94. R. A. Higgins, *Greek Terracottas*, 69; *MTSP²*, 138.

III. 1, 2

Copenhagen, National Museum, Inv. 597.
Attic red-figured skyphos by the Penelope Painter; c. 440 B.C.

A: Two women at a tomb inscribed AGAMEM(non). The tomb has been decorated with a circlet of leaves high up, and low down by a dark fillet; a small jug, a wreath, and a spray have been placed on the steps. The woman on the left, wearing her himation as a veil, is going to tie a fillet round the shaft of the tomb. The woman on the right looks intensely at her and holds a basket of offerings. The painter has adapted an ordinary 'visit to a tomb' to this special scene by naming the tomb Agamemnon's. He thinks of Elektra and a member of the chorus. He has written KALO(s) against the woman on the right: *kalos*, 'beautiful', without a name attached refers to one of the figures in the scene; as it is masculine, the painter shows that he thinks of a chorusman performing a female part.
B. Two young men with spears, cloaks (*chlamys*) and large hats (*petasos*) watching. KALOS is written between them. They are Orestes and Pylades.

ARV², 1301, no. 5; *CVA* 8, pl. 351; *MTSP²*, 138.

III.1,2 (Copenhagen). Aeschylus, *Choephoroi*

41

III. 1, 3-6

3. Syracuse 36334.
Sicilian red-figured kalyx-krater by the Dirce Painter; *c.* 380–370 B.C.

4. Munich 3266.
Lucanian hydria by the Choephoroi Painter; *c.* 350 B.C.

5. Paris, Louvre K 544.
Lucanian pelike by the Choephoroi Painter; *c.* 350 B.C.

6. Boston 99.540.
Paestan neck-amphora by the Boston Orestes Painter; *c.* 330 B.C.

The meeting of Orestes and Elektra at the tomb of Agamemnon is a very popular subject with South Italian vase-painters throughout the fourth century B.C. The number of figures represented varies considerably, but the central group is fairly constant and generally shows Orestes, often with Pylades, and Elektra, who is seated beside the tomb-monument of Agamemnon, which takes the form of a stele or column on a stepped basis.

On the krater in Syracuse (no. 3) Elektra is seated on an altar in front of the monument, and behind her stands a woman holding a white fillet in her hand and carrying a large basket of offerings on top of her head. Although more strictly a canephoros rather than a choephoros, she is probably to be interpreted as a member of the chorus; her stance and detached look suggest that she is not playing an active rôle in the drama. To left is a youth wearing a petasos and holding a spear and a staff; he is Pylades, the companion of Orestes. Orestes himself stands on the right, sheathed sword hanging from a baldric by his side, staff in hand, talking to Elektra, who looks at him with slightly upturned head.

The Munich hydria (no. 4) presents a rather fuller version of the story, the depiction of which is almost a specialty of the artist who painted this vase: he repeats it with variations no fewer than seven times (cf. no. 5) and has, in consequence, been given the name of the Choephoroi Painter. Here Elektra is shown seated in the typical attitude of dejection on the steps of the grave-monument, on which are seen a variety of offerings to the departed – a hydria, a kalyx-krater, a tall lekythos, a fillet, an egg and a pomegranate. To the left is Orestes, who approaches with a spear in one hand and in the other a small oenochoe, from which he seems about to pour a libation onto the outstretched hand of Elektra. To the right stands a youth, wearing a petasos, resting his left hand upon a herald's staff (*kerykeion*) and holding up a wreath in his right. He is most probably meant to represent Hermes Psychopompos, to whom

III.1,5 (Paris). Aeschylus, *Choephoroi*

III.1,4 (Munich). Aeschylus, *Choephoroi*

III.1,3 (Syracuse). Aeschylus, *Choephoroi*

III.1,6 (Boston). Aeschylus, *Choephoroi*

Orestes addresses himself in the opening lines of the play and whose presence would have been indicated, at least in symbolic form, on the stage. Beneath the handle, to left, is a seated bearded man on a travel-pack, with a boy in attendance and to the right a woman with a cista seated on a chest, with a girl standing beside her. The bearded man, who is also present in a similar scene on a hydria by the same painter in Naples (2858; Séchan, fig. 27; *LCS* 120, no. 600, pl. 60, 3 with bibliography) can hardly be Pylades, since he appears elsewhere on that vase together with a regal, bearded figure in whom Webster plausibly sees the ghost of Agamemnon (*MTSP*[2], 81); he is possibly the paidagogos or an attendant of Orestes, just as the balancing figures must be attendants of Elektra.

The Louvre pelike (no. 5), which is also by the Choephoroi Painter, shows an abridgement of the scene on 4 with only Orestes and Elektra, and the figure of Hermes, almost identical with that on the preceeding vase, to the right.

An interesting variant on the theme appears on two Paestan vases, on which two Furies are shown in the background above the main scene. A prototype may be found on an amphora of the Asteas Group, formerly in the Fienga collection at Nocera (*PPSupp*, no. 133 bis), which shows a woman wearing a black tunic meeting a youth with offerings at a grave stele, and the busts of two women in the corners above; the two principal figures are probably Orestes and Elektra, but there is nothing to indicate the busts as those of Furies. On a fragmentary squat lekythos attributed to Asteas (*PAdd*, p. 3, no. A10; to which some more fragments have now been added), probably the companion piece to his lekythos with the purification of Orestes (III. 1, 12), the busts above are, as there, certainly Furies, since some letters of the inscriptions which identified them still survive – ΤΕ[ΙΣΙΦΟΝΗ] to right and [ΜΕΓΑ]ΙΡΑ to left. Elektra was wearing a black chiton and Orestes stood behind her, with another woman, perhaps a member of chorus, to left. On the Boston vase (III. 1, 6), which is by a later follower of Asteas, the two Furies appear above, presumably Megaira to left and Teisiphone, winged, to right as on the fragments, Elektra in a black chiton with a fillet and a hydria standing beside the Ionic monument, Orestes and Pylades to left.

For the treatment of the subject in general see Séchan, 86 ff.; Goldman, *HSCP* 21, 1910, 127 ff.; Trendall, *Studies Robinson* II, 114 ff.; Jacobsthal, *Die melischen Reliefs*, 16; Webster, *MTSP*[2], 138–9, where many of the other South Italian vases with this theme are listed; Guerrini, s.v. Oreste in *EAA* v, 741–3.

3. *LCS* 203, no. 206.

4. *LCS* 120, no. 603; *RM* 62, 1955, 128, pl. 48, 2 gives details of the seated figure below the l. handle.

5. *LCS* 120, no. 599.

6. *Paestan Pottery*, pl. 29; *PPSupp*, no. 351; *Greek Etruscan and Roman Art* (MFA, Boston), 150, fig. 129; *Trojan War in Greek Art* (MFA, Boston), fig. 43.

III. 1, 7

London, British Museum 1958. 2–14. 1.
Lucanian squat lekythos (top missing), by the Primato Painter; third quarter of the fourth century B.C.

The decoration consists of a tragic mask above a simple stage platform supported by posts or crossbeams; on the left is a tall stele, on the right a laurel tree grows beneath a hanging fillet. The mask is that of a woman with long hair, smooth brow, and a down-turned mouth, wearing a diadem with three spikes. The features strongly recall those of Elektra on the Louvre pelike (III. 1, 5), and the mask may well represent her, in which case the stele could stand for the tomb of Agamemnon and the laurel tree would be an allusion to Apollo and his oracle. The vase might have been a votive offering by the actor who played the part of Elektra and wished to record the fact in the briefest possible terms.

Webster, *BMQ* 29, 1959, 100–1, pl. 35; *MTSP*[2], 81–2, LV 3, pl. 5a; *LCS* 175, no. 1021.

III.1,7 (London). Aeschylus, *Choephoroi* (?)

III.1,8 (London). Aeschylus, *Eumenides*

III.1,9 (Perugia). Aeschylus, *Eumenides*

Eumenides

III. 1, 8

London, British Museum 1923. 10–16. 10.
Attic red-figured column-krater by the Orestes Painter; *c.* 440 B.C.

At the end of Aeschylus' *Choephoroi* Orestes rushes off the stage pursued by the Furies of his mother. At the beginning of the next play, *Eumenides*, the priestess comes at dawn to open the temple of Apollo at Delphi. When she has gone in, she immediately starts out again in horror. She has seen Orestes with drawn sword and a suppliant branch sitting on the omphalos with the Furies sitting round him asleep. When she retires, the *ekkyklema* rolls out to show this tableau. Apollo tells Orestes to fly to Athens, where he will be tried and Apollo will help him.

Four Attic vases, contemporary with the earliest Attic *Choephoroi* picture, show Orestes arriving at Delphi and Apollo interposing himself in front of the pursuing Furies. One vase, somewhat irrelevantly, adds Artemis because she is the sister of Apollo. Another adds Athena because she will preside over the court which will try Orestes. On the London vase Orestes with cloak (*chlamys*), hat (*petasos*), sword and two spears, takes refuge on an altar of rough-hewn stone. The painter thinks of the great stone altar built outside the temple of Apollo by the Chians after the Persian Wars, 479 B.C. Apollo raises his right hand to curse the Furies (*Eum.* 179 ff.). The single Fury is winged (unlike the priestess' description,

Eum. 51), has snakes in her hair, and wears a short chiton. She runs up pointing to Orestes, as the chorus do later in the play when they chase him to Athens (*Eum.* 257).

ARV², 1112, no. 5; *MTSP²*, 140 (with references to the other Attic vases).

III. 1, 9

Perugia, Museo Etrusco-Romano.
Attic red-figured pelike; *c.* 380–360 B.C.

Orestes kneels on the omphalos with a drawn sword in his right hand and the scabbard in his left. He looks back at a Fury on the left who runs up with a torch held in both hands. On the right a Fury dances up with a torch in her right hand. Both Furies wear peploi with long Attic overfall, and have snakes in their hair.

This is the first Attic vase to show Orestes seated on the omphalos (as in *Eum.* 42) instead of on the stone altar. (Earlier South Italian vases, show him seated *beside* the omphalos, and there is no reason to assume any common ancestor other than Aeschylus.) Secondly, this painter is unique in giving the Furies long peploi, instead of short chitons; he probably thinks of them as dancing like maenads, who habitually wear long skirts. When he draws them, he thinks rather of their dance round Orestes in Athens (*Eum.* 307 ff.) than their appearance in Delphi.

M. Bock, *AA*, 1938, 877; *MTSP²*, 140.

III.1,10 (Leningrad). Aeschylus, *Eumenides*

III. 1, 10

Leningrad St. 349.
Gnathia kalyx-krater by the Konnakis Painter; 360–350 B.C.

The painter has shown on the right the priestess flying from the temple holding the temple key in her left hand. Inside the temple, Orestes is seated beside the omphalos with drawn sword (as in *Eum.* 42) and *chlamys*. Five white-haired Furies in short chitons sleep round the steps (they do not sit, as in *Eum.* 47). The temple is a wooden Ionic building with pediment and palmette akroteria; the painter is thinking of the stage-building at Taras rather than of the marble temple at Delphi. The shield hung in the background is presumably thought of as a dedication to Apollo.

*MTSP*², GV 2 and pp. 129, 140; *BICS* 15, 1968, 5; Dyer, *JHS* 89, 1969, 53, pl. 5, fig. 7.

III. 1, 11

London, British Museum 1917. 12–10. 1.
Paestan bell-krater by Python; 350–340 B.C.

This vase gives one of the fullest representations of Orestes at Delphi. He is seen in the centre, kneeling before the omphalos, two spears resting against his left shoulder, the drawn sword still clutched in his right hand. His head is turned left to look up at Athena, who stands in full panoply, resting her left foot on a column-base and gazing at him with an air of compassion. Behind the omphalos rises the huge Delphic tripod and to right is Apollo himself, wearing a laurel wreath and resting one hand against a laurel-tree, from the branches of which hang fillets and two votive tablets. Beside him, somewhat squeezed into the picture, is a Fury, in hunting costume, her wings rising up behind her and a large snake in her left hand. Above the tripod is the bust of another Fury, snakes hissing in her hair and round her shoulders, looking down malevolently in the direction of Apollo, who turns to face the other Fury. In the corners above are the busts of a woman wearing a crown with a veil and of a youth with pilos and spear, probably Pylades. The former was once thought to be the spirit of Clytemnestra, but in the light of the similarly-garbed figure inscribed Leto on the newly-discovered squat lekythos in Paestum (III. 1, 12), it is preferable to regard her as the mother of Apollo.

Paestan Pottery, 61, pl. 17; *PPSupp*, no. 147; Bieber, *History*², fig. 97; *MTSP*², 141 (where a list of other vases with similar scenes is given).

III.1,11 (London). Aeschylus, *Eumenides*

III.1, 12 (Paestum). Aeschylus, *Eumenides*

III. 1, 12

Paestum 4794, from Contrada Gaudo, Tomb 2.
Paestan squat lekythos, by Asteas; *c.* 350–340 B.C.

The scene now changes to the purification of Orestes at Delphi, which would seem to have been carried out by Apollo with the blood of a pig (*Eum.* 283). Several Apulian vases illustrate this purification (Dyer, *JHS* 89, 1969, 51–2), but the fullest version appears on this recently-discovered Paestan squat lekythos which may be attributed to Asteas, and which identifies the various participants by inscriptions. In the centre, seated on an altar, in front of a column which stands for the temple of Apollo, is Orestes, drawn sword in hand, the pilos hanging down behind his neck. From the left Apollo approaches him, laurel-branch in one hand, white piglet in the other, to carry out the ritual of purification. Above are the busts of two Furies, identified by the inscriptions as Teisiphone and Megaira (cf. the fragmentary vase by Asteas with the meeting of Orestes and Elektra referred to above, p. 44). Both are represented with snakes entwined around their bodies and in their hair, and they wear red tunics patterned in white with rosettes and dotted stripes. To left stands a goddess, with sceptre, crown and veil; she is Leto (ΛΑΤΩ), mother of Apollo (cf. no. 11); to right are the figures of Artemis, his sister, in huntress garb with spear and bow, and a white hound at her feet, and of the priestess Manto (ΜΑΝΤΩ) with a filleted wreath in one hand and a phiale in the other.

It is worth noting that Aeschylus does not give names to either the Furies or the priestess. Teisiphone and Megaira are named for the first time on this vase and its companion piece; the third Fury, Allecto, is named on a hydria (III. 3, 46) by Asteas, who seems to have had a particular interest in them. Alexandrian scholarship often invented names for minor characters in plays who were otherwise anonymous, e.g. the daughter of Teiresias in the *Phoenissae* is called Manto, and much the same process seems to have been at work on these vases (cf. also Astyanassa on III. 3, 46).

Sestieri, 'Riflessi di drammi eschilei nella ceramica pestana', in *Dioniso*, 22, 1959, 40–51, figs. 3–5; Dyer, *loc. cit.*, pl. 4, fig. 6; Trendall, *PAdd*, 2, no. A 3; *Italy's Life* 26, 1961, ill. in colour on p. 31.

Edonoi

III. 1, 13–16

Aeschylus wrote a Lycurgus trilogy. It was in the first play, the *Edonoi*, called after the Thracian tribe of which Lycurgus was king, that Lycurgus, who had imprisoned the maenads of Dionysos, was driven mad by Dionysos so that he killed his own son Dryas, mistaking him for a vine. The madness of Lycurgus, though comparatively rare in Attic vase-painting, is more popular in South Italy, where it is represented in varying detail, showing either the murder of Dryas or his attack on his wife, sometimes in the presence of Dionysos.

Séchan, 63 ff.; K. Deichgräber, *Die Lykurgie des Aischylos* (Nachrichten v. d. Gesellschaft der Wiss. Göttingen, Phil.-hist. Kl. III, 8, 1939); *MTSP*[2], 139–40 (where the vases are listed).

13. Cracow, National Museum (ex Czartoryski) 1225.
Attic red-figured hydria by a late Mannerist; third quarter fifth century B.C.

On the left, Lycurgus in short chiton, patterned Thracian cloak, and boots, runs up with an axe held in both hands; behind him a torch; in front of him, a woman runs towards an altar, tearing her hair; a naked youth seated on the altar raises his hands in supplication. On the right of the altar is Dionysos, bearded, in long chiton and himation, holding a thyrsos in his left hand and a vine in his right. Beyond him, a maenad dances to a satyr playing the flute, who is seated on a rock; she looks back towards Dionysos. The lamenting woman must be the wife of Lycurgus, the boy on the altar his son Dryas. The vine which Dionysos holds over him shows the form that the madness took. In the play Lycurgus mocks Dionysos' effeminate clothes, and Dionysos may have worn long chiton and elaborate himation as on the vase.

ARV[2], 1121, no. 17; *CVA*, Poland 2, pl. 12, 1; Deichgräber, *op. cit.*, pl. 1; *MTSP*[2], 139.
Text: Loeb Classical Library, Aeschylus, II, 398.

14. Reggio Cal. 5013.
Lucanian kalyx-krater, Locri Group; *c.* 370–360 B.C.

This vase shows only one episode of the story – Lycurgus, double-axe held up in his right hand, pursues a woman, doubtless his wife, who is running off to right but turns her head to look in his direction with terror in her eyes. Lycurgus is in hunting garb, with a cloak and boots, much as on the preceding vase. Behind him is Dionysos, here shown as a youth with long curly ringlets falling down onto his shoulder; in his extended right hand is a bell, which he is tinkling, in his left is a thyrsus, and behind him an ivy-trail.

NSc, 1917, 108–9, fig. 11; *LCS* 74, no. 374, pl. 35, 5; *MTSP*[2], 140.

15. London, British Museum F 271.
Apulian kalyx-krater by the Lycurgus Painter; *c.* 360–350 B.C.

III.1,13 (Cracow). Aeschylus, *Edonoi*

III.1,14 (Reggio Calabria). Aeschylus, *Edonoi*

III.1,16 (Naples). Aeschylus, *Edonoi*

III.1,15 (London). Aeschylus, *Edonoi*

The scene on this vase, as commonly on Apulian kraters with mythological or dramatic representation, is divided into two registers. Above are several of the gods, notably Apollo and Hermes, who are not very directly concerned with the events taking place below, where Lycurgus, bearded, wearing a Thracian cap, his short cloak flapping out behind him, pauses in his attack upon his wife with the double-axe he holds in his right hand to look upwards to the winged figure, who is swooping down upon him from above with a goad in her hand. She is surrounded by a radiate nimbus and is therefore more likely to be Lyssa, the personification of Madness (cf. III. 1, 28), rather than one of the Furies, despite the snakes coiled around her left arm. The wife of Lycurgus has already been smitten, since blood flows from a wound above her breast; her furrowed brow signifies her anguish, as she struggles vainly to free herself from his grip of her hair. To right a young woman and a youth carry off the dead body of Dryas, from a wound in whose chest a stream of blood is pouring; to left a youth tears his hair and raises one hand in a gesture of despair, unable to prevent the massacre, and behind him comes up the aged paidagogos, with white hair and beard, and wrinkled face, carrying a crooked stick in his right hand. He is a stock character in dramatic scenes, and his presence here connects the scene with a stage representation.

Deichgräber, *op. cit.*, pl. 4, fig. 5; Schmidt, *Der Dareiosmaler*, pl. 2; *EAA* iv, 750, fig. 909; Borda, *Ceramiche apule*, pl. 7 (colour); *MTSP*², 128, TV 46.
A very similar representation occurs on an earlier Apulian fragment in Amsterdam (2563), on which Dionysos appears as well.

16. Naples 3237 (inv. 82123).
Lucanian volute-krater by the Brooklyn-Budapest Painter; *c.* 360–350 B.C.

This vase is by a Lucanian artist, the Brooklyn-Budapest Painter, who was strongly under the influence of Apulian vase-painting; it has several elements in common with the Lycurgus Painter's krater, notably the presence of Lyssa with the nimbus behind her. In the centre is Lycurgus, double-axe raised in his right hand, ready to deal the fatal blow to his wife, who sits, dishevelled with bared breast, before him, as he grasps her hair and rests his knee against her thigh to give him better purchase for the blow. To the left the dead body of Dryas is supported by a woman; above to the right the flying figure of Lyssa strikes down at Lycurgus with her goad. The Dionysiac element, completely absent on the preceding vase, may be seen in the bust of the maenad above the left, holding a tambourine in her left hand, and in the satyr-boy kneeling behind a tree in the right-hand corner and spying on the proceedings. The treatment of Lyssa, Lycurgus and his wife has so much in common with that on the preceding vase that one

is tempted to see its influence upon this one, unless both look back to a common original.

Séchan, fig. 22; Deichgräber, *op. cit.*, pl. 3, fig. 4; Pickard-Cambridge, *Festivals*¹, fig. 182; Simon, *JÖAI* 42, 1955, 15, fig. 5; *LCS* 114, no. 593, pl. 59, 7; *MTSP*², 139–40.

Europa

III. 1, 17

New York 16.140.
Early Apulian bell-krater by the Sarpedon Painter; *c.* 400–380 B.C.

The theme of the *Carians or Europa* of Aeschylus seems to have been connected with the fate of Sarpedon, King of Lycia and son of Zeus and Europa, who was slain by Patroclus in the Trojan War and whose body was conveyed back to his mother in Lycia by Sleep and Death, since in the longest surviving fragment of the play Europa expresses her deep anxiety about him (Nauck, fr. 99; Loeb edition, Aeschylus, II, fr. 50, lines 15 ff.).
On one side of the New York vases is a scene which may well be associated with this play. It shows Europa in tragic costume with an oriental head-dress seated upon a throne in a doorway, highly reminiscent of stage architecture, while above to the right Sleep and Death fly back with the body of her dead son, Sarpedon. Below, two Lycians, also in stage costume, look up with wonder at the sight. To the left, seated beside Europa is another woman, also gazing upwards, and to the right a maid with a phiale. The bringing back of the body would have been done on the stage with the use of the *mechane*. This theme is repeated on one of the hydriai from the Policoro tomb (see above, p. 11), unfortunately in a bad state of preservation. It shows the bearded figure of Death holding the legs of Sarpedon (inscribed) while Sleep presumably grasped him by the shoulders, but that portion of the vase is completely missing. It may be noted that on this vase they are carrying the body in the opposite direction, and as the scene below represents an Amazonomachy, we may assume that the Policoro Painter is representing the moment of departure from Troy and not the return home as on the New York vase. The reverse design of our vase, which used to be interpreted as Thetis asking Hephaistos for the arms of Achilles, more probably represents another aspect of the Europa story, when she is discussing the fate of Sarpedon with Zeus and Hera, who are seated on a couch in the centre, the one holding a sceptre crowned by Nike, the other wearing a remarkable head-dress consisting of a chariot driven by Nike. Beside Hera stands Hypnos (Sleep), who will help to convey the body of Sarpedon back to Lycia; the woman beside him may be Sarpedon's wife Pasithea. With the exception of Hypnos the

III.1,17 (New York). Aeschylus, *Europa*

characters all wear elaborate costumes, especially Europa and Pasithea, and the porch behind Zeus also recalls typical stage architecture.

Messerschmidt, *RM* 47, 1932, 138, figs. 5–7; Richter, *Metr. Mus. Hdbk*⁷, 116, pl. 96c; Bieber, *History*², fig. 283; Pickard-Cambridge, *Theatre*, 100, figs. 30–31; Picard, *CRAI*, 1953, 103–20; *MTSP*², 76, TV 16.
For the Policoro hydria see Degrassi, *BdA* 50, 1965, 5–7, figs. 1, 5–7; *RM*, Ergänzungsheft 11, 1967, 197–202, pls. 50, 59, 61; *LCS* 57, no. 285, pls. 26, 2 and 27, 2.

Myrmidons – Nereids – Phrygians

III. 1, 18–19

Vienna University 505.
Attic red-figured kalyx-krater by Polygnotos; 450–440 B.C.

Aeschylus wrote three tragedies on the theme of the *Iliad*. The *Myrmidons* took the story from the Embassy to Achilles to the death of Patroclus and Achilles' lamentation for him. The *Nereids*, named after the chorus, continued the story to the death of Hector. In the *Phrygians* Priam came to Achilles' tent and Achilles accepted the weight of Hector's body in gold as a ransom. It is reasonably assumed that this was a connected trilogy but the only evidence is the Vienna vase which combines scenes from all three plays and does not depend directly on Homer because in Homer (I) it is Thetis alone, and not the Nereids, who brings Achilles' new arms from Hephaistos, and (2) Talthybios, whose name is inscribed on the vase, does not visit Achilles.
The fragments come from a kalyx-krater which had an upper and lower band of decoration. In the upper band Thetis and the Nereids on sea-monsters bring Achilles his arms. Names are given fr. 6, THE(tis), KY(mothoe?); fr. 10 (Ps)AMATHE and may have been quoted by Aeschylus. On fr. 1 one Nereid

carries Achilles' helmet, another his shield, and a third one of his greaves. The theme of the Nereids on dolphins or sea-monsters is immensely popular in later Greek art but is not found before 460 B.C. The original artist was inspired by Aeschylus' chorus, of which an early line in anapaests is preserved 'crossing the dolphin-bearing plain of the sea' (150N); Aeschylus himself seems to have adapted to his new needs the traditional chorus of dolphin-riders (cf. I, 11, 14, 15, the last with inscription in anapaests).
Of the lower band there remains A, fr. 9, at the left a figure seated facing right, in front of a bier, on which a man lies, the back of his head alone remaining; a woman approaches; outside the tent, indicated by framework and cloth roof, TALTHYBIOS (inscribed), with herald's staff, travelling hat (*pilos*), *chlamys*, and boots (cf. III. 1, 28), strides up. The seated man is Achilles and the man on the bier is Patroclus. Achilles certainly lamented Patroclus at the end of the *Myrmidons*, and this must be the main allusion of this side of the vase.
The woman is unlikely to be Thetis because Thetis appears in the upper band (fr. 6) wearing different clothes. She must then be Briseis. In the *Iliad* (19, 278 ff.) Achilles receives Briseis back much later after he has been given the new arms and after a council of the Greek chiefs. Aeschylus may have altered the order and may have opened the *Nereids* with a prologue in which Talthybios brought back Briseis: a papyrus fragment may preserve the opening words, praying for reconciliation among the Greek leaders. Of the other side of the lower band enough remains (frr. 10, 12, 13) to show that it illustrated Priam arriving with a mule cart, on which a bier was arranged, to ransom Hector. This was the subject of the third play *Hector's Ransom or Phrygians* (who formed the chorus).

*ARV*², 1030, no. 33; *CVA*, Vienna 1, pl. 24; *MTSP*², 141 f. (with references for earliest representations of Nereids bringing the arms of Achilles); *Greek Chorus*, 29.
Text: Loeb Classical Library, Aeschylus, II², pp. 422 ff. with p. 590, pp. 429 ff. with p. 582 (suggested prologue of *Nereids*), pp. 470 ff.

Fr.1

III.1,18 (Vienna). Aeschylus, *Myrmidons – Nereids – Phrygians*

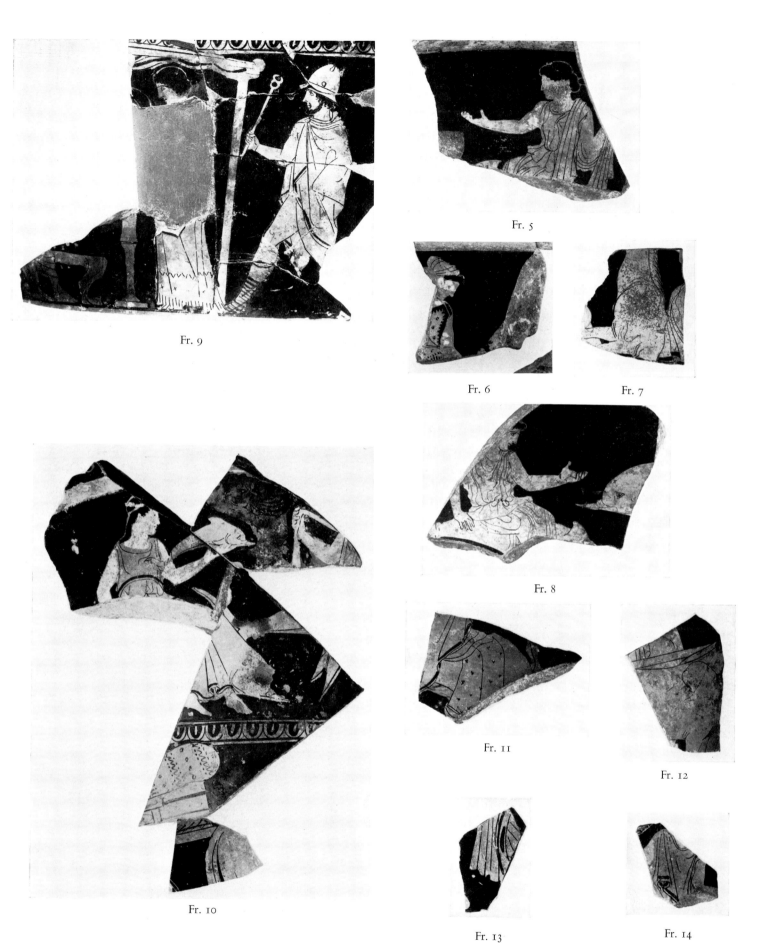

Fr. 9

Fr. 5

Fr. 6

Fr. 7

Fr. 8

Fr. 10

Fr. 11

Fr. 12

Fr. 13

Fr. 14

III.1,19 (Vienna). Aeschylus, *Myrmidons – Nereids – Phrygians*

III.1,20 (Toronto). Aeschylus, *Phrygians*

III.1,21 (New York). Aeschylus, *Phrygians*

III.1,22 (Copenhagen). Aeschylus, *Phrygians*

III. 1, 20

Toronto, Royal Ontario Museum 926.32.
Melian relief; 450–440 B.C.

In the *Phrygians* the gold brought by Priam as Hector's ransom was weighed out against the body. This scene first appears on the Melian relief illustrated, one of the same class as the *Choephoroi* relief (III. 1, 1). Priam is on the right, his head veiled, and his hand to his forehead in mourning. He appears clean-shaven because his beard is cropped close: this was probably a feature of Priam's mask, as the comic poets invented the word 'I will be Priamed' as a synonym for 'I will be shaved'. Achilles on the left, wearing a corselet, has one band on the weighbeam and a helmet in the other. The young Myrmidon (rather than Trojan) on the right holds a gold dish. Below the weighbeam can be seen the chest in which Priam has brought the gold and Hector's body lying on the ground.

J. W. Graham, *AJA* 62, 1958, 313; *MTSP²*, 141.
Kock, *Comicorum Atticorum Fragmenta*, iii, no. 1123.

III. 1, 21

New York 20.195.
Fragment of an early Apulian kalyx-krater, Black Fury Group; *c.* 400–390 B.C.

This is one of the finest of all extant South Italian vase fragments and the complete krater, depicting the Ransom of Hector, must have been of exceptional quality, On the fragment we see the aged Priam, with white hair and a short white beard, kneeling beside what would have been the couch of Achilles in a building of which only part of one of the fluted columns now survives. Priam is richly dressed in oriental stage costumes; he wears a Phrygian cap decorated with rows of white dots, a long-sleeved garment with embroidered patterns which include palmettes, tri-coloured chequers, and white dots and zig-zags on black stripes, and shoes similarly decorated. His white beard has been shaved fairly close (cf. III. 1, 20). Behind him stands the youthful Hermes, wearing winged boots and a chlamys with border-patterns of palmettes, waves and rays; the upper portion of his body is missing, but the lower part of the shaft of his caduceus is probably to be seen just above his hand, between the first two fingers of which is a small round white object. He had acted as Priam's charioteer across the plain of Troy upon this occasion. Behind him is a fragment of a youth, perhaps one of the ransom-bearers. Above the head of Priam is part of the arm of another figure, probably that of Achilles seated upon a couch or a stool. Priam is not looking up at him, but down towards the ground, most likely at the body of the slain Hector.

A full version of the story appears on a much repainted volute-krater in Leningrad (inv. 1718, St. 422; Séchan, pl. 3; *AJA* 62, 1958, pl. 83, fig. 5), on which Priam is shown seated below the couch of Achilles, watching two servants carrying in the dead body of Hector.

Bulas, *Eos* 34, 246, fig. 6; Trendall, *FI* 28, pl. 30 b; Charbonneaux, Martin and Villard, *La Grèce classique*, fig. 355; *MTSP²*, 141.

III. 1, 22

Copenhagen, National Museum.
Silver cup by Cheirisophos from Hoby; late first century B.C.

A pair of silver cups were found in 1920 in the tomb of a chieftain at Hoby in Denmark. Close, and in part mechanical, copies of both have been identified in Arretine ware dated to the Augustan period. The central figure of the other cup has been connected stylistically with the Philoctetes by the late fifth-century painter Parrhasios. The style of the central pair on this cup suggests that it derives from an original of the same date: transmission could be either by moulds from fifth-century cups or by drawings, since according to Pliny, writing in the second half of the first century A.D., 'many traces of his (Parrhasios) draughtsmanship remain both in pictures and on parchments'.
Priam in oriental tiara and long robes kisses the hand of the seated Achilles as in *Iliad*, 24, 478. Two young Myrmidons sit on the right, and two women on the left.

K. Friis Johansen, *Nordiske Fortidsminder*, II, 3, 1923, 119; *Acta Archaeologica*, 31, 1960, 185; Vagn Poulsen, *Antike Plastik*, viii, 69 ff., pl. 47; D. E. Strong, *Greek and Roman Silver Plate*, 136, pl. 35b; Webster, *MTSP²*, 141.
Drawings of Parrhasios, Pliny, *N.H.*, 35, 68.

III.1,23 (Market). Aeschylus, *Niobe*

Niobe

III. 1, 23

Italian Market.
Campanian hydria of the Libation Group; *c.* 340–330 B.C.

The lost *Niobe* was one of the most famous tragedies of Aeschylus, who seems to have treated the theme quite differently from Sophocles, and for the greater part of the play to have shown Niobe in grief-stricken silence at the tomb of her children. She had boasted of being a more prolific mother than Leto, who had borne only Apollo and Artemis, whereupon they, at their mother's request, shot down with their arrows all the children of Niobe, an event represented in both vase-painting and sculpture. In the Aeschylean play it would seem that Tantalus, the father of Niobe, finally persuaded her to break her silence, and this episode in the drama is depicted on several South Italian vases, of which this Campanian hydria gives one of the best illustrations. In the centre, in a small naiskos representing the tomb of her children, stands Niobe, wearing a veil and with her hand on her head in the conventional gesture of mourning. The lower part of her body is painted white (cf. Bonn 99 and Taranto 8928), perhaps to suggest the stone into which she is to be transformed. To the left, hands stretched out in entreaty, is an aged king, elaborately garbed and bearing a sceptre, presumably Niobe's father Tantalus, who is supported by a youth wearing a white *pilos*. On the other side is a woman seated on the base of the tomb, resting her veiled head on one hand in the typical attitude of dejection; she must be the mother either of Niobe or of her husband Amphion. In front are various offer-

ings brought to the tomb, and above to left is a woman (Leto?) seated on rising ground, and to right, Apollo with a laurel-branch.

A very similar scene is shown on an Apulian loutrophoros in Naples (3246; Séchan, 82 ff., fig. 24; Borda, *Ceramiche apule*, fig. 35) attributed to the Varrese Painter, and variations of it appear on amphorae in Bonn (99; Schauenburg, *RM* 64, 1957, pl. 37, 1–2) and in Taranto (8935; Schauenburg, *l.c.*, pl. 44, 1; Arias, *Storia*, pl. 163, 2; Paribeni, *Immagini*, pl. 19) by the same painter, and on a late Apulian dish, also in Taranto (8928; Phillips, *AJA* 72, 1968, pl. 10, fig. 23; Schauenburg, *Perseus*, pl. 25, 1), where it appears in the lower register beneath a representation of Andromeda.

All these vase-paintings probably give us a distant reflection of the Aeschylean drama, since, apart from the fact that Niobe is usually shown standing and not seated (as in fr. 157 and on Taranto 8935), they correspond well with what we know of the play from the few fragments which survive.

On Niobe see Lesky in *RE* xvii, 673–706 and R. M. Cook, *Niobe and her children* (with a list of the monuments on pp. 41–53).
Text: Loeb Classical Library, Aeschylus, II², 430–5 and 556–62.

Phineus

III. 1, 24

Copenhagen, National Museum, inv. Chr. VIII, 8.
Attic red-figure stamnos by the Painter of the Yale oinochoe; 470–450 B.C.

In 472 B.C. Aeschylus produced the *Phineus* with the *Persae*, *Glaukos of Potniai*, and the satyr-play *Prometheus Pyrkaeus* (cf. II, 4). Phineus was blind and the Harpies flew down and snatched away his food until Zetes and Kalais, the winged sons of Boreas, drove them away and killed them. Four Attic vases painted in the twenty years after the play was produced have been associated with it. On the first (British Museum E 291) a bald blind man, with a sceptre behind him, raises his hands saying 'O gods, gods' before a table with food on it. He is probably Phineus, but there is nothing to clinch the identification. On the second (Louvre G 364) an old man holding a sceptre, seated on an elaborate throne with a table of food in front of him, seems to greet a bearded winged man who approaches swiftly with hands stretched out. He is a Boread and this makes the identification of the old man with Phineus certain. Behind the old man a young man in short chiton, chlamys, and boots brandishes a spear; he must be thought of as threatening the Harpies rather than the Boread.

The third is the Copenhagen stamnos, which is badly preserved and therefore difficult to interpret. The bearded winged figure on the left, holding a sceptre, is a Boread. The second Boread is on the right, with wings spread out; he also holds a sceptre. Beyond him a man in a Thracian cloak

III.1,24 (Copenhagen). Aeschylus, *Phineus*

III.1,25 (London). Aeschylus, *Phineus*

appears with a table of food. In the centre under a column a seated figure. Here bad preservation is particularly unfortunate. The figure certainly has a covering over the head but this does not exclude Phineus (cf. III. 1, 25). Possibly then this is Phineus greeting the Boreads after their victory and preparing for a meal. The reverse shows Nike (Victory) between a young man with a sceptre and a bearded man with a stick; if the two sides are connected, the man will be Aeschylus and the youth Pericles, who was responsible for the production.

ARV², 502, no. 7; *CVA*, pl. 150, 2; *MTSP²*, 144, with references to other vases.
Text: Loeb Classical Library, Aeschylus, II, 468

III. 1, 25

London, British Museum E 302.
Attic red-figured neck-amphora by the Nikon Painter; 470–450 B.C.

Phineus seated with a sceptre in his left hand. A Harpy runs away with food, which she has taken off the table. On the other side of the vase is a similar Harpy, but wearing a more elaborately patterned chiton, running with food in her hands. For the flying run of the Harpies, compare the Furies on III. 1, 8 and the Cocks of I, 12. The Harpies are labelled *kalos* ('beautiful', masculine), which must refer to the young men who play the parts, cf. on III. 1, 2. Phineus wears a mask, shown by the line connecting beard to ear, by the stylization of the beard itself and by the open lips. He wears a woman's headdress (cf. on III. 1, 24). Phineus is included in Pollux' list of special masks (4, 141), and this rather than blindness may be its special characteristic; it recurs again on an Apulian red-figure fragment, whereas Phineus on III. 1, 26 wears an oriental tiara. As the Nikon Painter so clearly thinks of tragedy, the very large square footstool on which his feet rest may allude to the *ekkyklema*, which Pollux (iv, 128), presumably with reference to some particular play, defines as a high base with a throne on it.

ARV², 652, no. 2; *CVA* 5, III Ic, pl. 53, 2; *MTSP²*, 144 (including reference to the Apulian fragment in Amsterdam); *Greek Chorus*, 22 and 251.

III.1,26 (Ruvo, Jatta coll.). Aeschylus, *Phineus*

III.1,27 (Berlin). Aeschylus, *Prometheus Lyomenos*

III. 1, 26

Ruvo, Jatta coll. 1095.
Early Lucanian volute-krater by the Amykos Painter; late fifth century B.C.

This vase gives the fullest version of the story of Phineus and the Harpies. The blind Phineus, holding a sceptre in his right hand and wearing oriental stage-costume, is shown seated beside a partly overturned table with remains of food still upon it. Two Harpies fly off to right, one with some food clutched to her bosom, the other with a wine-cup she has snatched up; they are attacked by the two winged Boreads, Zetes and Kalais, one with a sword, the other with a spear. Around are grouped a number of the Argonauts, and below the handle of the vase the prow of the ship Argo appears in the distance, with several other Argonauts resting beside a fountain. According to the legend (Apollodorus 1.9.21), they were given advice about their voyage by Phineus in return for ridding him of the Harpies. That the scene takes place out of doors is shown by the numerous lines representing rising ground and by the pile of stones.

FR, pl. 60; Sichtermann, *Gr. Vasen aus Unteritalien*, 36, K 40 (where bibliography), pls. 62–3; *LCS* 47, no. 243, pl. 19; *La Grèce classique*, figs. 338–9.

Prometheus Lyomenos

III. 1, 27

Berlin 1969.9.
Apulian kalyx-krater by the Branca Painter (workshop of the Darius Painter); third quarter fourth century B.C.

The scene on this vase is unique in South Italian vase-painting and must be associated with the *Prometheus Lyomenos* of Aeschylus, in which Prometheus, fettered to a rock in the remote Caucasus, is tormented by the eagle of Zeus, which feeds upon his liver, until Herakles shoots the bird and frees Prometheus, who tells him of his future wanderings. The central figure on the vase, dominating the picture, is Prometheus fettered at the wrists to a large rock, which is almost certainly stage-inspired since similar rocks appear on other vases with dramatic themes, especially Andromeda (cf. III. 3, 13). He is long-haired and bearded, draped in a long, thin garment, which covers only the lower part of his body and is drawn up in a tight roll over his right shoulder. His eyes turn towards Herakles, who stands beside the rock to the left, club in hand, lion-skin over his shoulder, and bow in added white behind his left arm. Farther to the left sits Athena, a long spear in one hand, a leafy wreath in the other, perhaps symbolic of the one to be worn by Prometheus after he has been set free. To the right is a draped woman, probably Gaia, the mother of Prometheus, who had a part in this play. Then, balancing Athena on the other side, comes Apollo, to whom Herakles prayed to guide his arrow straight (fr. 200). Beneath Prometheus the eagle of Zeus falls in death, pierced by the shaft of Herakles in the breast, which is stained red with blood. Beside the eagle is a woman holding a cross-bow torch; she is probably Persephone, in which case the seated figure on the left should be Demeter. To the right is a seated Fury, with red-edged wings and snakes in her hair. From the ground spring numerous plants, often coloured red, which may be an allusion to the herb *prometheion* which sprang from the blood of Prometheus shed by the eagle and was used by Medea for her enchantments (Ap. Rhod. iii, 845).

The picture is not so much a specific scene from the play, as a general representation of the legend, introducing characters not actually in the drama but having some connection with it, like Apollo and Athena, who can also be taken as personifying Athens, which will later honour Prometheus by establishing the Prometheia in his name.

Trendall, *Jahrbuch Berliner Museen* 12, 1970, 168 ff., figs. 10 and 12.
Text: Loeb Classical Library, Aeschylus, II, pp. 446 ff.
For the treatment of the rock see W. Jobst, *Die Höhle im gr. Theater* (Vienna, 1970), 120 ff.

III.1,28 (Boston). Aeschylus, *Toxotides*

Toxotides

III. 1, 28

Boston 00.346.
Attic red-figured bell-krater by Lykaon Painter; 440 B.C.

In the centre AKTAION is being torn to pieces by his hounds, which are being driven on by LYSSA. On the left, ZEUS looks on; on the right ARTEMIS stands with flaming torch in her right hand, a bow in her left, and a quiver over her shoulder. The addition of Zeus and Lyssa distinguishes this from all earlier pictures of the myth. Lyssa (madness) with her sleeved garment, short chiton, and boots suggests a stage figure (cf. III. 1, 15): Aeschylus put Lyssa on the stage to drive the maenads mad in the *Xantriai*. Here the hound's head above her head shows that she drove the hounds mad. Aktaion's hair is stylized as animal's fur and he has a deer's ear and horns; Pollux lists among his special masks (4, 141) 'Aktaion with horns'.

Aeschylus wrote a *Toxotides* (archer-nymphs of Artemis, who presumably formed the chorus) and the rending of Aktaion was told in a messenger speech. That Zeus should ultimately be responsible is thoroughly Aeschylean; if Lyssa was a stage

figure (and not merely described in the messenger speech), a dialogue in which Artemis urged her to action is probable, like the later scene between Iris and Lyssa in the *Hercules Furens* of Euripides. The presence of Zeus has suggested to some the version of the story in which Aktaion wooed Semele, but the fragments of the play suggest that he was a chaste hunter, and the fact that the same hound-names occurred both in Aeschylus and in the Fable of Hyginus (181) which recounts that he was punished for seeing Artemis bathing may mean that this was Aeschylus' story. Zeus was the father of Artemis and in any case ultimately responsible for all that happens.

Above the figure of Aktaion is written EUAION. Euaion was the son of Aeschylus; he is called *tragikos* by the Suda lexicon, which can mean actor as well as poet. He may have acted in the original production or in a revival of his father's play (cf. also on III. 2, 1 and 9).

ARV², 1045, no. 7; *MTSP²*, 145. Pickard-Cambridge, *Festivals²*, fig. 59; Jobst, *op. cit.*, fig. 13.
Text: Loeb Classical Library, Aeschylus, II, 463.
On Aktaion in Greek vase-painting see P. Jacobsthal, *Aktaions Tod* (*Marburger Jahrb. Kunstwissenschaft* 5, 1929, 1 ff.) and K. Schauenburg, *JdI* 84, 1969, 29–46.

2. Sophocles

Andromeda

III. 2, 1–3

1. Agrigento, Museo Nazionale.
Attic white-ground kalyx-krater by the Phiale Painter; 450–440 B.C.
2. Boston 63.2663.
Attic red-figured pelike; 450–440 B.C.
3. London, British Museum E 169.
Attic red-figured hydria; 450–440 B.C.

These three contemporary vases have the same subject, Perseus and Andromeda (attested by the inscription on III. 2, 1). The only previous preserved illustration of the subject is on a Corinthian vase of the mid-sixth century. Some new impulse must have caused this interest, an impulse active some forty years earlier than the production of Euripides' *Andromeda* in 412 B.C. (cf. below III. 3, 10). Sophocles wrote an *Andromeda*: few fragments survive, but someone drives someone else to work with a lash; there is a mention of ointment vases; an oriental king; an oriental garment; the sacrifice of Andromeda; and the arrival of Perseus. This play probably inspired the vases, which are too divergent in detail to be copies of a common original painting but could well represent memories of the same production. Three essential differences separate these scenes from the vases which give the truest representation of the Euripidean play; Andromeda was tied up on the stage (like Prometheus in the Aeschylean *Prometheus Vinctus*, cf. III. 1, 27) instead of being shown to the audience already bound; she was tied to a stake or stakes instead of a rock in front of a cave; she wore oriental dress instead of Greek dress (with an oriental tiara sometimes).

The London hydria (III. 2, 3) has the largest number of figures. We can perhaps distinguish three scenes: (a) on the right, Kepheus, in tiara, long chiton, decorated over-garment, himation, shoes, is seated with his hands on a long, crooked stick, watching three Aithiopians making preparations to put in two posts; (b) Andromeda, in tiara, oriental sleeved and trousered garment, short chiton, shoes, is supported by two Aithiopians; behind her, three Aithiopians bring offerings suitable for the dead, a stool, a scarf, a mirror, an ointment vase, a perfume vase, a box; (c) on the extreme right, Perseus stands with his hand to his forehead looking on; he wears winged petasos, chlamys, high boots (perhaps thought of as winged), and holds two spears. The Boston pelike (III. 2, 2) gives on one side Andromeda, dressed as on III. 2, 3, but with the pattern of the oriental garment clearly marked, with her right arm tied to a post, and her left arm being tied by an Aithiopian to an invisible post. On the other side Kepheus, with white beard, and snub nose, dressed as on III. 2, 3 but

III.2, 1 (Agrigento). Sophocles, *Andromeda*

63

III.2,2 (Boston). Sophocles, *Andromeda*

III.2,3 (London). Sophocles, *Andromeda*

III.2,4 (London). Sophocles, *Antigone*

with oriental sleeves and a sceptre instead of a stick, looks back at an Aithiopian carrying stool and perfume vase (cf. III. 2, 3). On the Agrigento kalyx-krater (III. 2, 1) the scene is reduced to two figures. Perseus (inscribed) in short chiton, winged sandals, winged petasos, with two spears in his right hand, stands with his left foot on a rock. His chin is on his left hand as he stares at Andromeda (inscribed) as if she were a vision. She has a post behind her, and her hands are tied to two side-posts; she is dressed as on III. 2, 3. The Phiale Painter only represents the scene after the binding; Andromeda is tied up, Kepheus has departed, and Perseus arrives and contemplates her. He also has written beside Perseus' head EUAION KALOS AISCHYLOU. 'Euaion is beautiful, son of Aeschylus'. The occurrence of this name attached to a particular figure here, on the *Toxotides* bell-krater (III. 1, 28) and on the Thamyras hydria (III. 2, 9) suggests that in each case he is the actor who plays the character by whom his name is written. The play was parodied in a comedy illustrated below (IV, 1).

MTSP[2], AV 53-6 and p. 147; K. Schauenburg, *AuA* 13, 1967, 1 ff. Kyle M. Phillips Jr., *AJA* 72, 1968, 1 ff.; Webster, *Sophocles*[2], 203 ff.; Berger, *AntK* 11, 1968, 63 (with illustration of Andromeda vase in Basel, pl. 18, 6).
(1) *ARV*[2], 1017, no. 53; Phillips, *loc. cit.*, pl. 7, fig. 15; Griffo and Zirretta, *Il Museo Civico*, 89–90.
(2) H. Hoffman, *Boston Museum Bulletin*, 61, 1963, 108; Phillips, pl. 7, fig. 13; Snowden, *Blacks in Antiquity*, fig. 90.
(3) *ARV*[2], 1062; *CVA*, pl. 76, 1; Phillips, pl. 6, figs. 11–12; Snowden, *Blacks in Antiquity*, fig. 26.
Fragments: R. C. Jebb and A. C. Pearson, *Fragments of Sophocles*, I, 78; *POxy.* 2453, fr. 49.

Antigone

III. 2, 4

London, British Museum F 175.
Lucanian nestoris by the Dolon Painter; *c.* 380–370 B.C.

The figured scenes on this vase appear on two separate registers on each side; those on the reverse, representing a battle and a komos, are certainly not connected, and there is therefore no particular reason why the two on the obverse should be associated. The upper panel shows the arrival of Paris in Sparta and his meeting with Helen, the lower a scene which has sometimes been interpreted as Paris presenting Helen to Priam in Troy, but also, and perhaps more plausibly, as Antigone brought by two guards before Kreon. The two guards, appropriately clad in short tunics, both carry spears, and Antigone stands between them, her cloak drawn up over her head to serve as a veil, her gaze steadfast but downcast. One hand is concealed in the folds of her drapery, perhaps to hide the vessel from which she sprinkled the earth on the body of her brother Polynices. Kreon is seated on a stool, his feet resting on a footstool in front of it, and holds a sceptre. He wears what looks to be an oriental head-dress (cf. the phlyax vase IV, 29) and listens to the explanation of the guard as in *Antigone* 384 ff.

Trendall, *LCS* 103, no. 539; Webster, *MTSP*[2], 147–8.
For the interpretation see in particular: Séchan, 141–2 (fig. 43); Ehrenberg, *Sophocles and Pericles*, 110 (pl. 1); Ghali-Kahil, *Hélène*, 184 (pl. 27); Clairmont, *JHS* 79, 1959, 210.

Elektra

III. 2, 5

Vienna 689 (SK 195, 69).
Lucanian bell-krater by the Sydney Painter; *c.* 360–350 B.C.

The scene shows Pylades and Orestes advancing towards Elektra; Orestes holds out in his right hand the urn reputedly containing his own ashes, which Elektra contemplates with a slightly worried look, touching her chin with her first finger in a typical gesture of doubt or anxiety. The inspiration has probably come from the *Elektra* of Sophocles (lines 1098 ff.), although the vase-painter has taken a slight liberty in giving the urn to Orestes himself to carry instead of showing it, as in the play (l. 1122), in the hands of an attendant. There can, however, be little doubt as to the interpretation of the picture on the vase.

Séchan, 142–3, fig. 44; Trendall, *LCS* 128, no. 650, pl. 63, 1.

Nausikaa

III. 2, 6

Munich 2322.
Attic red-figured neck-amphora by Nausikaa Painter; 450–440 B.C.

Sophocles' *Nausikaa* was an early play as he acted Nausikaa himself, which means that it was produced before 449 B.C., when Herakleides was his chief actor. The fragments suggest that Sophocles followed the Sixth Book of the *Odyssey* closely, and we are told that he himself was extremely successful when he acted Nausikaa playing with the ball. The great painter Polygnotos had some close connection with Sophocles (cf. on III. 2, 9 and 10), and he painted a picture 'of Odysseus at the river approaching the maidens who are washing clothes with Nausikaa, just as Homer described the scene', which Pausanias (1, 22, 6) saw in the Pinakotheke, where it had been moved from its original location in a Kimonian building. Three vases, painted between 450 and 425 B.C., probably go back to this painting, and one figure on one of them, III. 2, 7, suggests that Polygnotos was inspired by Sophocles' play rather than by Homer directly.
The painter of the Munich amphora gives Odysseus coming out, naked with suppliant branches in his hands and hair, then Athena looking towards him, then two girls running, both with diadems in their hair, then three girls dealing with the washing, and a tree on which the washing is hung, which also does duty for the bush protecting the sleeping Odysseus.

*ARV*², 1107, no. 2; *MTSP*², 149; *CVA*, pls. 213–14; E. Simon, *AJA* 67, 1963, 59, pl. 12; Webster, *Sophocles*², 198, 200.
Text: Jebb-Pearson, II, 92.

III. 2, 7

Boston 04.18.
Attic red-figured pyxis-lid by Aison; 450–425 B.C.

Aison has arranged his figures differently from the Nausikaa Painter and his arrangement may be nearer the original and Sophocles, but he has reduced the girls dealing with the washing to one. Odysseus starts forth from the bush on the seashore; the thin scarf round his neck must be the *kredemnon* given him by Ino-Leukothea, which in the *Odyssey* (6, 333 ff., 458 ff.) he threw back into the river when he landed. Athena points the way towards Nausikaa. Two girls run away from Odysseus, looking back at him, one beyond the bush, the other beyond Athena. The girl beyond Athena wears a sleeved garment over her chiton, and this suggests tragedy: she is presumably the leader of the chorus. All the girls have wreaths in their hair, but Nausikaa has a more elaborate diadem, and a decorated garment over her chiton, which again suggests tragedy, but the lines on her arms are bracelets rather than the ends of sleeves.
In the play Odysseus' sleeping place must have been the central door (with the *ekkyklema* to bring out the bush). Athena may have spoken the prologue. The parodos must have been the arrival of Nausikaa and her girls, who had perhaps finished their washing and arrived to play ball. Odysseus certainly told his story (fr. 440P) but whether now or, with a change of scene (as in the *Ajax*), to the King and Queen of Phaeacia, is unknown.

*ARV*², 1177, no. 48; *MTSP*², 149; *Greek Chorus*, 29.

Oedipus Tyrannus

III. 2, 8

Syracuse 66557, from Syracuse.
Sicilian kalyx-krater (fragmentary) by the Capodarso Painter; third quarter fourth century B.C.

This remarkable vase, found near the Ospedale in Syracuse in 1969 in fragments, represents a performance of the *Oedipus* on a stage and is by the same painter as the krater in Caltanissetta (III. 6, 2) which shows a scene from an as yet unidentified tragedy upon a much simpler type of stage. On the Syracuse vase the floor of the stage and the posts which support it are clearly visible; the stage background is represented by four tall white Doric columns, decorated with a palmette pattern at the top of the shaft. The scene appears to be that in which the Messenger relates the death of Polybus (*Oedipus*, 924 ff.), leading up to the moment when Jocasta, realizing the full import of what has been said, rushes into the palace after

III.2, 5 (Vienna). Sophocles, *Elektra*

III.2, 6 (Munich). Sophocles, *Nausikaa*

III.2, 7 (Boston). Sophocles, *Nausikaa*

III.2, 8 (Syracuse). Sophocles, *Oedipus Tyrannus*

entreating Oedipus to pursue the matter no further (l. 1071). The principal characters, all of whom wear colourful or embroidered stage-costumes, stand between the columns; to the left is the Messenger, white-haired and bearded, wearing a short yellow tunic with a chlamys, and high boots (cf. the messenger on the krater in Caltanissetta, III. 6, 2) and carrying a staff. He looks fixedly in front of him, and might even be taken for Teiresias, such is the almost blind intensity of his gaze. Beside him is Oedipus, tall and bearded, wearing a cloak over his long-sleeved yellow robe. He plucks at his beard in a typical gesture of perplexity, not fully comprehending the significance of what the dialogue with the messenger has revealed and determined to pursue his quest for the truth. Jocasta, however, has grasped the import of the messenger's words and draws up her veil to hide her face in anguish; beside her, another woman, presumably her attendant, wearing a white cloak with yellow fold-lines, turns her head away in despair. In front, on a smaller scale, are the two daughters of Oedipus and Jocasta, Antigone and Ismene, one in an orange-pink cloak, with downturned head in profile to left, the other in a white and yellow cloak, with her head in three-quarter face to right. There is no hint of their presence in the Sophoclean tragedy until the last scene, but their identity seems reasonably certain, and the vase-painter may well have included them to heighten the pathos of the scene, unless he is following some other version of the tragedy of which we have no record.

Arch Reps 16, 1969–70, 46; *LCS, Suppl. I*, 105.

Thamyras

III. 2, 9

Rome, Vatican, inv. 16549.
Attic red-figured hydria by the Phiale Painter; 450–440 B.C.

Sophocles' *Thamyras* was an early play because he played Thamyras himself. According to the ancient life (4) 'he played the lyre in this play only, for which reason he was painted with a lyre in the Stoa Poikile'. The Stoa Poikile was finished about 460 B.C., and a picture there of a scene from the Sack of Troy, which also echoed a Sophoclean play, was by Polygnotos. It has therefore been suggested that Polygnotos painted Sophocles as Thamyras. This is credible as in his picture of the Underworld in Delphi Polygnotos painted Thamyras as 'blinded, and dishevelled, his lyre thrown at his feet, its arms broken and its strings snapped', which coincides with a description in Sophocles (244P). One Attic vase of about 425 B.C. has been connected with Polygnotos' picture in the Stoa Poikile; the two illustrated here can be connected with the play itself.

The fragments of the play show that someone, presumably not the Muses, who were challenged by Thamyras, defeated him in song, and punished him, described the exciting effect of Thamyras' music (240, 245P) and later described him breaking his lyre (244P). The lexicographer Pollux (4, 141) lists among the special masks (like Phineus and Aktaion) a Thamyras mask with one bright or blue and one black eye, and an ancient commentator on Pseudo-Euripides *Rhesus* 916, obviously inspired by this, says that Thamyras' right eye was blue and his left eye black. Of our two vases one shows the right profile before Thamyras was blinded, the other the left profile after Thamyras was blinded, so that they reproduce the stage usage. If Sophocles had this special mask made, it must mean that Thamyras was struck blind by the Muses on the stage; Oedipus in the *Oedipus Tyrannus* puts out his eyes off-stage and can therefore come on again wearing another, blind mask.

On the Vatican hydria THAMYRAS (inscribed) is seated on a rock, playing his lyre. He wears Thracian headdress, crowned with a laurel wreath, Thracian chlamys, short chiton, and boots. The locality is marked as sacred to the Muses by the three little figures above his head. On the right a white-haired woman dances up to him, holding a spray or wreath in her hand. Her speedy movements would suit either the resolved trochaics or the ionics of the fragments describing the effect of Thamyras' music (240, 245P). The face with its curved nose and furrowed brow is repeated in the mask on a fourth-century relief in Copenhagen (*MTSP²*, AS 4); it is, therefore, stylized on the theatre-mask. The woman is probably Argiope, Thamyras' mother; she joins other heroic mothers whose pride was disastrous for their children, Kassiopeia and Niobe. Above her head is written EUAION KALOS, so that we may conjecture that Euaion played her part, as he played Perseus in the *Andromeda*. On the left two stately women with earrings and laurel-wreaths looking on: they are inscribed CHORONIKA 'victorious in the chorus' (dual). Another hydria by the Phiale Painter, in Naples, puts Argiope on the left of Thamyras and the two women on the right: there they are identified as Muses, as one holds a flute and the other a lyre. With the inscription on the Vatican hydria it is almost certain that the Muses formed the chorus (it is one of the curious conventions of tragedy that a chorus of twelve (Aeschylus) can represent fifty daughters of Danaos, or a chorus of fifteen (Sophocles, Euripides) nine Muses or seven (or more accurately five) mothers of the Seven against Thebes.)

ARV², 1020, no. 92; Schefold, *Bildnisse*, 58; Séchan, fig. 61; *MTSP²*, AV 58 and p. 152; Webster, *Greek Chorus*, 29, 131: *Sophocles²*, 200, 203; *EAA* ii, 149, fig. 223.

Text: Jebb-Pearson, I, 176.

Polygnotos: most recently M. Robertson ap. L. H. Jeffery, *BSA* 60, 1965, 43 n. 12, 45 n. 17. The mask: A. Lesky, *Gesammelte Schriften*, 169 (=*Anz.Öst.Akad.*, 1951, 100).

III.2,9 (Vatican). Sophocles, *Thamyras*

III.2,10 (Oxford). Sophocles, *Thamyras*

III. 2, 10

Oxford G 291 (530).
Attic red-figured hydria from the group of Polygnotos; 440–430 B.C.

Thamyras seated on a rock, his left hand is on the rock, his right hand has just dropped the lyre. He is already blind. On the right a Muse muffled in her cloak, with her lyre in her left hand; the dress and posture recall the dithyramb-singers of the Copenhagen bell-krater (I, 17); the painter thinks of the stately song in which the Muses defeated Thamyras. On the left, Thamyras' mother tearing her hair and moving into the lament from which the aeolic fragment (244P) comes: 'Breaking the gold-bound arm, breaking the joinery of the strung lyre'.

*ARV*², 1061, no. 152; *CVA* 1, pl. 32, 1 and 2, p. vii; Bieber, *History*², fig. 105; Séchan, fig. 60; Pickard-Cambridge, *Festivals*², fig. 66; *MTSP*², AV 59, and p. 152.

III.2, 12 (Basel, H. A. Cahn coll.). Sophocles, *Trachiniae*

Trachiniae

III. 2, 11 (no illustration available)

Lipari inv. 9341, from Tomb 658.
Sicilian kalyx-krater; mid-fourth century B.C.

To left is Deianira (ΔΗΙΑΝΕΙΡΑ) seated on a cushion-covered stool holding three phialai in her hand; her attendant stands behind her. Above to right is Nike (NIKH) with a piece of drapery over her legs in the typical Sicilian manner, looking down at the crown she holds in her hands. In the centre of the picture stands the youthful Herakles (HPA-ΚΛΗΣ), holding his club, with the lion-skin, painted red on the inside, over his arm. He looks down to the white-haired figure of Oineus (OINEΥΣ), father of Deianeira, who is seated at his feet, and above whom sits Acheloös (AXEΛΩIOΣ), horned as befits a river-god, holding a wreath.

The picture admirably illustrates the opening of Deianeira's speech at the beginning of the *Trachiniae*.

'I, who in the house of my father Oineus, while yet I dwelt at Pleuron, had such fear of bridals as never vexed any maiden of Aetolia. For my wooer was a river-god, Acheloös, who was ever asking me from my sire . . . But at last, to my joy, came the glorious son of Zeus and Alkmene, who closed with him in combat, and delivered me . . .' (lines 6–9, 17–21).

It is unique so far in Greek vase-painting, giving much the fullest representation of the story, with Nike present to indicate the ultimate victory of Herakles. It would have made an admirable poster for the play.

The reverse of the vase further illustrates the painter's concern with dramatic performances, since it shows Thalia (ΘAΛIA), the Muse of Comedy, playing the flute, to the accompaniment of which a papposilen (ΣΙΜΟΣ) is dancing, while a satyr (ΣΚΡΓΟΣ) moves off to right.

The vase, which has only recently been excavated, is the work of a Sicilian artist of considerable ability, but, as yet, no other works specifically attributable to his hand have been discovered.

Arch Reps 16, 1969–70, 48.

III. 2, 12

Basel, H. A. Cahn coll. 229.
Fragment of Apulian bell-krater from the workshop of the Darius Painter; *c.* 330–320 B.C.

The interpretation of this small fragment poses many problems, but Dr. Margot Schmidt has plausibly connected it with the *Trachiniae*. In the background is a large portion of one of the columns of a temple or sanctuary and a slight trace of a second. To right, the youthful figure of Hyllos (ΥΛΛΟΣ), one of the sons of Herakles, advances from the right holding a bucranion above his head, as if to use it as a weapon. To the left, a man, with a petasos behind his head, a short cloak flapping behind his back, and a sheathed sword beneath his arm, seems to be tearing the drapery from another figure, of whom almost nothing remains. This may be an illustration of the scene in the *Trachiniae* following that where Herakles, driven mad by the pain of the poisoned shirt which is consuming his flesh, hurls Lichas, who had unwittingly brought him the fatal garment from Deianeira, to his death, while Hyllos stands helplessly by; thereafter one of his comrades, perhaps Philoctetes, endeavours to tear the devouring robe from the body of Herakles, and Hyllos, seizing the first object that he sees on the walls of the temple, rushes to his assistance.

Margot Schmidt, *Festschrift Karl Schefold* (*AntK*, Beiheft 4, 1967), 182–5, pl. 59, 4.

III.3,1 (New York). Euripides, *Aigeus*

3. Euripides

Aigeus

III. 3, 1

New York, Metropolitan Museum 56.171.48.
Attic red-figured kalyx-krater not far from Polygnotos; 450–425 B.C.

Euripides' *Aigeus* was probably produced soon after 450 B.C. The fragments suggest that Theseus arrived in Athens, his father Aigeus was persuaded by his second wife Medea to send him to catch the bull at Marathon; to Medea's consternation he captured the bull and brought it back to Athens; she then persuaded Aigeus to put poison in Theseus' cup at a banquet which celebrated his success; as Theseus was going to drink he gave Aigeus his sword, Aigeus recognized the sword as the one that he had left in Troizen for the infant Theseus. Together father and son banished Medea.
A series of vases illustrating this story has been put together by B. B. Shefton. The kalyx-krater in New York is one of the earliest. Theseus has grasped the bull's left horn with his left hand and raises the club with his right. It does not greatly matter whether the painter was thinking of the first capture or some later moment on the way to Athens when the bull grew restive. He has added Aigeus, a tall solemn watching figure, on the left, and a woman running away but looking back in horror, who holds a jug and a phiale (libation saucer). On two vases with much the same scheme painted after 430 B.C. she is identified as Medea by her tiara and oriental decorated sleeves. It is very likely that Medea was first dressed as an oriental in Euripides' *Medea* in 431 B.C., and after that date she normally appeared as an oriental in any story in which she had a part. The absence of oriental costume is therefore no argument against recognizing Medea on the New York krater. She sees that Theseus is victorious and makes haste to prepare her poison.

ARV[2], 1057, no. 104; B. B. Shefton, *AJA* 60, 1956, 159 ff.; Webster, *Tragedies of Euripides*, 77; *MTSP*[2], 153.

III. 3, 2

Florence P 80, from Populonia.
Attic red-figured skyphos; 430 B.C.

On one side, the bull tied up to a tree; Theseus stands in front of him, leaning on his club and holding his hat. On the other side, Medea, in oriental patterned sleeves and an overgarment over her chiton, approaches Aigeus, who is seated holding a sceptre, persuasively with the box of poisons in her left hand.

B. B. Shefton, *AJA* 60, 1956, 162, pl. 61.

III. 3, 3

Adolphseck, Schloss Fasanerie 179.
Apulian bell-krater by the Adolphseck Painter; early fourth century B.C.

III.3,2 (Florence). Euripides, *Aigeus*

III.3,3 (Adolphseck). Euripides, *Aigeus*

Here the scene shows the recognition of Theseus by Aigeus, which takes place not at a banquet but beside an altar. To left is Medea, wearing an embroidered peplos, with a shawl draped across the front of her body and pulled up on to her head like a veil. She starts back with a gesture of astonishment and, in her terror at the revelation of Theseus' true identity, drops the jug, which is shown falling to the ground. In the centre, the youthful Theseus, resting his left hand upon his club, pours wine from a phiale on to an altar; this may well be the poisoned draught prepared for him by Medea, which his father Aigeus, convinced by the tokens that it is his own son Theseus, tells him not to drink. Aigeus stands to right of the altar; he has white hair and beard (the added white now mostly vanished, giving him a bald effect), wears an elabor-

ately patterned tunic beneath his cloak, and holds a sceptre. In his hands are the sword and bonnet (*pilos*), which have led to the recognition of his son. It looks as if in one version of the story the *pilos* took the place of the sandals as one of the tokens; it is referred to by Bacchylides (XVIII, 46 ff.) in his description of the arrival of Theseus in Attica (illustrated on a fourth-century Attic bell-krater in Sydney; 49.04, *JHS* 56, 1936, pl. 5) and appears again on some vases (e.g. on another fragment of III. 3, 2) representing Theseus' fight with the bull. On our vase it must play a special rôle since Theseus is already wearing a *petasos* and would not need a *pilos* as well.

H. Möbius in *Antiken in deutschem Privatbesitz*, 42–3, no. 181, pl. 80; *CVA* 2, pl. 80; *APS*, 19–20, no. 1; Webster, *MTSP*², 153; *Tragedies of Euripides*, 77–80 and 298.

Aiolos

III. 3, 4

Bari 1535, from Canosa.
Early Lucanian hydria by the Amykos Painter; *c.* 410 B.C.

The *Aiolos* of Euripides, which was produced before 423 B.C. and possibly in the same year as the *Hecuba*, dealt with the incestuous love of Macareus, son of Aiolos, for his sister Canace. She tried to conceal the birth of their child by feigning illness; Macareus persuaded his father to let his sons marry his daughters and Aiolos drew lots, which unfortunately gave Canace to another of the sons. In some fashion not clear from the *hypothesis* or the surviving fragments, Aiolos learnt the truth and sent Canace a sword, with which she committed suicide. Macareus finally won Aiolos over, but came too late to save Canace and committed suicide himself.

The scene on the shoulder of the Bari hydria, painted little more than a decade after the production of the play in Athens, shows the suicide of Canace. She occupies the centre of the picture, lying on a couch, drooping in death, the fatal sword still clasped in her right hand. At the head of the couch stands the white-haired figure of Aiolos, pointing with his staff and hurling reproaches at Macareus, who stands at the left with his hands bound behind his back and with down-turned head and a look of guilt in his downcast eyes. Beside him is a youth, presumably one of his brothers, who is doing something to his bound hands. Behind Aiolos is an elderly woman, seated on an altar, with her cloak drawn over her head like a veil; this is grasped by a spear-bearer, and it looks as if the woman is to be identified as the aged nurse, who is about to be punished for her part in the affair. The three young women on the left are probably sisters of Canace, the more elderly woman to the right, perhaps her mother.

LCS 45, no. 221, pl. 18; *MTSP²*, 157–60 and 303; *EAA* iii, 353, fig. 429; *La Grèce classique*, fig. 336.

III.3,4 (Bari). Euripides, *Aiolos*

III.3,5 (Basel). Euripides, *Alkestis*

Alkestis

III. 3, 5

Basel, Antikenmuseum, Loan S. 21.
Apulian loutrophoros, by a forerunner of the Ganymede Painter; third quarter fourth century B.C.

In the tetralogy produced by Euripides in 438 B.C., which won the second prize, the *Alkestis* was the fourth play and of particular note as departing from the normal satyric tradition, although it strikes something of the note of a satyr-play in the character of Herakles. Apollo, banished for a season from Olympus for having slain the Cyclopes, who forged the thunderbolts of Zeus with which his son Asklepios had been smitten, and condemned to serve a mortal, became herdsman to Admetos, King of Pherae in Thessaly. Out of regard for his taskmaster he won from the Fates the boon that, when the day of Admetos' death came, he might escape if he could find a willing substitute. Only his wife Alkestis consented to take his place, and the day comes when she must yield up her life for him. After taking a long leave of him and her children, she descends to Hades, whence she is brought back by Herakles, who wrestles for her with Death. She is presented veiled to Admetos by Herakles, who asks him to look after her, and then throwing back her veil, she reveals her true identity to bring the play a happy ending.

Representations of the *Alkestis* in vase-painting are very rare, and, until the discovery of this vase, confined to an Etruscan krater (Cab. Méd. 918; Séchan, fig. 72; Beazley, *EVP* 133), showing two demons of the underworld come to fetch Admetos while Alkestis interposes to offer her life for his, and an Attic *onos* by the Eretria Painter showing Alkestis as a bride among her handmaids (Athens 1629; *ARV*², 1250, no. 34; Arias-Hirmer-Shefton, pl. 203). The new vase gives an admirable illustration of the farewell scene and the emotions reflected in the features of the principal characters emphasize the sorrow and fear inspired by the nearness of death. Alkestis (inscribed) is seated upon the couch in the palace, her head slightly turned towards Admetos, who stands beside her, his head bowed in grief and resting against his left hand, as he looks down to Alkestis. She is fondling her two children; her son Eumelos, wrapped in a cloak, looks up sorrowfully at her, while his sister stretches out both her hands in a gesture of entreaty. To right stands an aged woman, the mother of Admetos, who rests her chin upon her left hand and extends her right towards Alkestis; behind her is the aged retainer, in the typical stage costume for such persons, leaning on his stick beside a column, on top of which is a vase, with a bucrane to right. On the other side are two of the handmaids of Alkestis, one holding up a wool-basket, the other with a fillet and a fan. The appearance of Alkestis on the couch was probably brought about by the use of the *ekkyklema*; it would have been wheeled inside after her death.

For the play see A. M. Dale, *Euripides Alcestis* (Oxford, 1954); Webster, *The Tragedies of Euripides*, 48–52.

III.3,6 (Taranto). Euripides, *Alkmene*

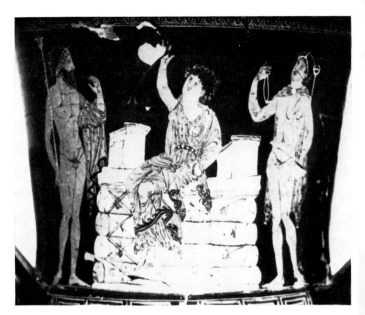

III.3,7 (Lipari). Euripides, *Alkmene*

Alkmene

III. 3, 6

Taranto, I.G. 4600.
Apulian kalyx-krater by the Painter of the Birth of Dionysos;
c. 400–390 B.C.

The action of Euripides' play seems to have taken place on the day that Alkmene gave birth to Herakles and Iphikles. The presence of Hermes on our vase, in the upper register with Zeus (who probably spoke the epilogue) and Eros, but on the right, suggests that he spoke the prologue. Amphitryon returned and suspected that his wife had been seduced by a rich lover. He threatened her with death, and when she took refuge on an altar inside the house, he followed her to burn her off the altar. What the audience heard next, presumably near the end of a chorus, was a thunderclap, then they saw Amphitryon staggering out of the house, then the messenger related the whole story: how Amphitryon tried to burn her off the altar, which is shown on the vase with the logs piled round it; how Zeus quenched the pyre with a thunderstorm and drove Amphitryon out – shown by the thunderbolt between Alkmene and Amphitryon; how Zeus then turned Alkmene's room into a bower (this is the meaning of the golden rain on III. 3, 8, which is recorded earlier by Pindar) and she gave birth to Herakles and Iphikles.

A. Cambitoglou and A. D. Trendall, *Mélanges Michalowski*, 676, no. 6, figs. 14–15; Schauenburg, *AuA* 10, 1961, pl. 13, fig. 25; Paribeni, *Immagini di vasi apuli*, pl. 14 (colour); Degrassi, *BdA* 50, 1965, fig. 54; Webster, *MTSP²*, TV 42 and p. 154; *Tragedies of Euripides*, 92; O. Skutsch, *CR*, n.s. 17, 1967, 11; *HSCP* 71, 1966, 129 (on the prologue in Ennius's adaptation).

III. 3, 7

Lipari 9405, from Tomb 730.

Early Sicilian kalyx-krater; second quarter fourth century B.C.

On this vase Alkmene is shown seated on the altar, with the pyre in front of it, one hand raised to heaven in a moving gesture of supplication. In response to her entreaty both Zeus and Hermes appear, as they did on the previous vase, but here one stands on each side of Alkmene with no one else present. We thus have the principal character in the drama shown between the probable speakers of the prologue and the epilogue, one to explain the situation, the other its ultimate resolution.

III. 3, 8

London, British Museum F 149, from St. Agata dei Goti.
Paestan bell-krater, signed by Python; third quarter fourth century B.C.

This famous vase gives the fullest version of the story, and shows Amphitryon with his helper Antenor setting fire to the pyre of logs in front of the altar, on which Alkmene is seated. As on the Lipari vase, she raises an arm in supplication to Zeus, who here appears as a bust in the top left-hand corner. He has hurled his thunderbolts, which may be seen beside the pyre, and now sends the Clouds to quench the flames with rain; they are shown pouring down water from the jars they are holding and creating the remarkable rainbow effect behind Alkmene. From the opposite corner Eos looks down upon the scene. All the characters, with the exception of the Clouds, are inscribed, and the three principals wear elaborately patterned costumes, which must reflect stage influence.

Trendall, *Paestan Pottery*, 56, pl. 15 and *PPSupp*, no. 146; Hinks, *Myth and Allegory*, 33, pl. 3a; Beazley, *EVP* 105; *La Grèce classique*; fig. 373 (colour); Séchan, 242 ff., pl. 5; Gigante, *Teatro Greco*, 86, pl. 3.
For references to the play see no. III. 3, 6.

III.3,8 (London). Euripides, *Alkmene*

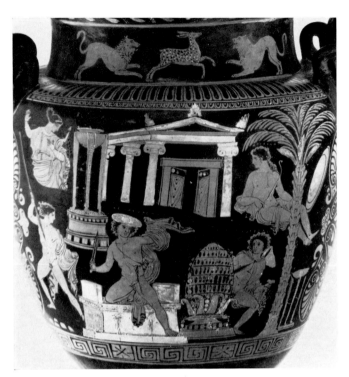

III.3,9 (Milan, Torno coll.). Euripides, *Andromache*

Andromache

III. 3, 9

Milan, Torno coll. (ex Ruvo, Caputi 239).
Apulian volute-krater by the Iliupersis Painter; *c.* 370 B.C.

The representation on this vase of the slaying of Neoptolemos at Delphi provides a good illustration to the description of it given by the Messenger in his speech in the *Andromache* (lines 1085 ff.). In the upper register are the Delphic tripod and the temple of Apollo, beside which the god himself (inscribed) is seated on the right, with the Pythian priestess on the left, clutching the temple key. In front, below, is an altar, on which Neoptolemos (inscribed) is kneeling, sword in hand, with blood pouring from a wound in his side. Nearby is the omphalos, behind which Orestes (inscribed) is lurking with drawn sword; to the left one of the men of Delphi, who assisted in the murder, stands with poised spear. The location is further defined by a tall palm-tree on the right of the scene, which probably represents the bronze palm dedicated by the Athenians after the battle of Eurymedon; beside it is a smaller tripod, probably a votive offering, and above, a shield, which may be an allusion to the shield which Neoptolemos grabbed from the temple to defend himself (lines 1121–2).

Séchan, 253–5, fig. 75; Cook, *Zeus* ii, 170 n. 2, fig. 117; Pouilloux and Roux, *Énigmes à Delphes*, 119, n. 3, pl. 21, 1; Gemma Sena Chiesa in *Acme* 21, 1968, 328 ff., no. 1, pl. 1.
Webster, *Tragedies of Euripides*, 118-21; *MTSP²*, 154.

Andromeda

III. 3, 10

Berlin, Staatliche Museen, inv. 3237, from Capua.
Attic red-figured kalyx-krater; soon after 400 B.C.

Euripides' *Andromeda* in 412 B.C. began with a monody in which Andromeda, tied to a rock, and waiting in the night for the monster to come and devour her, lamented her fate; she is only answered by Echo in the cave behind her, until the chorus of friendly girls come to comfort her. Later Perseus arrives. To produce Andromeda on her rock as the opening of the play was a startling innovation, and can only have been done with the *ekkyklema*; the doorway behind would then be Echo's cave.

The Berlin krater shows ANDROMEDA (inscribed) standing on a rock with hands stretched out as if bound to the rocks, from which the bushes to left and right grow. She wears a tiara but otherwise normal tragic costume, with himation, chiton, sleeved and decorated overgarment, *not* the oriental dress of the Sophoclean Andromeda (III. 2, 1–3). The chests above and below are offerings to the dead; possibly the chorus brought them. They are represented by the Aithiopian girl in oriental trousered, sleeved garment and short chiton, seated on a rock to the extreme left of the picture. Next to her on the upper level is HERMES (inscribed) walking away and looking back. He wears petasos and chlamys and holds his caduceus in his right hand. Probably his only function in the story was to have guided Perseus safely through the Gorgon adventure, and he looks back at Perseus. Between Hermes and Andromeda, KEPHEUS (inscribed) is seated, wearing tiara and himation and holding a sceptre in his right hand. He looks back at Perseus, and in fact he later objected to Perseus' proposal to marry Andromeda. On the right PERSEUS (inscribed) enters and stops entranced by Andromeda. He wears pilos (wreathed for victory), chlamys, and boots; he holds the *harpe* in his right hand and the bag hung over his right shoulder contains the Gorgon's head. Behind him and to the right APHRODITE (inscribed) holds a wreath over his head, so that the painter clearly alludes to the famous love-scene between Perseus and Andromeda, of which fragments survive. It is possible also that Aphrodite spoke the epilogue. Beyond Aphrodite (and corresponding to the Aithiopian girl on the left) a large altar with fire on it: this must have some relation to the story but what relation is unknown.

ARV², 1336, 1690; *MTSP²*, AV 34 and pp. 116, 154; Séchan, 356; Bieber, *History²*, 31; Webster, *Tragedies of Euripides*, 192, 304; Pickard-Cambridge, *Festivals²*, fig. 60; Mingazzini, *Rend Pont Acc* 38, 1965–6, 71, fig. 3; Phillips, *AJA* 72, 1968, pl. 6, fig. 17 and pl. 7, fig. 16; W. Jobst, *Die Höhle im gr. Theater*, figs. 19–20.

III. 3, 11–12

11. Naples 3225 (inv. 82266), from Canosa.
12. Matera 12538, from Irsina.
Apulian loutrophoros and kalyx-krater by the Darius Painter; third quarter of the fourth century B.C.

The South Italian representations of Andromeda, which are fairly numerous (see Phillips, *AJA* 72, 1968, 8 ff.), fall into three main groups. In the first she is shown bound to posts or columns (e.g. Phillips, pls. 8–9, figs. 18–21),[1] in the second to posts consisting of freshly-cut trees, still retaining the stumps of their branches and an occasional leafy spray (Phillips, pls. 10–11, figs. 23–29), and in the third to a rock, which often looks like the mouth of a cave or grotto, but is more probably a stage prop, since it serves also for Prometheus on III. 1, 27. The two vases here illustrated belong to the second group, though each gives a rather different treatment of the theme. On the Naples loutrophoros Andromeda appears in the centre of the upper register, her hands bound to two tall tree-trunks, from the upper part of which spring a few small leafy branches. To the left, seated in dejection upon a hydria, is a woman, over whose head a maid is holding a parasol; she is probably Cassiopeia, Andromeda's mother. To right, is her father Kepheus, supported by a servant in oriental garb, behind whom stands a sorrowing woman, perhaps one of Andromeda's sisters. Below, separated not inappropriately by a narrow band of fish and sea-creatures, Perseus, wearing a winged cap with the gorgoneion as an emblem, grapples with the sea-monster in the presence of five Nereids, mounted on dolphins or hippocamps, while a small Eros flies towards him, with the victor's crown in one hand and a magic love-wheel (iynx) held by its ribbons in the other. The same theme is repeated with minor variations, such as the presence of Aphrodite and more oriental attendants, on a large pelike in Naples (Stg. 708; Phillips, fig. 25) by a later follower of the Darius Painter, who drew his inspiration either from this vase or from the same monumental source.
The Matera krater, also by the Darius Painter, may be regarded as a sort of sequel to the Naples loutrophoros. Here Perseus has slain the monster and set Andromeda free. The now empty straps which fettered her hands to the tree-trunks hang down with the nails still attached to them. She looks down affectionately at Perseus, who moves away to the right wearing his winged cap and carrying the *harpe* in one hand and the gorgon's head in a satchel in the other. Flanking Andromeda are various divinities – Paniskos, Aphrodite with an iynx, Poseidon and another Pan, this time in human form

apart from the goat-horns, holding syrinx and pedum. Below, Kepheus in regal costume, with sceptre, stands beside the elaborate throne of Cassiopeia, in front of which a small Eros is placing a footstool. To right, a veiled Cassiopeia looks up towards Andromeda, a large hydria at her feet. The presence of Poseidon is natural, since it was he who sent the sea-monster to devour Andromeda, because her mother had taunted the sea-nymphs with her beauty; Aphrodite, love-charm in hand, ensures the transference of Andromeda's affections to Perseus, with all the complications that followed in consequence; the Pans suggest an outdoor or rustic setting, which is further emphasized by the tree on the right and the pebbly ground-lines.

11. Séchan, 259, pl. 6; Schauenburg, *Perseus*, pl. 24, 2; Phillips, *op. cit.* 10, fig. 24; Schmidt, *Dareiosmaler*, pl. 13; Rocco, *Arch Class*, 5, 1953, pls. 81–3; Webster, *MTSP*², 154; *Tragedies of Euripides*, 192 ff. and 304 (with list of representations).
12. Phillips, *op. cit.*, 10, figs. 27–9; *MTSP*², 155.

III. 3, 13

Caltagirone, Museo Civico.
Sicilian kalyx-krater by the Hecate Painter; third quarter of the fourth century B.C.

The third group of Andromeda vases makes use of a slightly different setting, in which the posts or tree-trunks are replaced by a rock – in one instance shown as a solid mass (Berlin 3238; *LCS* 227, no. 8, pl. 89, 1–3; Phillips, *op. cit.*, pl. 13, fig. 37), but more commonly drawn in outline like the mouth of a cave or grotto, sometimes with small plants growing on it, similar to the leafy sprays on the tree-trunks (cf. Phillips, figs. 30–2). This seems to represent a different convention in the stage production of the play, perhaps more in keeping with the description given by Perseus in one of the surviving fragments (124 N):
'What is this cliff I see, washed around by sea-foam? There is the image of a maiden, wrought from the very stuff of the rock, the sculpture of a skilled hand.'
To the four vases listed by Phillips as showing this background (*op. cit.*, pl. 2, figs. 30–2 and pl. 12, fig. 34) must now be added a large Apulian loutrophoros of the late fourth century at present on the European market, on which Perseus battles with the sea-monster beneath Andromeda, who is fastened to a rock very like that to which Prometheus is bound on III. 1, 27. Otherwise in this context Perseus is usually represented as about to set Andromeda free, having already slain the monster, which does not appear. The surrounding figures generally include members of Andromeda's family or servants and the Sicilian krater is of special interest as showing instead Phineus, her fiancé, who appears holding a spear (cf. the figure on the Halle fragments; Séchan, fig. 79

---

[1] An interesting variant of the 'column' type (cf. B.M. F 185; Phillips, fig. 19) appears on an Apulian bell-krater of *c.* 360 B.C. (Christchurch, N.Z., 116/71, ex Sotheby's, *Sale Cat.*, 29 March 1971, no. 80, ill. opp. p. 22), which shows Andromeda bound to the columns of an Ionic naiskos between Perseus and Kepheus.

III.3, 10 (Berlin). Euripides, *Andromeda*

III.3, 12 (Matera). Euripides, *Andromeda*

III.3,11 (Naples). Euripides, *Andromeda*

III.3,13 (Caltagirone). Euripides, *Andromeda*

III.3,14 (Policoro). Euripides, *Antiope*

2; Phillips, fig. 34), looking downcast on the left, while Perseus, in heroic nudity with flying hair, on the right, the *harpe* in one hand, the satchel with the gorgon's head slung over his shoulder on a baldric, his chlamys flapping out behind him, his hat in mid-air beside his head, and wearing the winged sandals, looks triumphant as he turns his head toward Andromeda. The simplicity of this representation contrasts with the more elaborate scenes on the Apulian vases; here we see the three people most affected by the development of the story. We do not know exactly what part Phineus played in the drama, but he seems to have conspired with Kepheus to dispose of his rival and Perseus may have threatened to petrify him. The rocky or cliff background found favour with later painters and reappears on several Pompeian wall-paintings (e.g. Phillips, figs. 2–7).

Arias, *Dioniso* 36, 1962, 50 ff., pls. 1–3, figs. 1–4; *LCS* 590, no. 29, pl. 228, 5–6; Phillips, *op. cit.*, 11, pl. 2, fig. 31; *MTSP²*, 155; W. Jobst, *Die Höhle im gr. Theater*, fig. 23.

Antiope

III. 3, 14–15

14. Policoro, Museo Nazionale della Siritide.
Early Lucanian pelike by the Policoro Painter; *c.* 400 B.C.
15. Berlin F 3296, from Palazzolo.
Early Sicilian kalyx-krater by the Dirce Painter; *c.* 380–370 B.C.

The *Antiope*, probably produced *c.* 410 B.C., was one of the more famous plays of Euripides and extensive fragments of it survive. The setting was probably outside a cave near Eleutherai, where Zeus had raped Antiope and where she had given birth to the twins Amphion and Zethos, who had been brought up by a shepherd, while their mother was held in captivity and maltreated by Lykos and his wife Dirce. Antiope escapes back to the cave and through the shepherd is reunited with her sons, who take revenge upon Dirce, when she comes in at the head of a band of maenads to celebrate the rites of Dionysos, by binding her upon the back of a wild bull, and are later about to kill Lykos, whom they have lured into the cave, when Hermes appears as *deus ex machina* to save him and to prophesy the future of the twins and provide for Dirce to be honoured by having a spring named after her.

Two vases illustrate what must have been highly dramatic moments in the drama. The Policoro pelike, found in 1963, shows Zethos and Amphion about to bind Dirce onto the bull, an episode which would have been narrated in the Messenger's speech. The vase gives a very spirited representation of the scene, with the huge figure of the bull dominating the composition, and Dirce lying dishevelled on the stony ground beside it, grasping one of its forelegs with her left hand, and raising the other in a gesture of supplication to the twins, each with a goad in hand, and one holding the cords with which Dirce is to be bound on to the animal's back.

The Berlin vase (III. 3, 15) gives us the next act in the drama. Lykos appears, is induced to enter the cave, and then the *ekkyklema* would roll out showing Amphion and Zethos standing over him ready to deliver the fatal blow. At that

III.3,15 (Berlin). Euripides, *Antiope*

moment Hermes appears to stop the murder and bring the play to a conclusion with appropriate forecasts of the future. This is the scene on the vase. Above to left is Dirce lying dead, fallen from the back of the bull which now gallops off; below in the herdsman's cave, the mouth of which is shown by two trees bent over to form an arch (cf. the trees on the Andromeda vases, III. 3, 11–12 above) and the floor by a mass of stones, Amphion and Zethos stand over Lykos, who has been forced to his knees, and threaten him with their swords, while Antiope flees to right. Looking down from above is Hermes, half concealed by rising ground, who is about to intervene and bring the play to its conclusion. From the top of the cave hangs a panther-skin, which suggests that it may have been sacred to Dionysos, and it is worth noting that Zeus had raped Antiope in the guise of a satyr (cf. fr. 203); to the left is a tree, indicative of a rustic setting.

For the *Antiope* see Séchan, 290–307; Webster, *Tragedies of Euripides*, 205–11 and 305; *MTSP²*, 155–6.
14. *LCS* 5⁸, no. 288, pl. 27, 4; Degrassi, *BdA* 50, 1965, 18, fig. 43, and *RM*, Ergänzungsheft 11, 1967, pl. 65, 1 and pls. 74–5; *AA* 83, 1968, 789, fig. 42; Neutsch, *Siris ed Heraclea*, fig. 34.
15. *LCS* 203, no. 27; Phillips, *AJA* 72, 1968, pl. 2, fig. 33; Greifenhagen, *Führer durch die Antikenabteilung* (1968), 107, pl. 95; Jobst, *op. cit.*, fig. 17.

Chrysippos

III. 3, 16–18

16. Berlin 1968. 12.
Apulian bell-krater by the Darius Painter; third quarter of the fourth century B.C.
17. Naples 1769 (inv. 81942).
Apulian amphora by the Darius Painter; third quarter of the fourth century B.C.
18. Melbourne D 87/1969.
Faliscan volute-krater; second quarter of the fourth century B.C.

In the play by Euripides, Chrysippos was the true son of Pelops and Hippodameia, and not his illegitimate offspring by a nymph. While staying with Pelops during his exile from Thebes, Laios was attracted by the exceptional beauty of the boy, and, unable to control his overwhelming passion, carried him off in a chariot, probably during the games at Olympia. Thereafter, the course of events is obscure, but it seems that Chrysippos committed suicide out of shame, and Pelops called down upon Laios the curse that he should perish by the hand of his own son.

The rape of Chrysippos is not a popular subject with vase-painters and so far only four representations of it are known. Of these the fullest is that on the Berlin krater. On the lower register we see Laios in his four-horse chariot driving off with the young Chrysippos, who stretches out his hands, imploringly but vainly, to his father Pelops, who comes running up from the right, wearing a long-sleeved, embroidered tunic, with a flapping cloak fastened at his throat by a brooch, high laced boots and a Phrygian cap. To the left two nude youths with spears in their hands confront each other; perhaps Atreus and Thyestes, the older brothers of Chrysippos, preparing to intervene. Above is a row of divinities, Pan, Apollo, Athena, and Aphrodite with a small Eros, which concludes somewhat unexpectedly with the paidagogos, who is shown tearing his white hair in a gesture of despair, and wearing the usual short tunic, with cloak, petasos and high boots. A somewhat similar version of the scene appears on an amphora in Berlin (F 3239; Séchan, fig. 91), from the school of the Darius Painter, except that here a small Eros flies with a wreath towards Laios, and a youth with two spears tries to halt the chariot.

The Naples amphora (III. 3, 17), also by the Darius Painter, who seems fond of this theme, gives a slightly different version, combining elements of both vases. Here the erotic element is emphasized by the presence of two Erotes, one holding the bridle of the leading horse, the other flying with crown and fillet towards the couple in the chariot. Chrysippos

III.3,16 (Berlin). Euripides, *Chrysippos*

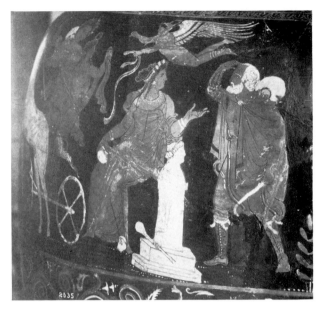

III.3,17 (Naples). Euripides, *Chrysippos*

III.3,18 (Melbourne). Euripides, *Chrysippos*

no longer holds out his arms in entreaty, but seems to be look-ing towards the approaching Eros. The place of Pelops is taken by the old paidagogos, who is almost a replica of the one in the Berlin vase, but here Aphrodite appears between him and the chariot, seated by a herm, looking as if she were trying to explain the situation to him and calm his doubts. To left is Pan, seated on a piece of drapery, holding syrinx and lagobolon; his presence, together with the plants and the dog biting at a small snake, indicates the rustic setting.

The third vase (III. 3, 18) is a Faliscan krater, formerly in the Pulszky collection, then lost to sight for many years, until it turned up in Melbourne and was acquired by the National Gallery in 1969. It gives a much reduced version of the episode, in which only Laios and Chrysippos in the chariot, with the bust of a woman above, are shown. Chrysippos is stretching out his arms towards an absent Pelops, which suggests that the vase-painter was drawing on an original similar to III. 3, 16. The identity of the woman who appears above the chariot is problematic; her open mouth, as if about to utter a cry, and her gestures suggest surprise or anguish and she may well be Hippodameia, the mother of Chrysippos in the play.

III.3, 19 (London). Euripides, *Hecuba*

On the play see Robert, *Oidipus*, I, 400 ff. and *JdI* 29, 1914, 168 ff.; Séchan, 311–18 and 588; Webster, *Tragedies of Euripides*, 111–13 and 298; *MTSP²*, 156–7.

16. *Jahrb. Berl. Museen*, 12, 1970, 154 ff., figs. 1, 3–4.
17. *JdI* 29, 1914, 168 ff., figs. 1–2 and pl. 11; Séchan, fig. 92; Schmidt, *Dareiosmaler*, pl. 14a and 15a.
18. *Wiener Vorlegeblätter*, VI, pl. 11 = Roscher, *ML* i, 903 = Séchan, fig. 90 = Stella, *Mitologia greca*, ill. on p. 632. Trendall, *Jahrb. Berl. Mus.* 12, 1970, 160, fig. 5, and *Art Bulletin of Victoria*, 1970–71, 7 ff., figs. 11–12.

Hecuba

III. 3, 19

London, British Museum 1900. 5–19. 1.
Apulian loutrophoros from the workshop of the Darius Painter and probably by his hand; third quarter of the fourth century B.C.

The last scenes of the *Hecuba* give us the terrible picture of the vengeance of the grief-crazed Hecuba upon Polymestor, King of the Thracian Chersonese, who had murdered her son Polydorus for the sake of the gold he had brought with him to provide for Priam's children if Troy were to fall. After enticing the king into her tent with the lure of further treasure and assuring him, in words of calculated dramatic irony, that he will be safe within, Hecuba with the aid of her attendants puts out his eyes and kills his children. Soon afterwards Hecuba emerges in triumph (l. 1046) to tell the chorus that they will soon see Polymestor groping his blind way (l. 1050) and the bodies of his slain sons, which are presumably brought out on the *ekkyklema* while she is speaking. In answer to Polymestor's shouts Agamemnon comes up and, after listening to both sides, passes judgement in favour of Hecuba. The scene on our vase shows Polymestor staggering forward in his blindness, vainly trying to feel his way with his outstretched hands, between Agamemnon on one side and Hecuba on the other. Polymestor wears a short ornamental chiton, with cloak and Phrygian cap; his now useless sword lies on the ground at his feet. On the left stands Agamemnon, sceptre in hand, attended by a youthful spear-bearer, and on the right is the aged Hecuba, her ravaged face lined with sorrow. She leans upon a staff and is supported by one of her attendants, who puts her arm around her shoulder, no doubt to comfort and encourage her during Polymestor's threats and long tirade (lines 1124 ff.).

Séchan, 321, fig. 95; Pickard-Cambridge, *Festivals*¹, 222, fig. 185; Webster, *Tragedies of Euripides*, 121–4; *MTSP²*, 157.

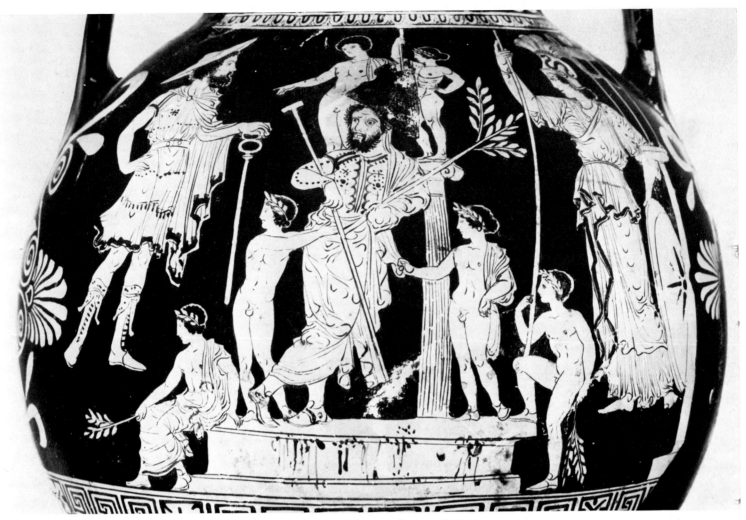

III.3,20 (Policoro). Euripides, *Herakleidai*

Herakleidai

III. 3, 20

Policoro, Museo Nazionale della Siritide, from Policoro.
Early Lucanian pelike, Policoro Group; *c.* 400 B.C.

The discovery of this vase in 1963 has provided us with an excellent illustration of the opening scene in the *Herakleidai*, a play which must have been originally produced early in the Peloponnesian War. Persecuted by Eurystheus, Iolaos, with Alkmene and the children of Herakles, has sought refuge in the sanctuary of Zeus near Marathon in Attica, in the hope that Demophon will grant them asylum in Athens. At the sight of the approaching herald of Eurystheus, Iolaos bids the younger children (who are with him in the sanctuary while Hyllos and their older brothers have gone to seek an alternative refuge in case Athens will not accept them) grasp his robes (ll. 48–50). This is the scene shown on the vase. In the centre is Iolaos, in stage costume, in the sanctuary represented by an altar and an Ionic column with the cult-statue of the god, who looks more like Apollo than Zeus, though this may be the vase-painter's fault; he holds a suppliant bough in one hand and around him are grouped four of the young children,

the two nearest grasping his robes as he directed, the other two with boughs in their hands. All these are wreathed; not so the slightly older-looking boy who stands behind Iolaos, one hand pointing in the direction of the herald Copreus, who comes up from the left, dressed in a short tunic with a cloak fastened by a brooch at the neck, wearing a petasos and high boots, and carrying a herald's staff. To right stands Athena, who is present to indicate that the location of the setting is in Attica; she looks down with sympathetic eyes towards the suppliants.

There can be little doubt that the scene has been directly inspired by the Euripidean play, which, in view of the close association between its title and Herakleia, the ancient name of the city (Policoro) where it was found, may well have been performed there.

Trendall, *Arch Reps.* 10, 1963–4, 35; *LCS* 55, no. 283, pl. 25, 5; Degrassi, *BdA* 50, 1965, 12–14, figs. 33 and 39–40, and *RM*, Ergänzungsheft 11, 1967, pls. 64, 76–7 and 79,2; *AA* 81, 1966, p. 303, fig. 61, and 83, 1968, p. 787, fig. 40; Schmidt, *Festschrift Karl Schefold* (*AntK*, Beiheft 4, 1967), pl. 59, 2; Neutsch, *Siris ed Heraclea*, figs. 35–6; Webster, *Apollo*, Aug. 1967, p. 100, fig. 15; *The Tragedies of Euripides*, 102–5; *MTSP²*, 130, LV 6.
On the setting see G. Zuntz, *The Political Plays of Euripides*, 97 ff.

III.3,21 (Berlin). Euripides, *Herakleidai*

III. 3, 21

Berlin 1969.6.
Early Lucanian column-krater, end of the fifth century B.C.

This vase, also of recent discovery and closely connected in style with the Policoro Group, provides a further illustration of the *Herakleidai*. The scene is again the sanctuary of Zeus near Marathon, and Iolaos, dressed in an elaborately patterned stage costume, appears seated upon the altar. This time greater emphasis is properly placed upon his age, since both hair and beard are white and he holds a staff, in preparation for his miraculous rejuvenation later in the play (847 ff.). Only two of the young children are shown, both naked and standing beside him. Resting one foot upon the altar is a nude youth, naked except for a chlamys down his back, who places one hand on the shoulder of Iolaos and holds a herald's staff in the other. He may well be Copreus, the herald of Eurystheus, despite his youthful appearance as compared with the preceding vase, who lays hands upon Iolaos (68 ff.), just before the arrival of Demophon and Akamas (118 ff.), who are here shown riding up on their horses, one raising his hand in a gesture either of greeting or possibly of warning to the herald

to proceed no further. Akamas has no speaking part in the play, but Demophon, after listening to the arguments of Copreus and Iolaos, offers the latter asylum (236 ff.) and later joins battle with the Argives on his behalf. Greifenhagen prefers to identify the herald with the retainer of Hyllos, who arrives with the joyful tidings (630 ff.) and brings comfort to the depressed Iolaos, who calls forth Alkmene from within the temple to hear the good news.

Above to left, is a woman seated upon a stone block, holding on her lap a cult image of Zeus with the thunderbolt. She is probably Alkmene, and Greifenhagen has ingeniously suggested, following Wilamowitz, that what she is sitting on may be the boundary stone (ὅρος) between the Tetrapolis and Athens, which would have appeared on the stage to define the location of the setting and would have been under the divine protection of Zeus.

The vase-painter seems to be giving a free interpretation of the opening of the play and may well have intended this vase, which is more or less contemporary with the Policoro pelike and may even be a product of the same workshop, to complement the other (or vice versa).

Greifenhagen, 123 *BWPr*, 1969, 5–23, pls. 1–3, fig. 2.

III.3,22 (Taranto.) Euripides, *First Hippolytus*

Hippolytus

III. 3, 22

Taranto, from Altamura.

Apulian pyxis, school of the Darius Painter; mid-fourth century B.C.

On the lid of this vase is a scene not easy of interpretation.[1] It represents a bearded man, holding a sheathed sword, in earnest converse with a seated figure in an attitude of despair, wearing a long-sleeved tunic with a cloak and contemplating a sword sticking point downwards in the ground. The sex of this figure is difficult to determine, but if, as seems not unlikely, it is a woman, then the scene might well have been inspired by the *First Hippolytus* of Euripides. We know comparatively little about this play except that it did not meet with approval when produced, and was later (in 428 B.C.) rewritten in a revised form in which, according to the Hypothesis, 'all that was unseemly and worthy of condemnation had been corrected'. It is this version of the play which we possess. In the first play Phaedra seems to have offered herself to Hippolytus (hence Aeschylus' reference to her being made into a whore in *Frogs* 1043), who covered his head to avoid being polluted by her approach (hence its title *Hippolytos Kalyptomenos*), and she subsequently accused him to save herself. In Seneca's play Theseus finds her contemplating suicide with the sword Hippolytus had cast aside as polluted when

[1] Dr. Mario Napoli has suggested that it may represent the identification by Odysseus of Achilles when disguised as one of the daughters of King Lycomedes.

she grasped it in supplication, and, recognizing the weapon, accepts her story. This version may well have derived from Euripides, and the vase provides a good illustration of it. The bearded man, with the slightly admonitory gesture, could then be identified as Theseus; the seated figure, with appropriately dishevelled hair and tormented look, would be Phaedra meditating suicide with the sword of Hippolytus, which occupies such a prominent place in the picture and which provides Theseus with what he regards as convincing evidence of guilt (cf. l. 896 in Seneca's *Hippolytus* – 'hic docet ensis').

Theseus calls down a curse upon Hippolytus, who is killed when the horses of the chariot he is driving along the sea-shore are terrified by the bull which Poseidon sends from the sea.

Arch Reps 16, 1969–70, 41, fig. 18.
On the play see W. S. Barrett, *Euripides: Hippolytos* (Oxford, 1964) 11–12, 18–22; Webster, *Tragedies of Euripides*, 66–71.

III. 3, 23–24

23. Lipari inv. 340 bis, from Tomb 229 bis.
Sicilian kalyx-krater by the Maron Painter; second quarter of the fourth century B.C.
24. London, British Museum F 279.
Apulian volute-krater, by the Darius Painter; third quarter of the fourth century B.C.

The manner of Hippolytus's death was common to both versions of the Euripidean play. As a result of the curse called down upon him by Theseus, Poseidon sent a bull from the sea, which terrified the horses of the chariot which Hippolytus was driving by the sea-shore so that he was thrown and fatally injured. In the extant play the scene is vividly described by the Messenger (1213 ff.), and the Lipari krater well illustrates the moment when 'wild panic fell upon the steeds' and Hippolytus uses all his might to control them, but in vain. The horses are shown rearing up in fright, one of the traces already broken and the chariot beginning to break apart. The sea is represented by a band of wave-pattern in the foreground, but the bull is not shown. Above, behind rising ground, appear Eros and Aphrodite, who contemplate with complete composure the disaster for which she is responsible. On an early Apulian bell-krater in Bari (5597) Hippolytus is shown in the chariot, while the horses rear up at the sight of the bull, but the fullest version appears on III. 3, 24, where on the lower level we see Hippolytus driving along in his chariot, as the bull emerges from the sea to frighten the horses, and to add to the terror of the scene the vase-painter has gratuitously included a Fury, snake in one hand and flaming torch in the other. Behind the chariot, one hand raised in a gesture of helpless horror, comes up the old retainer, dressed in the usual stage costume for this rôle (cf. III. 3, 17, 26), though on this

III.3,23 (Lipari). Euripides, *Hippolytus*

III.3,24 (London). Euripides, *Hippolytus*

occasion his cloak is white with a dark red border. He will later as the 'Messenger' tell how Hippolytus met his death (1153 ff.). The upper register contains, in accordance with the regular Apulian practice, a selection of divinities, not all of whom are connected directly with the play. From left to right we have Pan with syrinx and pedum (cf. III. 3, 17),

Apollo, Athena, Aphrodite with Eros, and Poseidon – only the last three being closely involved.

23. *Meligunis-Lipara* II, 78–9, pls. 80, 82–3; *LCS Suppl I*, 102; *MTSP*[2], 128, TV 44.
24. Séchan, fig. 99; Lippold, *RM* 60–1, 1953–4, 128 f., pl. 54, 1; Trendall, *SIVP*, pl. 9*a*; *MTSP*[2], 158.

III.3,25 (Leningrad). Euripides, *Hypsipyle*

III.3,26 (Naples). Euripides, *Hypsipyle*

Hypsipyle

III. 3, 25–26

25. Leningrad inv. 1714 (St. 523).
Apulian volute-krater, late work of the Lycurgus Painter; c. 350 B.C.
26. Naples 3255 (inv. 81394).
Apulian volute-krater, circle of the Darius Painter; c. 350–340 B.C.

Thanks to the discovery of extensive papyrus fragments (*Pap. Oxy.* vi. 852) it is possible to reconstruct the *Hypsipyle* with reasonable accuracy. It was one of Euripides' later plays, probably produced c. 410 B.C. The story tells of Hypsipyle, daughter of King Thoas of Lemnos, who, after bearing Jason twin sons (Euneos and Thoas), was driven out by the women of Lemnos for failing to kill her father, and who is now serving as nurse to the infant Opheltes in the palace of his parents Lycurgus and Eurydice, King and Queen of Nemea. Two young strangers, who are in fact her sons, although she does not recognize them, arrive and are admitted to the palace by Hypsipyle. Later Amphiaraos and his men pass through on their way to attack Thebes, and when she conducts him to a spring to obtain pure water for a sacrifice, a serpent kills the child Opheltes. Eurydice is about to put Hypsipyle to death, when Amphiaraos intervenes on her behalf and her life is spared. Amphiaraos sees in the death of the child, henceforth to be called Archemoros (beginner of woe), an omen for the fate of the Theban expedition, and decrees that the Nemean Games shall be established in his honour, and at the end of the play Hypsipyle is reunited with her children, who meantime have won a victory in the newly-founded games.

Two vases show the actual death of Opheltes, a very fragmentary Paestan kalyx-krater by Python (Bari 3581; *Paestan Pottery*, pl. 16a), on which the snake is devouring the infant, while the panic-stricken Hypsipyle has dropped her hydria and flees for help, and our vase (III. 3, 25) which gives the aftermath. Hypsipyle rushes up towards the dead body of Opheltes lying beside 'the shady fountain, where dwells a serpent that watches over it, . . . with a yellow crest quivering on his head' (163–6). Three of the warriors attack the snake with sword, spear and stone respectively, while a fourth, probably Amphiaraos himself, looks on as if drawing the dire omen from the event. The remaining figure, who holds a phiale of offerings in her hand, is probably Nemea or the nymph of the spring.

On the Naples krater (III. 3, 26) we see the events that followed the death of Opheltes, who is shown dead upon a funeral couch in front of the palace, already given his new name, Archemoros, in the inscription above him and mourned by a veiled woman, who is about to place a wreath on his head over which a maid is holding a parasol, and the paidagogos (inscribed; cf. III. 3, 17 and 24). To the right two male servants come up with tables of offerings on their heads. In the palace are Hypsipyle, Eurydice, and Amphiaraos (all inscribed), and this is clearly meant to represent the scene in which Hypsipyle tries to defend herself against the charges of Eurydice and is saved from death by the pleas of Amphiaraos. Around the palace are grouped several other figures – on the upper level, Dionysos (who was the father of King Thoas) and a satyr on the left, Zeus and Nemea (inscribed) on the right; below Dionysos is Euneos (inscribed) and the remains of another figure who would almost certainly have been Thoas, to the right are Parthenopaios and Capaneus (inscribed), two of the Seven against Thebes, who accompanied Amphiaraos.

The presence of the paidagogos, and the connection between the palace and the typical architecture of the stage background, especially in the treatment of the floor, argue a more direct stage inspiration for this vase than for the other, which merely provides an illustration of a narrated event in the drama.

On the *Hypsipyle*: Powell, *New Chapters in Greek Literature* III (1933), 120–9, figs. 7–9; Page, *Greek Literary Papyri* I, 76–109; Bond, *Euripides Hypsipyle*[2] (Oxford, 1968); Webster, *Tragedies of Euripides*, 211 ff. and 306; *MTSP*[2], 75, TV 8 and 158–9.
25. Séchan, 365, fig. 105.
26. Séchan, 361, fig. 103; details: Richter, *Furniture*[2], figs. 304 and 365.

Iphigenia in Tauris

III. 3, 27

Ferrara, Spina T 1145.
Attic red-figured kalyx-krater by the Iphigeneia Painter; 400–380 B.C.

The painter has composed various moments and characters from Euripides' *Iphigenia in Tauris* into a single picture dominated by the shrine of Artemis. In this simple wooden structure he is thinking more of the central door of the stage-building than of Euripides' description, which supposes an elaborate stone building. Inside the shrine the primitive idol of Artemis is shown because Iphigenia will take it back to Greece. Wreaths and fillets hanging in the background and a table of offerings in front show that it is a shrine. The wide steps on which it stands are the stage. Iphigenia stands on the left, wearing the sleeved tragic costume; she holds the key of the temple and her letter home, which brought about the recognition of Orestes as her brother (725 ff.). The attendant

III.3,27 (Ferrara). Euripides, *Iphigenia in Tauris*

III.3,28 (Naples). Euripides, *Iphigenia in Tauris*

on the right with libation bowl and basket of offerings may rather allude to the later scene when Iphigenia moves with the statue in solemn procession from the temple (1124). Iphigenia gives the letter to Pylades, he will give it to Orestes. Orestes and Pylades are seated naked on rocks; here the allusion is to the moment when Thoas' herdsman saw them seated on the shore (264); the young barbarian with his hand up in amazement in the top left corner is probably the herdsman. The painter also wanted to include Thoas, who had to be tricked into allowing Iphigenia and the Greeks to escape. He is seated on the right in the stage-costume of an oriental king with a fan-bearer behind him. But because Orestes has to be next him, Orestes' hand is raised towards him in supplication. On the left above Iphigenia is a seated woman – perhaps Artemis over her Crimean temple rather than a member of the chorus. A naked boy seated on the extreme right at the top, if he belongs to this picture rather than to the three young satyrs on the back, may represent Orestes' crew.

The picture is important because, as the play is preserved, we can see what liberties the painter took to get all the moments and characters he desired into the space at his disposal. The play was probably produced in 414 B.C. Revivals at the City Dionysia started in 386 B.C., which is perhaps not too late for our vase. Otherwise it may have been inspired by a revival at a theatre in one of the Attic demes, like the Andromeda krater (III. 3, 10), which has the same scheme and conventions.

*ARV*², 1440, no. 1; *MTSP*², AV 32 and p. 116, 159; S. Aurigemma, *Scavi di Spina*, I, 2, 1965, pl. 24–6.

III. 3, 28

Naples 3223 (inv. 82113).
Apulian volute-krater by the Iliupersis Painter; *c.* 370–360 B.C.

The *Iphigenia in Tauris* is represented on a number of South Italian vases, and several different episodes appear, in varying degrees of detail. On this vase, we have the scene where Iphigenia has been questioning Orestes, not yet of course identified as her brother, and moved by sympathy offers him deliverance if he will bear a letter for her to Argos. Orestes insists that Pylades take the letter and he be sacrificed; Iphigenia promises him a rich burial and goes into the temple to get the letter.

The temple of Artemis is shown in simple perspective in the background; its doors are slightly open, and it is partly obscured by rising ground. In the centre of the picture Orestes (inscribed) sits upon the altar, head bowed in dejection, with Pylades (inscribed) standing beside, and a laurel tree in the background to tell us the scene is out of doors. To the right is Iphigenia (inscribed) in stage costume, holding the temple key and gesturing with her right hand as if to tell Orestes to wait while she gets the letter; beside her is an attendant maid, a jug in one hand and the other supporting a tray of boughs above her head. To the left of the temple, above, are Apollo and Artemis, seemingly in converse together; the former is connected with the plot in that it was his oracle which sent Orestes to Taurica (85).

Séchan, 382–3, fig. 111; FR iii 165, fig. 79, and 349, pl. 148; Pickard-Cambridge, *Theatre*, fig. 19; White, *Perspective*, pl. 6a; Bieber, *History*², fig. 116; Richter, *Furniture*², fig. 654; *Perspective*, 43, fig. 176; *Letteratura e arte figurata nella Magna Grecia*, no. 129 (ill.); *MTSP*², 75, TV 6.

III. 3, 29

Leningrad inv. 1715 (St. 420).
Apulian volute-krater by the Baltimore Painter; *c.* 330–320 B.C.

This vase gives a rather more elaborate version of the same episode as the last. The temple is represented by a naiskos, seen

III.3,29 (Leningrad). Euripides, *Iphigenia in Tauris*

III.3,30(a). (Moscow). Euripides, *Iphigenia in Tauris*

III.3,30(b) (Sydney). Euripides, *Iphigenia in Tauris*

in perspective, with four Ionic columns; the altar stands inside it, and behind is the statue of Artemis, who holds a torch and a spear. Iphigenia in an embroidered stage costume stands in front of the altar; a long-handled patera, used for sacrificial purposes, is leaning against one of the columns of the temple beside her. She holds the temple-key in one hand and with the other makes a gesture to Pylades, towards whom she turns and slightly bends her head, as if to explain the situation. Orestes stands at a slightly lower level, leaning against a lustral basin, resting his head pensively on his left hand. In the upper level are various divinities – Iris and Athena, Artemis and Hermes; grouped around and below the temple are three warriors in oriental costume, perhaps the Scythian guards at rest; two are conversing with women, one is offering a leafy crown to a deer, perhaps a reminder that it is a sanctuary of Artemis.

Séchan, 385, fig. 113; *MTSP*², 74, TV 4; Pickard-Cambridge, *Theatre*, fig. 15.

III. 3, 30

(a) Moscow 504.
Apulian kalyx-krater, circle of the Darius Painter; *c.* 350–340 B.C.
(b) Sydney 51.17.
Campanian neck-amphora by the Libation Painter; third quarter of the fourth century B.C.

These two vases show the handing over of the letter to Pylades (728 ff.), the reading of which by Iphigenia as a precautionary device (760 ff.) brings about the recognition scene. On both the scene has been simplified to exclude Orestes, who was, however, present in the scene on a lost vase formerly in the Buckingham collection (Séchan, fig. 112). On the Moscow vase the temple is similar to that on III. 3, 29; Iphigenia, holding the temple key in her left hand, leans on an archaic-looking statue of Artemis, the letter ready in her other hand to give to Pylades, who stands beside the temple dressed for

III.3,31 (Paris). Euripides, *Iphigenia in Tauris*   III.3,32 (Leningrad). Euripides, *Iphigenia in Tauris*

travel, with petasos, short cloak, stick and sword. In front of the temple are various vessels, and to the right is Artemis seated upon the altar, with Apollo standing beside her. The altar is on the step of the temple and this may reflect the stage arrangement.

The Sydney amphora simplifies the scene still further. Here the temple is reduced to two Ionic columns, with the altar, on which a fire is blazing, between them, and a votive shield with fillet hanging from the roof. Iphigenia, wearing a tiara and a long crimson veil, has the key in one hand and holds out the letter to Pylades in the other. He is again dressed for travel, this time with a pilos on his head and a spear in his left hand, and holds out his right to take the letter from Iphigenia.

(a) Séchan, 386, fig. 114; Blavatsky, *History of ancient painted pottery* (in Russian), 228 (ill.); *MTSP*², 75, TV 5.
(b) *LCS* 406, no. 305, pl. 160, 4; *MTSP*², 160.

III. 3, 31

Paris, Louvre K 404.
Campanian bell-krater; school of the Errera Painter (near to the Painter of B.M. F 63); *c.* 330–320 B.C.

The scene on this vase seems to be the dialogue between Orestes and Iphigenia, in the presence of Pylades, as to how they shall steal the statue and make good their escape (1017 ff.), but its main interest lies in the way that the vase-painter has rendered the temple, giving it something of the effect of a stage background. Two separate doors are shown, in front of one is the statue of Artemis on a low base, on the threshold of the other is Iphigenia, not in stage costume, but with her cloak

drawn over her head to serve as a veil. The two doors are connected by a tiled roof, above what looks like a dark wall, in front of which stand Orestes and Pylades. The painter's attempt at perspective by drawing the half-open doors with receding lines is interesting, even though he has not succeeded in making the lines converge in the same direction.

LCS 321, no. 702; Lehmann-Hartleben, *JdI* 42, 1927, 30 ff., figs. 1–2; Bieber, *History*², 33, fig. 115, and 66, fig. 253; Jongkees, *BA Besch* 32, 1957, 51, fig. 2; Bulle, *Skenographie* 15, fig. 6; Pickard-Cambridge, *Theatre*, 171–2, fig. 58; Richter, *Furniture*², 137, fig. 652; *Perspective*, 44, fig. 187; Webster, *MTSP*², 84, NV 2.

III. 3, 32

Leningrad inv. 2080 (W. 1033), from Capua.
Campanian neck-amphora by the Ixion Painter; *c.* 330–320 B.C.

Here we have the escape of Orestes and Pylades with Iphigenia from the temple on a vase in which the figured scene is in added colour, giving it an unusually vivid effect. The temple dominates the picture, and is shown in much greater detail, with acroteria, pediment, and triglyph-metope frieze. Through the open doors the trio emerge – Pylades scans the horizon to see they are unobserved, both Iphigenia and Orestes look cautiously around as they step it out in a movement reminiscent of ballet. Above is a piece of hanging drapery and a severed head, no doubt to remind us of the fate Orestes has so narrowly escaped.

LCS 338, no. 790, pl. 131, 6; Beazley, *JHS* 63, 1943, pl. 1, 2; Blavatsky, *op. cit.*, ill. on p. 233; *MTSP*², 159.

III.3,33 (Berlin). Euripides, *Ixion*

Ixion

III. 3, 33

Berlin F 3023, from Cumae.
Campanian neck-amphora by the Ixion Painter; *c.* 330–320
B.C.

Of the *Ixion* of Euripides we know very little except that it
must have been produced shortly after 420 B.C. since it contained a reference to the death of Protagoras and that, in reply
to a criticism that he had portrayed Ixion as a sacrilegious
villain, Euripides said, 'I did not take him off the stage until I
had nailed him to the wheel' (Plutarch, *Moralia* 19e). In the
light of this remark it is tempting to see an illustration of
Euripides' drama on this vase, which shows Ixion, encircled
by two snakes which bite into his shoulders, bound on to the
fiery wheel. Below, to left, Hermes, the mandatory of Zeus,
turns his back upon the scene, but glances upward as if fasci-
nated by the sight; immediately below the wheel rises a Fury,
holding a torch, and to right Hephaistos, hammer in hand,
shades his eyes at the sight of his handiwork. Above on either
side of the wheel, which they gently touch, are two winged
female figures, perhaps the Clouds (Nephelai), but more likely
Aurai, the gentle zephyrs which are to support the wheel in
its flight.

The scene in the play might have been narrated in the
Messenger's speech, but could have been shown on stage, with
the use of the *ekkyklema* to carry the wheel, as for the binding
of Prometheus or Andromeda, and would have provided an
unusual spectacle.

The design on our vase is heightened by a considerable use
of added colour, especially for the flames on the wheel and
the wings, which gives it a very striking effect. The subject
appealed to the vase-painter who reproduced it with minor
variations on another amphora, now in Capua (7336; *CVA* I,
pl. 19); it is also found on the neck of a late Apulian volute-
krater in Leningrad (St. 424), where Zeus himself is present to
watch the proceedings.

LCS 338, no. 787 (with bibliography for the vase).
On the play: Webster, *Tragedies of Euripides*, 160–1 and 303.
On the subject: Cook, *Zeus* i, 198 ff.; Erika Simon, 'Ixion und die
Schlangen' in *JÖAI*, 42, 1955, 5–26; Séchan, 388–95.

III.3,34 (Policoro). Euripides, *Medas*

Medea

III. 3, 34

Policoro, Museo Nazionale della Siritide.
Early Lucanian hydria, by the Policoro Painter; *c.* 400 B.C.

Medea's Corinthian adventures were not represented in vase-painting until the end of the fifth century B.C. and it therefore seems reasonable to assume that the painters drew their inspiration from Euripides' play, which was produced in 431 B.C. Our vase, from the same tomb at Policoro (anc. Herakleia) that contained several others with dramatic themes (e.g. III. 3, 14 and 20) and may well have been that of a poet or an actor, gives the earliest representation of the conclusion of the play, and, since Medea is wearing stage costume, there can be little doubt of direct dramatic influence.

In the centre of the picture, Medea (inscribed) stands, ready to drive off to Athens in the snake-drawn chariot of the Sun, which would have appeared in the play on the *mechane* after line 1316. Below lie the bodies of her two slain children, mourned by the paidagogos on the left who kneels beside them in the conventional attitude of grief. From the right Jason rushes up, brandishing his sword and reviling Medea (1323 ff.) as a barbarian murderess. Above to left is the seated figure of a woman, looking into a mirror, balanced on the other side by Eros; she is probably Aphrodite.

LCS 58, no. 286, pls. 26, 3 and 27, 3; Degrassi, *BdA* 50, 1965, 8 ff., figs. 3, 8, 12 and *RM*, Ergänzungsheft 11, 1967, 204 ff., pls. 51, 58, 2, 60 and 79, 1; *AA* 83, 1968, 788, fig. 41; Neutsch, *Siris ed Heraclea*, figs. 32–3; Webster, *MTSI*[2], 129, LV 5, pl. 8 b.
On the play and its representations: Page, *Euripides Medea*, introd. xxi–xxx and lvii ff.; Simon, 'Die Typen der Medeadarstellung', in *Gymnasium*, 61, 1954, 203–27; Webster, *Tragedies of Euripides*, 52–7.

III.3,34 (Policoro). Euripides, *Medea*

III.3,35 (Paris). Euripides, *Medea*

III. 3, 35

Paris, Louvre CA 2193.
Lucanian bell-krater by the Dolon Painter; *c.* 400–380 B.C.

The subject of this vase is the presentation of Medea's fatal gifts to Creusa and must have been inspired by Euripides' play, in which the episode is mentioned twice (784 ff. and 947 ff.), although it does not take place on the stage. To left stands Kreon, in stage costume with sceptre, seemingly reassuring Creusa, who seems a little diffident about the gifts. She has put on the crown and mantle and is perhaps smitten by some foreboding of their dreadful powers; beside her stands the hand-maid, holding a closed jewel-box in one hand, and in the other a cloak, which perhaps Creusa has taken off when she donned the one sent by Medea. The maid looks at the new finery admiringly. The children of Medea are not present, but a retainer stands on the right, plucking his beard with a rather doubtful look; it will no doubt be he who later recounts the appalling fate of Creusa as the poison in the crown and robes began to take effect (1121 ff.). The vase-painter gives us a free, but natural, interpretation of the episode; in the play Kreon does not appear until Creusa is dead (1224), but his presence here is a reminder of his forthcoming involvement in his daughter's doom.

LCS 100, no. 517; Séchan, 398, pl. VII; *MTSP*², 130, LV 8; Margot Schmidt, *Gnomon* 42, 1970, 826.

III. 3, 36

Paris, Louvre K 300, from Cumae.
Campanian neck-amphora by the Ixion Painter; *c.* 330–320 B.C.

This vase gives a simplified version of the murder of the children. Only one of them, a boy, is shown, and Medea, identifiable by the long-sleeved tragic costume she is wearing, grasps his hair and is about to plunge the sword a second time into his bleeding body just below the arm he stretches out in a vain plea for mercy. Behind him is an altar in front of the cult-statue of a god, seemingly Apollo. In the background are two massive white columns, one Doric and one Ionic, perhaps representing palace and sanctuary, but also reminiscent of the stage background.

Séchan, fig. 120; *LCS* 338, no. 786, pl. 131, 3; *La Grèce classique*, fig. 375; Schmidt, *Gnomon* 42, 1970, 830.

III.3,36 (Paris). Euripides, *Medea*

Meleager

III. 3, 37–38

37. Vienna, IV 158.
Attic red-figured volute-krater by the Meleager Painter; 400–375 B.C.
38. Athens, N.M. 15113.
Attic red-figured neck-amphora by the Meleager Painter; 400–375 B.C.

Euripides' *Meleager* was probably produced in 416 B.C. The story ran from the preparations for the hunt of the Calydonian boar until the death of Meleager. The fury of his mother Althaia, which caused her to burn the torch and thereby kill Meleager, was roused by his passion for Atalanta, which led him not only to award her the hide of the boar but also to kill his uncles when they tried to prevent her getting the hide. Four vases with the hunters assembled and Atalanta prominent among them have been attributed to the Meleager Painter: this is a new version of the old Calydonian boar story and it was probably due to Euripides. The messenger who reported the boar-hunt gave the names of the hunters at the beginning, and this is the inspiration of these scenes.

Both vases have a central group of three figures distinguished by elaborately decorated chitons, which may recall tragic costume. Meleager and Atalanta can be certainly identified; the third is probably Tydeus, who in this version was Meleager's brother and supports Meleager in the death scene (III. 3, 40). They are inviting Atalanta to join the hunt. The central group is flanked by two seated men looking back. On the Vienna krater the one on the left is bearded and therefore is likely to be one of Meleager's uncles, and the one on the right holds a club, which identifies him as Theseus. The Athens amphora adds outside them two men standing with one foot on a rock, perhaps the other uncle on the left and a friend of Theseus on the right (Peirithoos, if Euripides included him). On the right the Athens amphora adds a hero running between two dancing heroes; he holds an ivy branch and is therefore Telamon, who in Euripides had vines in his hair in reference to the vines on Salamis. He also appears on the Vienna krater with nothing to identify him, and he is balanced by a similar figure on the extreme left.

37. *ARV*², 1408, no. 1; Webster, *MTSP*², 161; *Tragedies of Euripides*, 233, 306.
38. *ARV*², 1411, no. 39; *AE* 1924, pls. 1–2. The vase has been extensively repainted.

III. 3, 39

Bari 872, from Canosa.
Apulian amphora by the Painter of the Naples Europa Amphora; *c.* 330 B.C.

On the main picture on this vase is a representation of the restoration of the boar's hide by Meleager to Atalanta, as no doubt reported to Oineus by the messenger (cf. Page, *Greek Literary Papyri* no. 27, lines 7 ff.), and it is not uncharacteristic of later Apulian vase-painting to choose this more romantic episode from the story, rather than the actual boar-hunt. In the centre sits Atalanta dressed in the stage costume of a huntress, with her hound beside her; Meleager stands before her, offering her the boar's hide. Between them flies a small Eros with a wreath, behind Atalanta is Aphrodite with a magic wheel. The love-motif is therefore strongly emphasized by the painter. On the extreme left is a Fury with torch and sword, beside whom is an old retainer in the appropriate costume, who will later narrate the story to Oineus. At his feet is a curious object, which appears also on III. 3, 40; it must be the rolled-up net and stakes used in the trapping of the boar. To the right are two of Meleager's companions in the hunt.

Séchan, fig. 429; Paribeni, *Immagini di vasi apuli*, no. 16, pl. 18; *MTSP*², 161.

III. 3, 40;

Naples, Stg. 11.
Apulian volute-krater, Suckling Group; second quarter of the fourth century B.C.

When Oineus tells Althaia of Meleager's slaughter of his uncles and the return of the hide to Atalanta, she enters the house and extinguishes the torch, thus bringing Meleager's life to a close. On the Naples vase we see him brought dying into the house by Tydeus (inscribed), who is about to lay him down on a couch; his sister Deianeira (inscribed) rushes up to help, and another woman, probably Althaia, runs in with a gesture of astonishment, repenting too late of having brought about the death of her own son. Below the building Peleus and Theseus (both inscribed) sit in attitudes of deep dejection; their hounds are by their side, and also the rolled-up net and stakes, which we noted on the preceding vase. To the right of the building above sits Aphrodite (inscribed), a small winged boy inscribed ΦΘΟΝΟΣ standing by her side; below is Oineus (inscribed), bearded, holding a sceptre, and tearing his hair in the conventional gesture of sorrow.

Séchan, fig. 123; Stella, *Mitologia greca*, ill. on p. 551; *MTSP*², 161.

III.3,37 (Vienna). Euripides, *Meleager*

III.3,38 (Athens, N.M.). Euripides, *Meleager*

III.3,39 (Bari). Euripides, *Meleager*

III.3,40 (Naples). Euripides, *Meleager*

III.3,41 (London). Euripides, *Oineus*

Oineus

III. 3, 41

London, British Museum F 155.
Paestan hydria by Python; *c.* 340–330 B.C.

Of Euripides' play *Oineus* we know comparatively little; two early Latin tragedies, the *Periboea* of Pacuvius and the *Diomedes* of Accius, seem to have been based upon it and from the scanty fragments of these and the original it is possible to reconstruct something of the plot. Agrios and his sons shamefully maltreated the aged Oineus, whom they had robbed of his kingdom; when his grandson Diomedes returned from Troy, he rescued him from servitude and took revenge upon Agrios for the cruel treatment of him. This would appear to be the scene on the Paestan hydria, since the bound figure on the altar is inscribed ΑΓΡΙΟΣ and, as both he and the aged man to left are wearing tragic costume, it is reasonable to assume a dramatic source. It must be the dénouement of the play; Periboia, his second wife, brings along the aged Oineus, who has now resumed his royal rank, as costume and sceptre testify; his grandson Diomedes hands him the sword with which he may take vengeance on the helpless Agrios, who awaits his fate with a look of anxiety. Beside the altar rises a black Fury, brandishing a snake in one hand, with another coiled around her head: she emphasizes the vengeance about to be exacted.

Séchan, 445, fig. 125; *Paestan Pottery*, no. 154, pl. 16, 3; Simon, *JÖAI* 42, 1955, 10, fig. 4; *MTSP*², 83, PV 3.

Phoinix

III. 3, 42

Oklahoma, University C. 53. 455.
Fragment of Apulian kalyx-krater; mid-fourth century B.C.

This small fragment, which shows between trees Peleus (inscribed) leaning on a stick and talking to Phoinix (inscribed), who is seated on a rock and obviously blind, is of particular interest since it is the only scene in vase-painting which seems definitely to be associated with the lost *Phoinix* of Euripides. It clearly depicts the arrival of Peleus to take Phoinix to Cheiron for healing. Above are the remains of a seated figure, perhaps Athena, and weapons.

*MTSP*², 129, TV 52.

III.3,42 (Oklahoma). Euripides, *Phoinix*

III.3,43 (Würzburg). Euripides, *Stheneboia*

Stheneboia

III. 3, 43

Würzburg H 4696 + 4701.
Fragments of Gnathia bell-krater by the Konnakis Painter;
360–350 B.C.

Euripides' *Stheneboia* was an early play, and included startling
unrealities of time. Bellerophon was falsely accused by Proitos'
wife Stheneboia of trying to seduce her and was sent with a
letter to Iobates in Lycia, who sent him against the Chimaira.
He returned victorious to Proitos on the winged horse
Pegasos, and found that Stheneboia was still intent on seducing
him. He put her on Pegasos, and when they were over the
island of Melos pitched her into the sea. Fishermen brought
her body back to Proitos, and Bellerophon appeared on
Pegasos to tell Proitos that he had taken a fitting vengeance.
The Konnakis Painter, who learned his trade in one of the
great Apulian workshops of the second quarter of the fourth
century and started up on his own with the new technique of
polychrome painting on the black glaze ground, has given
two moments in the story. The clue is given by the akroteria,
the little figures on the top of the pediment of the palace
(probably the door on the right had a similar pediment with
identical akroteria). Bellerophon appears on Pegasos in the
centre; to the left a man running away in horror, to the right
a man storming against him. This must be the end of the play
when Bellerophon appeared on the *mechane* and Proitos
stormed against him as Jason stormed against Medea at the
end of the *Medea* (cf. III. 3, 34).

The main scene gives a woman listening through each of the
side doors while a young traveller in a dejected posture is
greeted by an elderly man holding a phiale. The most suitable
moment in the play is Bellerophon's return after killing the
Chimaira when he complained that Proitos had deceived him.
The two women are then Stheneboia and her nurse; the
artist may have put them there merely because they are characters in the play or one of them may actually have over-
heard Bellerophon's accusation and reported it to the other.

For the play and its representations: Webster, *Tragedies of Euripides*,
80–84 and 301–2; *MTSP²*, 163; Brommer, *Bellerophon* (*MWPr*
1954), 3 ff.; Schauenburg, *JdI* 71, 1956, 59–96 and *AA* 1958, cols. 21–
38; Séchan, 494–502; Bulle, *Skenographie*, pp. 1–4, pls. 1–2; Forti,
Ceramica di Gnathia, 98, pl. 13c; *BICS* 15, 1968, 5; *La Grèce classique*,
fig. 360; *MTSP²*, GV 1; Richter, *Perspective*, 46, fig. 196.

III.3,44 (Paestum). Euripides, *Stheneboia*

III. 3, 44–46

44. Paestum 20202, from Agropoli.
Paestan hydria by Asteas; *c.* 350–330 B.C.
45. Boston 00.349.
Early Apulian stamnos by the Ariadne Painter; *c.* 400–390 B.C.
46. Geneva, private coll.
Campanian bell-krater of the Libation Group; *c.* 330 B.C.

The adventures of Bellerophon, especially his fight with the Chimaira, were popular with South Italian vase-painters, who are also fond of showing his departure from the palace of Proitos with the letter for Iobates. There can be little doubt that this scene, as it appears on the recently discovered hydria signed by Asteas, draws its inspiration from a stage performance, since the characters all wear elaborate tragic costumes and are represented in a stage setting like that on the Madness of Herakles krater in Madrid by the same painter. Proitos is shown handing over the letter to Bellerophon in the presence of Stheneboia, who is seated, with her maid Astyanassa standing beside her. All four are inscribed, and this is the first time that the handmaid has been named; this was also the name of Helen's servant in Sparta, and Asteas, not always very strong on nomenclature, may have used it as a generally appropriate name for a maid, rather than taking it from Euripides. Above, in a sort of colonnaded loggia is the bust of Aphrodite (inscribed) between two Furies, one inscribed Allecto, the other inscription being now lost. It may be noted that Pegasos does not appear. The Boston stamnos shows the parting in a simpler form. Stheneboia stands at the door of the house, just touching Proitos' shoulder with her hand, as if wishing to give him pause; he carries a bird-crowned sceptre, and wears only a piece of drapery round the lower part of his body. Beside him stands Bellerophon, in the act of taking the letter from his hand, and Pegasos stands behind, one foreleg raised. A still simpler version is to be found on a Campanian hydria in Capua (*CVA* 1, pl. 9; *LCS* 308, no. 571) showing only Proitos with the letter, and Bellerophon standing beside Pegasos and pointing to it, as if anxious to depart.

The Geneva krater is unusual in that it shows Bellerophon already mounted on Pegasos and holding out his hand to take the letter from Proitos, behind whom Stheneboia is seated attended by a maid (cf. the Asteas hydria) holding a mirror and fan, while another maid sits below with a phiale.

The Boston and Geneva vases give illustrations prompted perhaps by a performance rather than of the play itself.

44. *Arch Reps* 16, 1969–70, 37, fig. 7; M. Napoli, *Il Museo di Paestum*, pl. 36, and *Paestum* (1970), fig. 97.
45. Trendall *FI*, pl. 23; *APS* 16; *MTSP²*, 127, TV 41.
46. We owe our knowledge of this vase to the kindness of M. J.-M. Moret, who will shortly publish it in detail in *AntK*.

III.3,45 (Boston). Euripides, *Stheneboia*

III.3,46 (Geneva, private coll.). Euripides, *Stheneboia*

Telephos

III. 3, 47

Berlin inv. 3974.
Attic red-figured kalyx-krater; 400–375 B.C.

Euripides produced the *Telephos* in 438 B.C. The play was frequently parodied, criticized, and alluded to in subsequent comedies. The Berlin krater is probably too early for a revival after 386 B.C. in the theatre of Dionysos but may be inspired by a revival in a deme theatre. Telephos had been wounded by Achilles' spear in the first unsuccessful attempt to get to Troy and could only be healed by the weapon which had wounded him. He came to Greece and found the Greeks assembling for another attempt on Troy. He seems to have won the confidence of Clytemnestra and she may have suggested the ultimate possibility of seizing the infant Orestes. At first Telephos seems to have been successful, pleading that the expedition should be called off. But Odysseus arrived and led a spy-hunt. Telephos fled to the sanctuary of the Lycian Apollo, where he knew that he would find Clytemnestra and Orestes. He seized the child and, from the safety of an altar, threatened to kill him.

This must have been related in a messenger speech, which is illustrated by the Berlin krater. The sanctuary is indicated by the seated figure of Apollo, the laurel tree with votive-tablets suspended from the branches, the bush, the altar, the basket. Telephos has taken refuge on the altar with Orestes in his left hand and a drawn sword in his right. On the right Agamemnon rushes up with a spear and a woman runs away

III.3,47 (Berlin). Euripides, *Telephos*

III.3,48 (Naples). Euripides, *Telephos*

III.3,49 (Boston). Euripides, *Telephos*

(perhaps the nurse from whom Telephos had snatched up the baby). On the left, a woman wearing diadem and shoes moves off looking back (Clytemnestra?). Above a young man watches, holding two spears. He must be Achilles, who arrives after this and consents to heal Telephos in return for Telephos' guidance of the expedition to Troy.

Webster, *MTSP²*, 164; *Tragedies of Euripides*, 43, 302; C. Austin, *Nova Fragmenta Euripidea*, 1968, 66; Metzger, *Representations*, pl. 39, 1. On the story see Beazley in Caskey-Beazley iii, 54 ff.

III. 3, 48

Naples RC 141 (inv. 86064), from Cumae.
Campanian hydria by the Ixion Painter; *c.* 330–320 B.C.

This vase gives an even more vivid representation of the scene than the last. In the centre, kneeling on the altar, is the bare-headed Telephos, grasping by his leg the infant Orestes, whom he holds head downward in his left hand, the drawn sword held menacingly in the other. The white bandage round his thigh is clearly visible, drawing attention to the wound, which played such an important part in the story. From the right, Agamemnon comes up, spear in hand, only to be restrained by Clytemnestra, who throws her arms about him in a dramatic gesture. On the left is a woman tearing her hair, and above to the right is the bust of a woman looking on with an anxious air – one will probably be the nurse of Orestes and the other a servant.

LCS 340, no. 804, pl. 133, 4; Séchan, 509, fig. 149; *MTSP²*, 164.

III. 3, 49

Boston 1970. 487 (gift of J. H. and C. A. Payne).
Faliscan kalyx-krater by the Nazzano Painter; second quarter fourth century B.C.

This Etruscan vase gives an elaborate version of the story, perhaps based on an Attic original, and, from the richly-decorated tragic costumes worn by the principal characters, derived from a stage production. In the centre of the lower register Telephos sits upon the altar, holding a drawn sword in his left hand, and encircling the legs of the infant Orestes with his right arm, hidden beneath the drapery. Orestes stretches out his hands in supplication to Agamemnon, who comes up from the left, sceptre in hand, turning his head towards another Greek, Menelaos or Odysseus, who follows him, pointing to the altar. On the other side the nurse drops her basket in horror and raises her hands, while Clytemnestra, veiled and holding a phiale, looks on. Above in the centre is Apollo, who gave the oracle concerning the healing of Telephos and in whose sanctuary at Argos the events are taking place; beside him is his sister, Artemis, with Zeus and Hermes to right. From the left Iris comes up towards him, messenger's staff in hand; behind her are Athena and Eros.

Art of Ancient Italy (Exhibition Catalogue, Emmerich Gallery, New York, 1970), 32–3, no. 45.

III.3,51 (Boston). Euripides, *Theseus*

Theseus

III. 3, 50

Syracuse 17427.
Attic red-figured kalyx-krater by the Kadmos Painter; 430–420 B.C.

Euripides' *Theseus* was an early play. The scene was Crete and dealt with the story of Theseus killing the Minotaur with the help of Ariadne. The chorus were the boys and girls who were sent as tribute to Minos. A fragment which says that sober men should love the pious and bid a long farewell to Aphrodite has been connected with the Syracuse krater by Professor Erika Simon, who sees in it a warning by Athena to Theseus to pursue his Athenian career and leave Ariadne on Naxos. It is perhaps more likely that the fragment is a warning delivered to Theseus by himself, but the Naxian story must have been prophesied by Athena in an epilogue speech and is illustrated on the Syracuse krater, which may be inspired by the play.

On the left Aphrodite sends Eros to beautify the sleeping Ariadne who is approached by Dionysos, a stately bearded figure carrying the thyrsus. Athena places a wreath on Theseus' head as he moves away looking back at Ariadne. Poseidon, his father, according to some accounts, appears above looking back, on the right a young man with a lyre (an allusion to the victory dance in which Theseus led the Athenian boys and girls on Crete after killing the Minotaur; perhaps this was the chorus after the messenger speech) is already climbing on to Theseus' ship.

ARV², 1184, no. 4; Webster, *MTSP²*, 165; *Tragedies of Euripides*, 105, 303; E. Simon, *AntK* 6, 1963, 14.
On the dance, K. Friis Johansen, *Thésée et la danse*, Danish Academy, 1945.

III.3,50 (Syracuse). Euripides, *Theseus*

III, 3. 51

Boston 00.349.
Apulian stamnos by the Ariadne Painter; *c.* 400–390 B.C.

Here we have a very clear picture of the desertion of Ariadne. She is shown stretched out half-naked on a couch, her head resting on the pillow, her eyes closed fast in sleep, thanks to the drops which the winged god of Sleep, Hypnos, has let fall upon her. To the left, Theseus, starting back at what must be the sight of Dionysos approaching, though he does not appear on the vase, makes for his ship, the prow of which can be seen behind him. In the background Athena is seated. Both shape and subject are rare in South Italian vase-painting; only three other stamnoi are so far known, and the desertion of Ariadne occurs only once again, on a fragmentary Apulian kalyx-krater (Taranto 52230; Paribeni, *Immagini*, pl. 13), which shows Dionysos arriving to comfort Ariadne, as Theseus departs, and is a decade or so later than our vase. The other side of this vase, showing Bellerophon, Stheneboia and Proitos, is discussed under III. 3, 45, and it is interesting to find two early Euripidean plays illustrated on the same vase.

APS, 16–17, no. 1; *MTSP²*, 127, TV 41 and 164; *Greek Gods and Heroes* (Boston, M.F.A., 1962), 83, fig. 70.

4. Other Tragedians

Astydamas (?), *Parthenopaios*

III. 4, 1

Milan, Civico Museo Archeologico. St. 6873.
Apulian kalyx-krater; school of the Lycurgus Painter and perhaps an early work by the painter himself; *c.* 360–50 B.C.

Two fourth-century tragedians, father and son, bore the name Astydamas, and there is considerable confusion as to which of the two some of the extant records refer. The elder produced his first play in 398 B.C., won his first victory in 372 (*Marmor Parium* 71) and is said to have lived to the age of sixty. The references in *Inscriptiones Graecae* ii², 2320 (Pickard-Cambridge, *Festivals*, 110 ff.) to victories at the festival of Dionysos in 341 and 340, on the latter occasion with the *Parthenopaios* and the *Lycaon*, must therefore refer to the son, and the ascription of the former play to the father in the Suda lexicon and by Photius must be an error.

The scene on the Milan vase which, both from the costumes and from the use as a frame for the picture of Ionic columns surmounted by tripods, seems certainly to be associated with a stage performance, and, since the seated youth, who appears to be the principal character, is identified by an inscription as Parthenopaios, possibly with a play of that name, cannot refer to the victorious play by the younger Astydamas, since the vase must be dated a decade or so earlier. It might, however, refer to an earlier, unrecorded play with the same subject, perhaps by the elder tragedian. On our vase Parthenopaios appears as a young man, seated upon a couch, which stands on a low platform, very reminiscent of the treatment of the stage on certain vases (e.g. III. 2, 8); he is listening to an aged man wearing the usual costume of a messenger or a paidagogos, who seems to be putting forward some argument which Parthenopaios tries to counter. It would be tempting to interpret him as Adrastos trying to persuade Parthenopaios to take part in the expedition of the Seven against Thebes. Behind Parthenopaios is Atalanta (inscribed), his mother; she wears a richly embroidered garment and seems from her attitude to be in doubt or anxiety, but as the lower part of her head is missing, we cannot be certain of her expression. She is balanced on the other side by another woman, also richly draped. Above are three gods – Hermes, Apollo with laurel-branch and lyre, beside whom is a large white swan, and finally Ares (inscribed) to whom the painter has given a rather Zeus-like aspect and who might have been difficult to identify but for the spear and the inscription. His presence may be due to his being the father of Parthenopaios in certain versions of the legend or to his interest as god of war in the Theban expedition.

Parthenopaios is represented as one of the Seven against Thebes on an Attic red-figured hydria (*c.* 470 B.C. by one of the earlier Mannerists), on which he is identified by an inscription, the other six not being named individually.

Stenico, *Finarte Cat.* 5 (14 March 1963), 75 ff., pl. 44; Belloni, *BdA* 49, 1964, 404, fig. 1; Webster, *MTSP*², 166.
Attic hydria (in a private collection): Richter, *AJA* 74, 1970, 331 ff., pls. 79–82.

Chaeremon, *Achilles*

III. 4, 2

Boston 03.804.
Apulian volute-krater; *c.* 350–340 B.C.

The scene on this vase, which represents Achilles and the slain Thersites, has certain stage connections (e.g. the costume of

III.4, 1 (Milan). Astydamas (?), *Parthenopaios*

III.4,2 (Boston). Chaeremon, *Achilles*

Agamemnon; the rendering of the building, which resembles the projecting central portion of the stage background) and may perhaps be associated with the *Achilles Thersitoktonos* of Chaeremon, a fourth-century dramatist.

All the characters are inscribed and so no doubts remain about their identification. In the foreground lies the dead body of Thersites, a little apart from its severed head, amid a collection of overturned vessels or other objects, including a lustral basin broken off from its support, suggestive of a violent struggle. To the left, Automedon, the friend of Achilles, kneels watchfully with spear and shield, as if guarding the corpse; to right a servant (ΔΜΩΣ) moves off. In the centre, in a structure which must represent the tent of Achilles, from the ceiling of which hang down various pieces of armour and two chariot-wheels, Achilles, spear in hand, sits upon a couch, with the aged Phoinix beside him in an attitude of dejection. On the left, Agamemnon, in tragic costume with sceptre, comes up followed by Phorbas; on the right Menelaos tries to restrain Diomedes, the cousin of Thersites, who is in the act of drawing his sword; behind him is a henchman, simply characterized as the Aetolian (ΑΙΤΩΛΟΣ). Above, Pan looks at a seated winged figure resembling a Fury, but inscribed

ΠΟΙΝΑ (Vengeance); to right is Athena seated on her shield, with Hermes standing beside her.

The story of Thersites was told in the *Aithiopis*, where he was slain in a fit of temper by Achilles, for taunting him with his love for the Amazon queen Penthesilea. This act of violence provoked serious dissension among the Greeks, which was appeased only when Achilles sailed for Lesbos to sacrifice to Apollo. Chaeremon probably took the theme of his tragedy from the epic poem and seems to have included a scene in which Diomedes threatened vengeance (Nauck, fr. 3), which would well accord with the picture on our vase and the presence of Poine. It would also seem that Achilles had refused the rites of burial to Thersites, hence the guard over his body, and that Phoinix and perhaps Agamemnon also tried to bring about a change of mind. Athena might have delivered the epilogue.

Séchan, 527 ff., fig. 156; Pickard-Cambridge, *Theatre*, fig. 17; *AntK* 5, 1962, p. 58, pl. 20; *Greek, Etruscan and Roman Art* (Boston MFA), 151, fig. 130; *The Trojan War in Greek Art*, pl. 31; Richter, *Furniture*[2], fig. 284; Webster, *MTSP*[2], 74, TV 2, *Art and Literature in fourth-century Athens*, 66, pl. 9, and *Hellenistic Poetry and Art*, 283.
On Chaeremon see C. Collard, *JHS* 90, 1970, 22 ff., esp. p. 26.

5. Plays by Unidentified Tragedians

Eriphyle

III. 5, 1–3

1. Lecce 570.
Attic red-figured pelike by the Chicago Painter; *c.* 460–450 B.C.
2. Taranto 6957, from Pisticci.
Early Lucanian kalyx-krater, by the Pisticci Painter; *c.* 430–420 B.C.
3. Policoro, Museo Nazionale della Siritide.
Early Lucanian pelike, by the Policoro Painter; *c.* 400 B.C.

On the Lecce pelike Polynices (inscribed), wearing pilos and short chiton, has taken the necklace of Harmonia from the jewel-box and is holding it out to Eriphyle (inscribed), who looks longingly in its direction and stretches out her right hand to take it, while with her left she makes a gesture of refusal. This theme appears suddenly in the red-figure vase-painting about the middle of the fifth century (cf. also vases by the Villa Giulia and Sabouroff Painters – *ARV*², 622, no. 47 and 844, no. 146), and its use may well have been inspired by this temptation scene in some lost drama.

The subject is repeated on an early Lucanian kalyx-krater by the Pisticci Painter about a generation later. Here Polynices is similarly dressed, if a little younger since his beard is hardly grown, and is shown taking the necklace out of the box, while Eriphyle stands beside her loom on the threshold of her dwelling, represented by an Ionic column with abacus supporting a roof. She turns her head away from the loom to look at Polynices and is just beginning to raise her hand, preparatory to stretching it out for the necklace, as on the preceding vase. On this occasion Polynices is accompanied by a young spear-bearer. Although the figures are not inscribed, there can be little doubt as to their identity (cf. also similar representations on Attic vases, *c.* 450–420 B.C. – e.g. *ARV*², 1065, no. 7; 1110, no. 1; 1206, no. 12). Our third vase comes from the same tomb in Policoro that yielded several others with dramatic subjects (e.g. III. 3, 14, 20, and 34), and this, if anything, would lead support to its theme also having a stage connection, though the interpretation is less certain. On the right is Eriphyle, looking at a box of jewels (no doubt the famous necklace), which seems to have been given to her by the youth on the left (Polynices), who wears a petasos and high-boots, and carries a spear and a jewel coffer. Between them, is a nude warrior carrying a spear; his eyes are wide open, as if in fear. He may be Amphiaraos, husband of Eriphyle, who, for the bribe of the necklace, will compel him to take part in the Theban expedition, in which he knows he will lose his life. To the left, at a somewhat higher level and therefore not directly concerned with the three main figures, is a woman wearing a black peplos and draped in a cloak. Her head is missing, so identification is uncertain, but she might well be Harmonia, the original owner of the necklace, who also possessed a famous robe, which the vase-painter may here have also wished to represent.

It is difficult to say what play may have inspired the vase-painters' sudden interest in the story of Polynices and Eriphyle. Sophocles wrote a satyr-play called *Amphiaraos*, which is certainly not relevant, and a tragedy on Eriphyle, which would seem to be too late in date to have influenced the vases. Other writers of tragedy (e.g. Carcinus and Cleophon) are also mentioned as having written an *Amphiaraos*, but we know virtually nothing of them, and it is safest to leave the matter open.

*MTSP*², 166.
1. *ARV*², 629, no. 23; *CVA* 1, pl. 1–4; Cook, *Greek Painted Pottery*, pl. 45.
2. *LCS* 21, no. 53; *CVA* 3, IV D, pl. 5.
3. *LCS* 58, no. 287, pl. 25, 5; *BdA* 50, 1965, 17, fig. 41; *RM*, Ergänzungsheft, 11, 1967, 221–3, pls. 65, 2 and 78, 2.

III.5,2 (Taranto). 'Polynices and Eriphyle'

III.5,1 (Lecce). 'Polynices and Eriphyle'

III.5,3 (Policoro). 'Polynices and Eriphyle'

III.5,5 (Bari). 'Merops and Klymene'

Medea

III. 5, 4

Munich 3296 (J. 810), from Canosa.
Apulian volute-krater by the Underworld Painter; *c.* 330–320 B.C.

This vase gives much the fullest version of Medea's Corinthian adventures (cf. III. 3, 34–6) and is undoubtedly inspired by a dramatic representation, though it can hardly be the tragedy by Euripides, since it contains several characters unconnected with that play, as well as divergencies from it, like the escape of one of the children; it is probably based on some fourth-century *Medea*, now completely lost. It would make an admirable poster for the play, showing not only the death of Kreon's daughter, but also Medea's murder of one of her children and the waiting snake-chariot of the sun. The tripod-crowned columns (cf. III. 4, 3) flanking the upper register seem again to associate the scene with a successful dramatic performance.

In the centre is the palace of Kreon, in which he, shown as a white-bearded old man in tragic costume, lets go his sceptre to tear his hair in anguish with one hand, while with the other he seeks to support his daughter (inscribed Kreonteia i.e. Kreon's daughter; the painter did not know her real name), already collapsing on her throne in death as the poisoned robe and tiara get to work. The empty jewel-box, which held the latter, is clearly visible at the foot of the steps. At either side of the palace appear two new characters, named by inscriptions – Merope dashes up on the left, tearing her hair with one hand and clutching one of the columns of the palace with the other; on the other side, Hippotes tries to tear the fatal crown from his sister's head. Behind him, the old nurse runs off, looking back with horror at the events in prgoress. Below, Medea, dressed in a richly decorated oriental stage costume, is about to murder one of her children; behind her, a spear-bearer is trying to arrange the escape of the other. On the other side Jason, accompanied by a spear-bearer who points to Medea, comes up with spear and sword. Between him and Medea is the chariot, driven by Oistros (inscribed), the personification of her frenzy, who holds a flaming torch in each hand; it is

ready to take her off to escape the vengeance which Jason threatens. Behind to the right stands the ghost of Aietes (ΕΙΔΩΛΟΝ ΑΗΤΟΥ) on a rock, richly costumed like Medea, watching the fulfilment of his curse as he stretches out his hand towards the scene in the lower register. On the upper level to the left are Herakles and Athena, balanced by the Dioskouroi on the other side; all are concerned with the expedition of the Argonauts, which set the train of events in motion. Behind Merope, at a slightly lower level, the aged paidagogos comes up to help, supported by a female attendant.

FR, pl. 90; Schmidt, *Dareiosmaler*, pl. 21; Séchan, 405 ff., pl. 8; Simon, *Gymnasium*, 61, 1954, 212 ff.; Webster, *MTSP*,[2] TV 9 and *Hellenistic Poetry and Art*, 283 (where the connections between the representation on the vase and the play by Pacuvius are discussed).

Merops

III. 5, 5

Bari 3648, from Ceglie del Campo.
Apulian volute-krater, by a late follower of the Iliupersis Painter; *c.* 360–350 B.C.

The scene on the neck of the obverse of this vase is undoubtedly of dramatic inspiration (cf. the costume of Merops with that of Agamemnon on III. 4, 4) but, although the characters are named, we do not know the play from which they come. On the left Merops, with drawn sword, followed by Klymene runs up towards Melanippos, who is collapsing in death behind a large tripod, beside which is an altar, on which the youth Stornyx is kneeling with a drawn sword; to the right, a woman, perhaps the priestess, is running away.

Merops and Klymene are the parents of Phaethon in Euripides' play of that name, and we may have here a scene from some later tragedy in which they played a part in a story which is now lost to us. Stornyx is known only from this vase, but it looks as if he has been responsible for the death of Melanippos and that Merops is approaching to take vengeance upon him and that he has fled for refuge to the altar.

Roscher, *ML* iv, 1538–9; *NSc*, 1900, 507; Pickard-Cambridge, *Fest.*[1], fig. 171; Bieber, *Skenika* (75 *BWPr*, 1915), fig. 1; *MTSP*[2], 75, TV 11 and 167; M. Schmidt, *AntK* 13, 1970, 71 n. 2, pl. 33.

III.5,4 (Munich). 'Medea'

III.5,6 (Naples). 'Persai'

Persai

III. 5, 6

Naples 3253 (inv. 81947), from Canosa.
Apulian volute-krater by the Darius Painter; *c.* 340–330 B.C.

The scene on this famous vase, the name-piece of the Darius Painter, is entitled *Persai*, and from the costumes of some of the figures in it (e.g. Darius) looks to have been inspired by some drama now lost to us, perhaps a fourth-century version of the famous play by Phrynichus.

The scene is in three registers. In the centre is Darius (inscribed) in council seated upon an elaborate throne; he is listening to a bearded man wearing the pilos of a traveller and dressed like the traditional tragic messenger, who stands upon a platform (bearing the inscription ΠΕΡΣΑΙ) and seems to be delivering a warning, perhaps after recounting the Persian defeat at Marathon. The members of the council, three of whom wear oriental dress, assume attitudes of surprise or alarm at his speech. Below, the royal treasurer, seated at a table inscribed with letters corresponding to our former £.s.d., arranges the counting pebbles in their appropriate columns, and holds up in his left hand a wax diptych inscribed '100 talents'. From both sides come up the Persian satraps, two with contributions of gold and plate, three empty-handed, kneeling in attitudes of grovelling submission. Above, the decision has already been made on Olympos; Athena leads Hellas up to Zeus, as the coming victor, in the presence of Apollo and

Artemis (on whose festival the battle of Marathon took place), while, on the right, Apate (Deception) endeavours to lure Asia away from the protection of the goddess on whose altar she is seated.

Cook, *Zeus* ii, 852-4, pl. 38; Schmidt, *Dareiosmaler*, 24 ff., pls. 4, 6–8; C. Anti, *Arch Cl* 4, 1952, 23–45, pls. 12–14 (with bibliography on p. 25); Anna Rocco, *Arch Cl* 5, 1953, 170 ff., pls. 76–9; Borda, *Ceramiche apule*, pls. 12–13; *EAA* iii, figs. 15–16; *MTSP*², 76, TV 15.

Rhesus

III. 5, 7–8

7. Naples 2910 (inv. 81863).
Apulian situla by the Lycurgus Painter; *c.* 360–350 B.C.
8. Berlin inv. 3157.
Apulian volute-krater; *c.* 350 B.C.

The *Rhesus* dramatizes an episode from Book X of the *Iliad*, in which Odysseus and Diomedes, after slaying the Trojan spy Dolon, enter the Trojan camp to steal the horses of Rhesus, the recently arrived King of Thrace, which they do after killing him and a dozen of his sleeping followers. The play has come down to us among the works of Euripides, but its authenticity has been strongly contested on linguistic, metrical and other grounds. Some scholars regard it as a very early work by Euripides himself (*c.* 455 B.C.); others as not

III.5,7 (Naples). 'Rhesus'

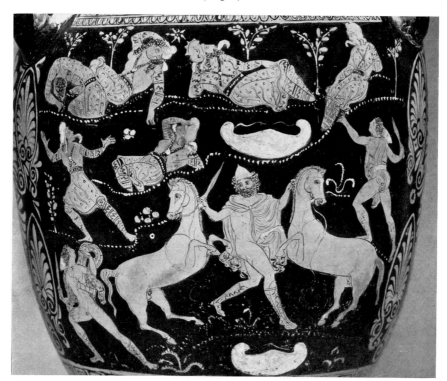

III.5,8 (Berlin). 'Rhesus'

by him, but perhaps by his son, the younger Euripides, who also wrote tragedies.

The first vase gives a spirited rendering of the theft of the horses. Above are the bodies of three of the murdered Thracians, dressed in elaborately-patterned local costume that may reflect stage influence; below, Diomedes and Odysseus each with drawn sword in hand, escape with the horses of Rhesus. Odysseus holds the two horses by the reins, while Diomedes with a gesture indicates the best line of escape. A similar treatment of the subject, with a little more detail, will be found on the second vase, which is slightly later in date, but from the same workshop as the first. Otherwise it is rarely treated.

For the play see in particular: W. Ritchie, *The Authenticity of the Rhesus of Euripides* (Cambridge, 1964) and the review by E. Fraenkel in *Gnomon* 87, 1965, 228; Lesky, *History of Greek Literature*, 631.
7. Schmidt, *Dareiosmaler*, pl. 1; *Letteratura ed arte figurata*, no. 14 (ill.); *BABesch* 41, 1966, 69, fig. 11.
8. Neugebauer, *Führer*, 160, pl. 81.

6. Plays with Unidentified Subjects

III. 6, 1

Caltanissetta, Museo Civico from Capodarso.
Sicilian kalyx-krater by the Capodarso Painter; third quarter of the fourth century B.C.

Until the discovery in 1969 of the Oedipus krater by the same painter (III. 2, 8), this was the only vase to show a tragic performance actually taking place upon a stage. A woman with short hair kneels with a gesture of appeal or supplication between two other women, dressed alike in long, embroidered tragic costumes with cloaks, one of whom turns away from the suppliant, while the other raises both hands, as if in horror, as she listens to the words of an old, white-haired man, wearing a pilos, who looks like the Messenger. The scene might be associated with the *Hypsipyle* of Euripides, where the messenger narrates the death of Opheltes to Eurydice, and Hypsipyle's appeal for mercy is ignored by the leader of the chorus. Certainty is hardly possible, but there can be no doubt of the tragic connotation of the scene.

LCS 601, no. 98, pl. 235, 2–3; Webster, *MTSP²*, 126, SV 2, and 168.

III. 6, 2

Lipari inv. 2297, from T. 402.
Sicilian kalyx-krater by the Maron Painter; mid-fourth century B.C.

The scene on this vase, which represents the Thracian Maron (inscribed) handing over to Odysseus (inscribed), in the presence of Opora and Ampelis (both inscribed), the skin of wine which he will subsequently use to intoxicate the Cyclops (cf. Euripides, *Cyclops*, 141, and II, 11), must be of dramatic inspiration, not only by reason of the stage costume worn by Maron, but also from the fact that the characters stand upon what looks to be the floor of a stage, rather than upon normal ground, which would be shown by dotted lines with small flowering plants, etc. The presence of Opora (the autumn or harvest) and Ampelis (the spirit of the vine) confirms this, since such personifications would be not uncommon in a fourth-century play, where they might well speak the prologue or epilogue. The play, which would hardly be a tragedy, would have been based upon the episode in *Odyssey*, ix, 196 ff., which gives the background to the adventure of Odysseus with the Cyclops. It might have been one of the *hilarotragedies*, popular in Magna Graecia in the fourth and early third centuries B.C. and raised to a literary form by Rhinthon.

Bernabò Brea, *Meligunis-Lipara*, ii, 142, pls. 84–5; *LCS, Suppl. I*, 102; *MTSP²*, 126, SV 1; Touchefeu-Meynier, *Thèmes odysséens*, 271, no. 500, pl. 39, 1.

III. 6, 3

Bonn 2667.
Lucanian nestoris by the Brooklyn-Budapest Painter; second quarter of the fourth century B.C.

On rocky ground at the foot of an Ionic column, a bearded man in stage costume is about to be slain by a negroid-looking youth with a sword. To the right, a woman and a youth run off with bits of furniture; to the left, a bearded man flees in terror, and another youth of negroid cast holds a chopper in his hand. The interpretation remains a problem. The details do not correspond with those in other representations of Herakles slaying Busiris; nor does the murder of Aegisthus seem very plausible, since the youth bears no resemblance to Orestes, and some of the other figures would be inexplicable in that context. The scene may perhaps be connected with the *Lynkeus* of Theodektes, a fourth-century tragedian; if so, Lynkeus (son of Aigyptos; hence possibly his foreign appearance) would be slaying Danaos, while Hypermnestra and a boy (Abas?) carry off pieces of his throne.
The scene remains an interesting puzzle.

LCS 113, no. 584, pl. 59, 1; Felletti Maj, *Riv Ist Arch*, 6, 1937–8, 220, n. 45, fig. 8; Schauenburg, *Perseus*, 102, n. 719, pl. 35, 1; *MTSP²*, 130, LV 9, and 166.

III.6,3 (Bonn). Scene from an unidentified tragedy, possibly Theodektes' *Lynkeus*

III.6, 1 (Caltanissetta). Scene from an unidentified tragedy

III.6, 2 (Lipari). 'Maron and Odysseus'

III.6,4 (Bari). Scene from an unidentified tragedy

III. 6, 4

Bari 6254.

Lucanian amphora by the Dolon Painter; *c.* 400–380 B.C.

In the centre on an altar a veiled woman is seated, with a nude boy beside her, resting one hand upon her lap. Beside him stands a woman, her right hand on his shoulder, her left holding an axe-like weapon. To the left, stands a nude youth with a pilos on his head and a cloak down his back, holding a staff or spear. It seems to be an asylum scene, like those which appear in some of the stepmother plays (e.g. the *Ino* or *Phrixos* of Euripides), but no convincing interpretation has yet been put forward.

LCS 103, no. 536, pl. 53, 2; *MTSP*², 168; *La Collezione Polese*, pl. 10, no. 31.

III. 6, 5

Sydney 53. 10.

Fragment of krater, near in style to the Lycurgus Painter; *c.* 360–350 B.C.

In the centre is a half-open door through which a bearded figure, dressed in tragic costume with an embroidered long-sleeved tunic, rushes with one arm flung out between the leaves of the door. To the left is a pile of overturned furniture and vessels, including a small table on which a foot is visible. It is certainly a scene of violence and confusion in which someone – perhaps a younger man, to judge from the foot on the table – attacks a king, who flees in terror.

*MTSP*², 75, TV 7.

III.6,5 (Sydney). Scene from an unidentified tragedy

IV. OLD AND MIDDLE COMEDY; PHLYAKES

IV, 1

Athens, Vlastos coll.
Attic red-figure chous from Anavysos; 420 B.C.

This is the only Attic vase with a picture of comedy which shows a stage. The stage is approached, like the stage on South Italian phlyax vases, by a short flight of steps. The two spectators sit on chairs watching: one is young and holds a stick, the other is bearded and wreathed with ivy. They may be choregos (producer) and poet. The curved lines at the side of the stage may represent a curtain, which decorates the background on either side of the stage-door: the use of a curtain as background is known from fourth-century and later comedy. Attic painters, as we have seen, are apt to paint characters rather than actors, but the lines on the wrist are the ends of the actor's tights and the phallos is looped up as on the Herakles of IV, 9. That the actor is playing Perseus is shown by the *harpe* and the bag for the Gorgon's head, and he has his hand raised towards his forehead like the Perseus on III. 2, 3. The comedy must have parodied Sophocles' *Andromeda*; the comic poet Phrynichos, in a play written well before 420 B.C., had a scene in which a monster was going to eat a woman – this sounds like a parody of the *Andromeda*.

*ARV*², 1215, no. 1 (Group of the Perseus Dancer); *PhV*², no. 1; Pickard-Cambridge, *Festivals*², fig. 76; Webster, *AE*, 1953–4, 199.
Curtain: *Rylands Bulletin*, 45, 1962, 262.
Phrynichos: see Aristophanes, *Clouds*, 556.

IV,1 (Athens, Vlastos). A parody of Sophocles, *Andromeda*

IV, 2

Paris, Louvre N3408, from Cyrene.
Attic red-figured chous by the Nikias Painter; 410 B.C.

Herakles stands on a chariot driven by Nike and pulled by four Centaurs; a wreathed man goes ahead holding two torches. The connection with comedy is given first by the mask-like faces. Nike's snub-nosed black-haired mask is repeated on IV, 4, below; Herakles is exactly like the Herakles of the New York set of actor-terracottas (IV, 9). The Centaurs' faces are very like the slave mask (B) on IV, 3, but they have equine ears. The torch-bearer's face recurs as a slave-mask (N) on a late Middle Comedy relief (IV, 8a). His body is stylized very like the body of Perseus (IV, 1), and his tights are shown by the wrinkles on the legs and the lines round the right wrist and ankle. Nike, Herakles, and the torch-bearer are presumably actors, and the Centaurs may be members of the chorus. Plato seems to have known of a drama with Centaurs, and the name has survived of a comedy called *Centaurs* by Apollophanes. (Herakles feasted in Aristophanes' *Dramata or Centaur*, but one would expect the singular Centaur to be Pholos, who provided Herakles with wine).

On a black-figured pyxis of the late sixth century Herakles drives a Centaur chariot; there is nothing specifically to connect this vase with comedy or pre-comedy except the fact that it anticipates the Louvre chous, just as the early Birds, Knights, and Titans have their later fifth-century successors. In this case we can perhaps see what gave the impulse to revive the old scheme. Here Nike drives the chariot and a torch-bearer runs ahead. On a rather earlier vase by the Kadmos Painter, Herakles is driven to heaven by Athena, while satyrs steal the arms on his pyre. This may have been inspired by a satyr-play, which was parodied by the writer of our comedy. In the comedy Herakles did not drive to heaven but to marriage, and so the forerunner is not Hermes (as on several vases with the drive to heaven), but a slave with torches like the old man in Euripides' *Helen* (723), who carried the torches beside Helen's marriage car (cf. IV, 28).

*ARV*², 1335, no. 34; *PhV*², no. 3; Pickard-Cambridge, *Festivals*², fig. 77; Snowden, *Blacks in Antiquity*, fig. 88.
Plato, *Politicus* 303*d*, cf. 291*a*.
Black-figured pyxis, Agora P1257, E. Vanderpool, *Hesperia* 7, 1938, 393, no. 31.
Kadmos Painter: *ARV*², 1186; cf. Webster, *Art and Literature in fourth-century Athens*, 34.

117

IV,2 (Paris). Scene from Old Comedy

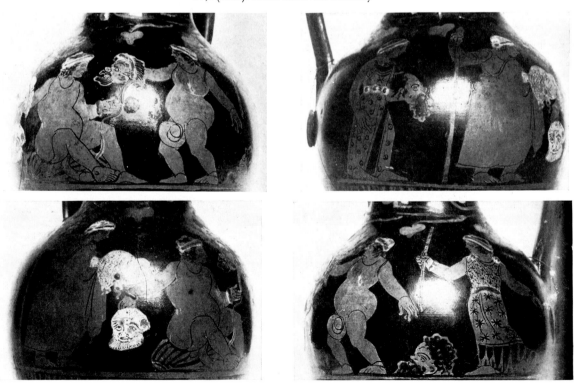

IV,3 (Leningrad). A children's comedy

IV, 3

Leningrad ΦA 1869.47, from Phanagoria, South Russia.
Attic red-figured chous from Meidias' workshop (J. R. Green);
410–400 B.C.

Five children concerned with comedy. There is no evidence
for children's comedy before the second century A.D. and no
likelihood that such existed. The chous was frequently (but
not exclusively) given as a present to children at the Anthesteria, and it was pleasing to decorate choes with children, not
only doing childish things but also doing grown-up things,
which children were not allowed to do. These children must
therefore be interpreted as if they were grown-ups.
The outside figures wear elaborate chitons: the right-hand one
has sleeves and a flute – the flute-player in proper dress
(cf. II, 1: contemporary satyr-play). The one on the left
carries a mask; we can only say that he is not an actor
because he is not in actor's costume; he may be poet,
choregos, or helping friend. There are five masks and three
actors, the statutory number of actors for comedy as for
tragedy. It looks as if the central actor has taken off the old
man's mask (E), which he holds in his right hand and is taking
the slave-mask (B) from the actor on the right. These two
actors wear tights, padding, phallos – bound up on the right-
hand actor and hanging down on the central actor. The central
actor sits on a bundle, which he has either just unstrapped from
his shoulders or is just going to strap up: similar bundles can
be seen on IV, 20 and 35. The actor on the left wears a large
himation over his tights like Oedipus on IV, 32, and holds a
sceptre. His white-haired, hook-nosed, bearded mask (G) has a
little crown on the top: the same mask and the same crown are
worn by Zeus on IV, 19. Zeus, however, on IV, 22 wears the
neat dark-haired mask (H), which lies on the ground on the
right of the Leningrad chous. The mask (F) held by the figure
on the left is worn by a man dancing along with two torches
on a rather earlier chous in the Louvre.
The mask (E) held by the centre actor is commonly worn by
old men, e.g. by Tyndareus on IV, 26. But in this mask the
pupils are indicated at the top of the eyeballs. If this is inten-
tional, it must mean that the character was blind. It is true
that the blind masks of Phineus (III. 1, 25) and Thamyras (III.
2, 10) show only the eyebrows and one lid, but somehow the
actor must have been able to see and he saw through a hole in
the eye of the mask. It was a possible convention to fit a blind
mask with the hole at the top of the eyeball instead of in the
centre. This appears again in a Hellenistic mask of a girl in
New Comedy. Aristophanes produced the first version of the
Ploutos in 408 B.C., and presumably the god of wealth was
blind in that play as in the second preserved version.

*PhV*², no. 3; Pickard-Cambridge, *Festivals*², fig. 78.
Children's comedy: E. J. Jory, *BICS* 14, 1967, 84.

Louvre chous: *PhV*², no. 2.
Hellenistic mask: *Griechische Bühnenaltertümer*, 31, pl. 5, 1.

IV, 4

Heidelberg B 134.
Attic red-figured bell-krater; early fourth century B.C.

Two members of the chorus of a comedy with a female
chorus. The chorus-man on the left is represented dancing.
The mask is the same as the mask worn by Nike on IV, 2. The
dress is a long chiton and a patterned himation worn over the
head. The posture recalls the Muse on III. 2, 10, and the
dithyramb-singers on I, 17, 19, 20. It has been suggested that
this was the posture and arrangement of clothes for a stately
song, which seems out of tune with comedy, but in fact one of
the choruses of Aristophanes' early fourth-century comedy
the *Ekklesiazousai* (571 ff.) is written in dactylo-epitrites, the
metre of some dithyrambs and tragic choruses, and a much
earlier example of a stately muffled comic chorus can be seen
in the Berlin Birds (quoted on I, 12).
The step of the other chorus-man is much more lively: one
bent leg and the other stretched straight out, like the satyr
Simos on the Oxford Prometheus krater (II, 4). This is appropriate for the lively song and dance with which the chorus
make their exit at the end of a comedy. This chorus-man has
thrown off his chiton (or the vase-painter has omitted it),
flung his himation over one shoulder, pushed his mask back
on his forehead, and picked up a torch. The need to maintain
dramatic illusion is over and so the chorus-man can show his
face. The moment might be either when the chorus dance off

IV,4 (Heidelberg). A chorus of a comedy

the stage at the end of the play (in the *Ekklesiazousai* an actor goes off at the end with a torch (1150) and an actor is shown dancing off with a torch on a rather earlier chous in the Louvre, noted on IV, 3), or when they danced in the procession which escorted the statue of Dionysos out of the theatre.

*PhV*², no. 7; Pickard-Cambridge, *Festivals*², fig. 85.

IV, 5–6

5. London, British Museum 98.2–27.1.
6. Athens, Agora P23900.
Attic choes, unglazed with painted polychrome decoration; 400–390 B.C.

In 1954 four oinochoai were excavated in a well in the Athenian Agora. They evidently formed a set specially painted in a unique technique for a party; a fifth, in the British Museum, may have belonged to the same set. The paint is very friable, but the designs can mostly be made out. The set may have been made to celebrate a victory with a comedy. On the British Museum chous a little fat man rows an enormous blue fish. He is in the tradition of the dolphin-riders (I, 11, 14, 15) and Aeschylus *Nereids* (III, 1, 19), and on a lost Apulian vase some thirty years later a comic actor rides a fish. Possibly men on fish were the chorus of this comedy, and in the actual performance the long oars may have been stilts between which the fish was swung (cf. I, 10). The first chous from the Agora set has a clean-shaven man with enormous ears running along with a stick in his right hand, a jug on his left arm, and possibly a lyre slung round his neck. He wears cuffed boots, and a small himation slung round his arms. He is naked (i.e. wears pink tights) and sexless. Clean-shaven figures for Aristophanes are effeminate and are often addressed as women; this explains the sexlessness. Large ears probably mean that he is stupid. He is running up to join in a party. On the second chous of the Agora set two bearded men, one with cuffed boots and a feminine headdress, carry an enormous cake on a

IV,6 (Athens, Agora). Scene from Old Comedy

spit; the scene is repeated on an Apulian bell-krater of 375–350 B.C., and 'Spit-cake carriers' is the title of a comedy by Ephippos, which seems to have been produced 380–370 B.C., perhaps too late for the Agora choes (a later comic poet may reproduce a successful turn from a predecessor's play). The third chous gives Dionysos with Phor (a thief?) or Phormio, and the fourth Neleus, Tyro, and Pelias; perhaps a parody of the recognition scene in Sophocles' *Tyro*: gods and heroic characters are indistinguishable in costume and mask from the ordinary characters of comedy.

*PhV*², nos. 9–13; Pickard-Cambridge, *Festivals*², figs. 82–4.
Agora choes: Sparkes and Talcott, *Athenian Agora* xii, 205.
Apulian fish-rider: *PhV*², no. 144; Cake-carriers, *PhV*², no. 34.

IV, 7a

Lyme Park, Stockport.
Attic grave-relief; *c.* 380 B.C.

This large grave-relief (preserved height, 3 ft 8½ ins.) was found in 1812 in the Kerameikos. It can be dated only by style, and comparison with other grave-reliefs suggests a date about 380 B.C. The man held a roll in his left hand, like the seated poet of the Pronomos vase (II, 1). He was therefore a comic poet, and this is the earliest of a series of representations of dramatic poets holding a mask or having a mask held in front of them, as they write a speech for a character. The wreath round the head was probably an ivy wreath (cf. IV, 1). The face is individual with deep cuts on either side of the nose and close-cut beard. The date would fit with Aristophanes and perhaps his baldness as a young man (*Knights*, 550; *Peace*, 767 f.; Eupolis 78K) need not have been emphasized in a grave-relief. The size of the relief implies a famous poet. The sadness of the poet contrasts with the gaiety of the slave-mask (B) on his lap. This mask is very common on South Italian comic

IV,5 (London). Scene from Old Comedy

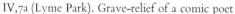

IV,7a (Lyme Park). Grave-relief of a comic poet

IV,7b (Madrid). Funerary vase of a comic poet

vases (e.g. IV, 26), as well as on Attic terracottas of comic actors. The old man's mask with the triangular beard (A), hanging on the wall, is much commoner in Attic art than in South Italian (cf., however, IV, 8b). These masks could have been worn by the slave Karion and his master Chremylos in Aristophanes' last surviving play, the second *Ploutos*.

Bieber, *History*[2], fig. 201; Webster, *OMC*, no. AS 1; Pickard-Cambridge, *Festivals*[2], fig. 88.
Poet and Mask: Webster, in *Classical Drama and its influence*, 1965, 5.

IV, 7b

Madrid 11223 (L. 346).
Apulian amphora, late work of the Iliupersis Painter; c. 360–350 B.C.

The large Apulian red-figured vases were commonly funerary vases and were often decorated on one side with a representation of a grave monument (*naiskos*) or relief. On the Madrid amphora the naiskos has hanging in the background, in the same position as the old man's mask on the Attic relief IV, 7a, the mask of a curly-haired young man, perhaps Hermes as the prologue-speaker of a comedy. The dead man, wearing a large red himation and carrying a stick, is brought a lyre by a boy, who is probably his slave. On the Pronomos vase (II, 1) the poet's lyre hangs behind him, and the lyre is an obvious attribute of the poet as writer of lyrics and trainer of choruses. Two other South Italian vases show the grave monument of a poet; both are Lucanian, by the Primato Painter (*LCS*, nos. 920 and 923), and represent a balding man holding a lyre.

Ossorio, *Cat.*, pl. 41; Leroux, *Cat.*, pl. 42; Pickard-Cambridge, *Theatre*, p. 100, fig. 32; *Museo Arch. Nacional*, pl. 26; *PhV*[2], no. (xxv).

IV,8a (Athens, Epigraphical Museum). Relief in honour of a choregos

IV, 8a

Athens, Epigraphical Museum 1338.
Marble relief; 340 B.C.

The relief consists of a pediment, an architrave decorated with five comic masks in relief, and a shaft decorated with a relief of a seated Dionysos approached by a satyr holding an oinochoe. Below this relief an inscription records that the local assembly of Aixone (an Attic deme on the coast southeast of Athens) had decreed honours for two successful producers (*choregoi*) in the archonship of Theophrastos. Unfortunately the archon was called Theophrastos both in 340/339 B.C. and in 313/312 B.C. The prosopography of the persons named, the style of the relief, and the types of mask suit the earlier date better than the later. This is the only relief honouring choregoi which is decorated with masks. The five masks are: (1) an old man with large square beard (M). This is a comparatively new mask and develops later into the standard mask for the stern father of New Comedy (cf. IV, 8c); (2) an elderly woman with an untidy mop of hair (R). This is worn by the old woman welcoming an unwilling man on IV, 16; (3) a slave with a beard with small point (N). This is the mask worn by the man who precedes the Centaur-chariot on the Louvre chous (IV, 2); (4) a beardless youth (O). This again is a comparatively new mask: to be clean-shaven is now respectable. It is worn by Oedipus on IV, 32; (5) a young woman with short hair (S). This is the Antigone mask of IV, 33.
The central position of the slave (N) suggests that he intrigued for the two young lovers (O and S) against their parents (M and R).

OMC, AS 2; Pickard-Cambridge, *Festivals*², fig. 25.

IV, 8b

Vatican AD 1 (inv. 17370).
Paestan bell-krater by Python; 350–325 B.C.

Three young men are having a party in an arbour. The wooden supports are shown at the side, an ivy-trail is strung under the roof and from it hang three masks. The tradition of such arbours goes on into the Hellenistic age; in the great Dionysiac procession of Ptolemy II Philadelphos, Dionysos appeared in a similar arbour, which was carried on a tableau-float. The young men are playing kottabos, flicking drops of wine on to the scale on the top of the tall stand. On the left, a flute-girl plays for them. On the right, a young satyr arrives with part of the kottabos-stand and a ladle. In the centre Papposilenos has gone to sleep, still holding his flutes. The presence of the satyr shows that Dionysos favours this party, and the young men may, therefore, be actors. And Papposilenos is depicted as an actor playing Papposilenos, since his tights are marked at ankles and feet (cf. I, 16; II, 1 and 5). He might also be an actor, who went to sleep at the party; but an actor would not wear mask and costume, so that he again is rather a bringer of Dionysos' goodwill. The masks are those of the slave B, the old man A (cf. IV, 7a) and the long-haired girl (SS, which appears twice in the background of IV, 14).

*PhV*², no. 172; Webster, *Rylands Bulletin*, 45, 1962, 247; *Hellenistic Poetry and Art*, 163.

IV, 8c

Delos, House of the Masks.
Mosaic; second century B.C.

Delos had a flourishing theatre from the fourth century B.C. until its sack in the early first century B.C. A large house built in the prosperous period of Athenian occupation in the second century has three mosaic floors connected with the theatre and has therefore been regarded as a kind of headquarters for visiting actors, but it must be remembered that theatre subjects are always appropriate to Dionysos, appropriate to him as god of the symposion or god of the dead as well as god of the theatre. The floor of the dining-room has a mosaic of perspective cubes in black, white, dark red, and light red. On two sides the mosaic has a border of five masks hanging from a trailer of fruited ivy. The design is in the same tradition as the arbour on the Paestan krater (IV, 8b), and elsewhere terracotta masks with suspension holes have been found in dining-rooms.

In each set four of the masks are standard masks of New Comedy: to these are added a Pan mask in one set and a

IV.8b (Vatican). Actors celebrating

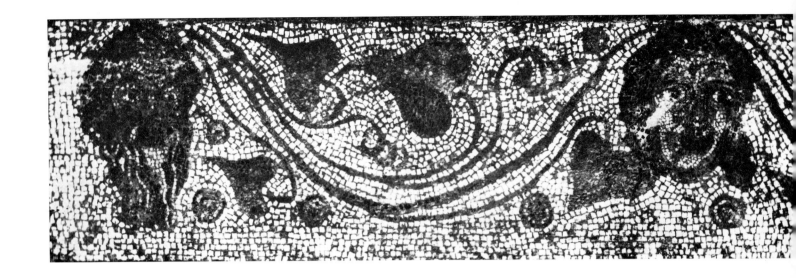

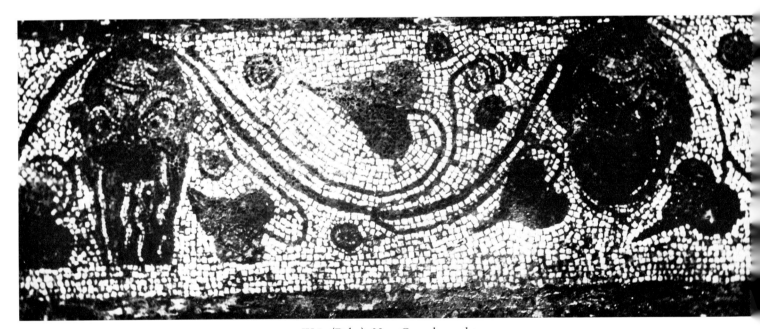

IV,8c (Delos). New Comedy masks

IV,8c (Delos). New Comedy masks

26 23 14

27 13 27 22

22 20 20

IV,9 (New York). Seven comic statuettes

Satyr mask in the other. The artist may have been thinking of them as prologue-speakers: Pan speaks the prologue of Menander's *Dyskolos*. On one side illustrated the first mask is the Satyr; the rest are standard masks of New Comedy: the 'dark' youth (probably worn by Charisios, the hero of Menander's *Epitrepontes*); the 'old man with wavy-hair' (the New Comedy successor of Middle Comedy mask L, cf. IV, 9, and worn by Kallippides in Menander's *Dyskolos*); the brothel-keeper; the leading slave, the New Comedy successor of Middle Comedy mask B (cf. IV, 7a).

Webster, *MNC* 69, DM 1; *Hellenistic Art*, 150; Chamonard, *Délos* XIV, pl. 4–6.

IV, 9

Metropolitan Museum, New York, 13.225. 13, 14, 20, 22, 23, 26, 27.
Attic terracotta statuettes; 375–350 B.C.

This set of seven terracottas was found in a tomb in Athens with another set of seven different comic types distinguished also by the colour of the fired clay, which is yellow for the first set and red for the second. The mould for one of the yellow set and a replica of one of the yellow set have been found in the Agora in Athens. We know about eighty types of comic terracottas which were manufactured in Athens in the second quarter of the fourth century; they were evidently extremely popular in replicas or imitations, and local variants have been found all over the Greek world, in Spain, North Africa, Egypt, South Russia, Italy, Lipari, Sicily, as well as mainland Greece itself.

The set illustrated gives the cast of an intrigue comedy which included Herakles and a baby. The Middle Comedy *Auge* by Eubulus is a possibility; it was to some extent a parody of Euripides' *Auge*, in which Auge sent her nurse to expose her child by Herakles, Telephos. Possibly the same comedy is illustrated on IV, 24. In the New York set the Nurse carrying the baby wears mask U, cf. the old woman on IV, 13. The young woman pulling her himation away from her face is Auge; she wears mask V, cf. IV, 24. Herakles wears his usual mask (cf. IV, 2) and has lion-skin, bow, and club. Then a man in the felt-hat of a traveller, evidently distressed; he wears mask L, which is the commonest mask for middle-aged as distinct from old men, cf. the traveller on IV, 20. In New Comedy it becomes the mask of the wavy-haired old man (cf. IV, 8c). A fragment of Eubulus' *Auge* (15K) says: 'Why are you still standing in the doorway? Why don't you go in? They have already torn the roast-goose to pieces . . .' In comedy Aleos, Auge's father, would be more distressed at the expense of the feast than at the rape of his daughter. Late arrival is a stock comic situation (cf. Kallippides in Menander's

Dyskolos, 775 ff.). Here the feast has been prepared by two slaves: one carrying a shopping basket, and one with a himation over his head carrying a hydria (lost) on his head. He is parodying the women water-carriers who walked in sacred processions. A third slave is seated on an altar, thinking out a plan to trick Aleos? The slaves all wear mask K, which recurs commonly on these Attic terracottas and is the ancestor of the New Comedy slave with wavy hair (V, 5).

OMC, AT 8–14; Pickard-Cambridge, *Festivals*², figs. 89–90; Bieber, *History*², figs. 185–91.
Eubulus *Auge*: Webster, *Later Greek Comedy*, 84 f.; Euripides *Auge*: Webster, *Tragedies of Euripides*, 240.

IV, 10

The Hague, Schneider-Herrmann coll. 19.
Paestan bell-krater by Python; third quarter fourth century B.C.

This vase is an excellent illustration of the association of Dionysos with a phlyax actor, a subject popular with the Paestan vase-painters of the school of Asteas and Python. To the left is a youthful Dionysos with a dish of offerings in his left hand and an egg in his right, which he holds out towards an actor dressed in phlyax costume, and also holding an egg and a thyrsus. He wears the typical Paestan tights with a seam down the legs and arms, and over them a short white chiton, with padding in front and a large red phallos. Above, hanging

IV,10 (The Hague, Schneider-Herrmann). Phlyax actor and Dionysos

from an ivy-trail, over which is looped a red fillet with white dots, is a white female mask (type XC) in profile.

G. Schneider-Herrmann, *BABesch*, 40, 1965, 75–9, figs. 1–4; *PhV²*, 31, no. 27, pl. 31.
Other examples of a phlyax actor with Dionysos: *PhV²*, nos. 28, 35, 38, 42, 43, 54, 64, 70, 140; or with Dionysos and a maenad, nos. 47, 90.
For Dionysos with a phlyax mask, cf. nos. 170–1.
Full bibliographies of each phlyax vase will be found in *PhV²* and are therefore not repeated for the individual entries.

IV, 11

Lipari inv. 927, from Lipari T. 367.
Paestan kalyx-krater near in style to, and probably an early work by, Asteas; *c*. 360–350 B.C.

On this vase a stage very similar to that on Asteas' signed krater in Berlin (IV, 14) is shown, except that the columns supporting it are hidden behind a pleated curtain with a black border. To the left, a youthful Dionysos seated on a chair watches a female tumbler performing acrobatics on a small table. To the right are two phlyakes, one white-haired (L) gazing with gloating eyes at the naked body of the tumbler, the other (B) looking on with a more blasé air, as he leans against the post, which, as usual, marks the boundary of the stage. Above, looking down from two windows, are two characters wearing comic female masks – the hetaira (XB) and the kore (S). The vase is of particular interest not only for its subject-matter but also for its style. Tumblers appear not

infrequently on vases, and a Paestan skyphos in Oxford (1945. 43; *PhV²*, no. 96) shows a phlyax working the turntable for one, with a female mask suspended above. Our vase further emphasizes the connection of Dionysos with the stage.

Two recently discovered kraters from Lipari are by the same painter as this vase (*Arch Reps* 16, 1969–70, 48 and *LCS, Suppl. I*, 32); one shows Dionysos in the company of two flute-players and a silen, with a female mask (SS) suspended above, the other a silen surprising a sleeping maenad in the presence of a papposilen, who reappears on another vase (Louvre K 240; *PhV²*, 92, pl. 14*c*) along with Dionysos, who holds a thyrsus, to which is tied a mask similar to that in the left-hand window of the Lipari vase (XB). These four vases, then, form a compact group in regard to both style and subject; the reverse designs likewise link them together and also with the Berlin kalyx-krater signed by Asteas, of which the Lipari vase might well be regarded as a prototype for the treatment of the stage and of the masks above. It is therefore very likely that all four are in fact early works by Asteas, thus strengthening the connection between Paestan and Sicilian vase-painting in the second quarter of the fourth century.

PhV², 52, no. 80, pl. 6b; Charbonneaux, Martin and Villard, *La Grèce classique*, fig. 371 (colour); Gigante, *Teatro Greco*, 114, pl. 6.

IV, 12

Ruvo, Jatta coll. 1402, from Ruvo.
Apulian askos; *c*. 380–360 B.C.

IV,11 (Lipari). Phlyax actors and Dionysos

IV,12 (Ruvo, Jatta coll.). Phlyax actor in thiasos

IV,12 (Ruvo, Jatta coll.). Dancing hag of negroid type

The figured scene running round the body of this vase, which is generally described as an askos from a fancied resemblance to a wine-skin, is an excellent illustration of the association between the phlyax actor and the Dionysiac thiasos. In the midst of a group of dancing maenads and satyrs, some holding torches and others tambourines, are two other figures, one a phlyax wearing the characteristic tights, over which is a short tunic, and a snub-nosed, short-bearded mask (B), the other a hag with negroid features and protruding breasts, who dances on one foot with hands extended.

PhV[2], 68, no. 135; detail of the dancing hag (in colour): *La Grèce classique*, fig. 369; Snowden, *Blacks in Antiquity*, figs. 94 and 2.

IV,13 (New York). 'Punishment of Thief' from Old Comedy

IV, 13

New York 24.97.104.
Apulian kalyx-krater by the Tarporley Painter; *c.* 400–390 B.C.

The Tarporley Painter, whose main period of activity lies in the first quarter of the fourth century B.C., has a decided preference for themes associated with actors (cf. II, 2) and the stage, and this must be regarded as one of his more important vases, since it presents us not only with one of the earliest of the series depicting phlyax plays but also with several metrical inscriptions which may well be quotations from the actual play. The vase depicts the 'Punishment of the Thief' (cf. IV, 15), who is shown in the middle of the picture with his hands bound above his head and beside him an inscription reading κατέδησ' ἄνω τὼ χεῖρε (he has bound my two hands above). To the left stands the policeman, stick in hand ready to beat the malefactor, and from his mouth runs the nonsense inscription NOPAPETTEBΛO, which is probably some bogus foreign language, since he might well be a Scythian or Thracian, as Whatmough has shown that he is not speaking Messapian. To the right, on a wooden proskenion, with an elaborate door with figured decoration leading in to her house, is the old woman whose possessions, a goose and a kid

in a wicker basket, the thief had tried to steal; she says ἐγὼ παρέξω (I shall hand him over) and stretches out her right hand in an appropriate gesture, with a look of anger on her wrinkled face. Above the central figures is a phlyax mask (B) and further to the left stands a youth inscribed TPAΓOIΔOΣ, who Beazley suggests may have been a tragic actor looking on at the comedy after his own performance was over.
The inscription may be arranged either as iambics:

A. κατέδησ' ἄνω τὼ χεῖρε   B. νωραρεττεβλω.
Γ. ἐγὼ παρέξω...

or, keeping them in the order in which they appear on the vase, as an iambic tetrameter catalectic:

A. νοραρεττεβλω. B. κατέδησ' ἄνω τὼ χεῖρε. Γ. ἐγὼ παρέξω . . .

and in either case are probably quotations from the play. It may be noted that they are in Attic and not Doric (as might be expected at Tarentum), and it is probably right to associate the vase with the performance of an Attic comedy and not a local farce.

*PhV*², 14 ff. and 53, no. 84; Gigante, *Teatro Greco*, 103 f.
On the interpretation of the inscription see especially:—Whatmough, *HSCP* 39, 1928, 1–6 and *Class Phil* 47, 1952, 26; Webster, *CQ* 42, 1948, 25 and *Festschrift Schweitzer*, 260; Beazley, *AJA* 56, 1952, 193; Cambitoglou and Trendall, *APS* 31–2.

IV,14 (Berlin). 'Robbing the Miser' from Middle Comedy

IV, 14

Berlin F 3044, from St. Agata dei Goti.
Paestan kalyx-krater, signed by Asteas; c. 350–340 B.C.

Theft of food, wine or money is another very popular theme in farce, and this vase by Asteas gives a vivid and realistic representation of "Robbing the Miser". A quite elaborate stage setting is shown; the floor, decorated with a frieze of dots perhaps to symbolize the ends of the cross-timbers (cf. IV, 11), is supposed by five fluted Doric columns in added white to signify marble; on either side are tall posts and to left a door opening inwards. Two rascals, Gymnilos and Kosilos, have dragged the miser (Charinos) out of his house on his strong-box, which is of a type still found at Pompeii four centuries later. He looks to have gone to sleep on it the better

to protect his wealth, and is now being rudely handled by the two intruders, while his cowardly slave (Karion) stands by in an attitude of helpless despair, hands stretched out in a gesture of fear, trembling at the knees. Above were two female masks (SS) in profile, facing in opposite directions beside a central wreath, but in the restoration of the vase the second has largely disappeared.

It may be noted that in the Mytilene mosaic of Menander's *Messenia* (*AntK*, Beiheft 6, 1970, pls. 4, 4 and 21, 2) a young man named Charinos is being dragged about by two slaves; the use of this name in such a contest may therefore be traditional.

PhV², 50, no. 76; Kahane, *Ancient and Classical Art*, colour-illustration on p. 160.

IV,15 (Berlin). 'Punishment of Slave' from Old Comedy   IV,16 (Cambridge, Mass.). 'Husband and wife' from Middle Comedy

IV, 15

Berlin F 3043.
Early Lucanian kalyx-krater by the Amykos Painter; late fifth century B.C.

This is one of the earliest phlyax vases to have come down to us from South Italy and seems to be a late work of the Amykos Painter, in which case it must be dated just before 400 B.C. The subject represents the punishment of a slave (cf. IV, 13), a popular theme in Greek comedy, which, though derided by Aristophanes in the *Peace* (746 ff.), continued at least until the time of Menander (cf. *Perinthia, Pap. Oxy.* 855). Here the overseer (B), with a long stick in his hand, is about to thrash the errant slave (B), whom he holds by a cord tied round his neck, and who crouches down as if to make the task as difficult as possible; above is the head of another slave (B), who mocks him by cocking a snook.

*PhV*², 49, no. 75.

IV, 16

Cambridge (Mass.), Harvard University – McDaniel coll.
Apulian bell-krater, near in style to the Painter of Perseus and Athena; first quarter fourth century B.C.

Only the floor to the stage is shown, with a Doric column to the left, and a door, opening inwards, on the right. To the left an old phlyax, with curly white hair and a snub nose (L), listens with resignation to the expostulations of a white-haired woman (R), who has emerged from the house in barefoot haste and is clearly lashing him with her tongue. Such husband and wife scenes obviously gave scope to the writers of phlyax plays for amusing dialogue and they are not infrequently represented (cf. Vienna 466; *PhV*², no. 66). Above hangs a phlyax mask of type B.

Anne Bromberg, *HSCP* 64, 1959, 237 ff., pl. 1; *PhV*², 30, no. 24.

IV, 17

London, British Museum F 189.
Paestan bell-krater by Python; third quarter fourth century B.C.

Here the scene takes place on a rather more elaborate stage, supported by three Doric columns with garlands and red fillets suspended between them, and with a tall post on each side, serving as a sort of frame for the picture. An older man, with a pointed white beard (L), holds a walking-stick in his left hand and with his right firmly grasps the arm of a younger man (B) who reels slightly backward; he holds a situla in one hand and a dish of eggs in the other. The scene has often been interpreted as the father dragging his reluctant son home after the banquet, but the young man would hardly be carrying his own pail and dish, and he is more likely to be the old man's slave, who has attended him to the feast, and has become drunk, as in various extant fragments of Greek comedy (e.g. Eubulus 126; Alexis 25).

*PhV*², 36, no. 39.

IV, 18

Milan, Moretti coll.
Apulian bell-krater; *c.* 380 B.C.

We have already looked at the reverse of this vase, which showed a scene from a satyr-play (II, 13). The obverse represents one of the most popular themes of Middle Comedy, food and the people who consume it or the slaves who steal it. The stage is supported by three short Doric columns, and to the left is a door of the usual type, opening inwards. On the stage, master and mistress are busy consuming dainties from a large tray, which they hold between them, while unobserved by them, so intent are they upon the food, the slave Xanthias (P) has stolen a large flat cake (*plakous*), which he secretes in his

IV,17 (London). 'Master and Servant' from Middle Comedy

ΦΙΛΟΤΙΜΙΔΗΣ   ΧΑΡΙΣ   ΞΑΝΘΙΑΣ

IV,18 (Milan, Moretti coll.). 'Eaters of Dainties' from Middle Comedy

garment as he makes his getaway, still casting a longing glance upon the food on the tray. The master is named Philotimides (note the Attic form) and the mistress Charis, though her looks, especially the wart on her nose, belie her name. Philotimides is white-haired (L) and holds up a piece of salami or the like with evident approval; Charis (T) is about to eat a cake, and on the tray are other varieties of cake and an egg. Above a wine-jug is suspended, and in front is a low table, from which the tray has been taken. The characterization of the three figures is particularly well done, their faces all betraying different emotions.

*PhV*², 38, no. 45, pl. 2; *MTSP*², 169.

IV, 19

Vatican U 19 (inv. 17106).
Paestan bell-krater by Asteas; *c.* 350–340 B.C.

This witty and colourful vase shows the art of Asteas at its best. It gives a parody of one of Zeus's many love-adventures, probably his wooing of Alkmene (cf. III. 3, 7), and represents the king of the gods as a very comic figure, his head with its tinsel crown poking through the rungs of the ladder, by means of which he hopes to gain access to his lady-love, who appears in profile in a window above. As it is dark, he is lighted on his way by the flame of a tiny lamp held by Hermes, who wears an orange petasos and carries a large caduceus, and plays the rôle of *amantis subparasitus* as in the *Amphitruo* of Plautus (l. 993). Both Zeus (G) and Hermes (Z) wear the typical Paestan seamed tights with heavily padded red jerkins over them; Hermes has an orange cloak flapping behind his back as well. The next stage in such an adventure as this appears on another Paestan bell-krater, also by Asteas, in the British Museum (F 151; *PhV*², no. 36) in which the lover is mounting the ladder with gifts for the lady in the window, though on this occasion he is not specifically identified as Zeus, nor his companion as Hermes.

*PhV*², 46, no. 65; Richter, *Perspective*, fig. 185; Gigante, *Teatro Greco*, 86, pl. 2.

IV, 20

Bari 2970, from Bitonto.
Apulian bell-krater; second quarter of the fourth century B.C.

To the left, seated on a platform supported by Ionic columns with a curtain draped between them and approached by a flight of steps at the side, is a white-haired phlyax (L), identifiable as Zeus from the eagle he holds by the neck, and most probably as Zeus Ammon from the palm-branch beside him. He turns to look at another old phlyax (G), who is cautiously

mounting the stairs with the aid of a stick and wears the pointed felt-hat (*pilos*) of the traveller. He has come to consult the oracle and is a little wary of it. On the ground below to the right stands his servant (C), a traveller's pack slung behind his back, who gazes with eyes of greedy wonder into a basket containing the gifts for the god, pondering no doubt how best he may appropriate them for his own use. The type of the sly and cunning servant, eager to turn things to his own advantage, appears very frequently in Attic comedy as well as upon phlyax vases.

*PhV*², 27, no. 17.
On Zeus Ammon see A. B. Cook, *Zeus* i, 361 ff., and for his oracles, H. W. Parke, *Oracles of Zeus*, 194 ff.

IV, 21

London, British Museum F 269.
Apulian kalyx-krater by the Varrese Painter; *c.* 350 B.C.

On a simple stage-platform supported by posts and approached by a flight of steps Hera (inscribed) is seated on a throne, sceptre in hand; to the left and right two comic warriors, one inscribed Daidalos and the other Enyalios, fight a duel with spears in front of her. The scene represents a comic version of the revenge of Hephaistos on his mother Hera for her mockery of him and for casting him out of Olympos. He sent her a magic throne, from which she was unable to rise, and Zeus offered the hand of Aphrodite to anyone who could set her free. Here Hephaistos, also named Daidalos (cf. Euripides, *Herc. Fur.* 471; Pindar, *Nemean*, iv, 59), with a basket-like cap on his head, fights with Ares (Enyalios), who wears a plumed and crested helmet in the *miles gloriosus* tradition (cf. also that of Herakles on the Asteas krater in Madrid; *Paestan Pottery*, pl. 7; *La Grèce classique*, fig. 372), but is quite clearly coming off second best. His presence is perhaps an allusion to his later love-affair with Aphrodite, after she had become the wife of Hephaestus, whose return to Olympus was a most popular theme with vase-painters (cf. I, 4).

The subject was originally treated by Epicharmus in *The Comasts or Hephaestus*, and both Plato and Eubulus wrote comedies entitled *Daidalos*, of which the vase may give an echo.

*PhV*², 52, no. 61; Gigante, *Teatro Greco*, 95, pl. 5.
For the Varrese Painter see *Jb. Berl. Mus.* 12, 1970, 175–7.

IV, 22

Leningrad inv. 299 (St. 1775; W. 1121), from Ruvo.
Apulian bell-krater; second quarter of the fourth century B.C.

IV,19 (Vatican). 'Zeus, Hermes and Alkmene' from a phlyax play

IV,20 (Bari). 'Consulting the Oracle of Zeus' from a phlyax play

IV,21 (London). 'Duel between Daidalos and Enyalios'
from a phlyax play

IV,22 (Leningrad). 'Herakles visiting Zeus' from a phlyax play

IV,23 (Taranto). 'Herakles and Eurystheus' from a phlyax play

On the stage, of which only the floor is shown, are three actors in an amusing parody of Herakles' visit to the temple of his father Zeus. On a high throne to the left is seated the king of the gods (H), wearing a crown and holding the eagle-sceptre in his left hand and a thunderbolt, poised for hurling, in his right. He is clearly beside himself with rage and kicks his legs in anger at the provocative and irreverent behaviour of Herakles (J), who may readily be identified by the lion-skin over his head. Herakles stands before him, blatantly eating the last of the sacrificial offerings from the now empty phiale, which he holds in his left hand, prudently out of reach of Zeus. To right, Iolaos (L), the companion of Herakles, pours a libation from an oenochoe on to a pillar-altar, his hand raised in a gesture of mock piety. The rendering is particularly animated and the vase-painter admirably contrasts the impotent wrath of Zeus with the contemptuous air of Herakles, who has consumed the offerings to Zeus and got away with his defiance.

*PhV*², 33, no. 31.

IV, 23

Taranto 56048, from Taranto.
Apulian chous; second quarter of the fourth century B.C.

This vase gives us a lively version of a hitherto unrecorded episode in the career of Herakles. He is seen in the centre of the picture, wearing his lion-skin, but having thrown away his club and bow, which lie on the ground at his feet. In their place he holds an iynx, or magic wheel, which serves as a love charm, and it is clear that he is now weary of his labours and wishes to take up the pursuit of love instead. To the left is king Eurystheus (D), wearing a comic crown and obviously beside himself with fury; to the right a white-haired phlyax (C), probably Iolaos (cf. IV, 22), points with an expressive gesture to the discarded weapons and tries to recall the hero to a sense of duty.

*PhV*², 64, no. 122, pl. 8a.

IV, 24

Lentini, Museo Archeologico, from Lentini.
Sicilian kalyx-krater, Manfria Group; *c.* 340–330 B.C.

The stage is of the type commonly found on Sicilian vases and looks rather like an empty rectangular box placed on its side, with a flight of steps in front. The temple background is indicated by four Ionic columns in white to simulate marble; in front of the stage are two incense-burners and four pendent fillets. The scene depicts Herakles and Auge. Auge (V), who has sought the protection of the goddess by whose statue behind an altar she is standing, is assailed by Herakles, identified by his lion-skin, who starts back at her unveiling; to the left an old man, presumably her father Aleos, looks on with disapproval, to the right an old woman (Y), probably the nurse, watches with a satisfied smirk. We know of two comedies entitled *Auge*, one by Philyllius in the fifth century, the other by Eubulus towards the middle of the fourth (cf. IV, 9), but the scene might well have been intended as a parody of an episode from the lost tragedy of Euripides.

*PhV*², 51, no. 79.

IV, 25

London, Victoria and Albert Museum 1776–1919.
Apulian bell-krater by the Iris Painter; *c.* 370–360 B.C.

The stage platform is here of the simplest form and is composed of logs fitted together. On it is a banqueter between two white-haired phlyakes, one holding a thyrsus and tambourine, the other a torch. The banqueter reclines upon a skin and helps himself to food from a dish beside him; in front are what look like the mangled remains of some animal. The scene is almost certainly a parody of the feasting Herakles, whose greed was proverbial, and who is often shown on vase-paintings being served by satyrs, for whom here the phlyakes are substituted, still, however, retaining in the thyrsus and tambourine typical Dionysiac elements.

*PhV*², 37, no. 41.

IV,24 (Lentini). 'Herakles and Auge' from a phlyax play

IV,25 (London, Victoria and Albert Museum). 'Banquet scene' from Middle Comedy

IV,26 (Bari). 'The Birth of Helen' from a phlyax play

IV,27 (Bari). Scene from a phlyax play

IV, 26

Bari 3899, from Bari.
Apulian bell-krater, Eton-Nika Group; second quarter of the fourth century B.C.

The scene represents a comic version of the birth of Helen from the egg of Nemesis. The subject of Leda and the Egg is treated upon several Attic vases, which mostly show the egg placed upon the altar of Zeus. On South Italian vases, however, the actual birth is depicted, and this theme may have drawn its inspiration from a lost play, of which our vase would be a parody. The action takes place upon a simple stage, supported by posts, with a curtain hanging between them. To the left, standing in a half-open door, is Leda, wearing a hideous mask (T) and anxiously looking on as a white-haired phlyax (E) raises his double-axe to deal the egg a second blow, since his upward glance suggests that he has not yet fully perceived the effects of the first, which has cleft the egg apart, allowing the infant Helen to emerge. She stretches out her right hand towards him as if to entreat him to take no further action. To the right is another phlyax (B), who raises his hand in a gesture of wonder at the event that has just taken place and who also seems to be saying 'Hold; enough!' The identity of these two figures is open to some question; as Beazley has pointed out, the phlyax on the right can hardly be Tyndareus, since even in low comedy kings do not look like slaves; he must be the servant, in which case the man wielding the axe is probably Tyndareus, which would perhaps explain his averted gaze. Here a basket with a piece of drapery in it is substituted for the altar of Zeus, and the scene is obviously taking place outside the house, of which the door and a window are shown.

*PhV*², 27, no. 18.
For the legend of Leda and the Egg and its representation in Greek vase-paintings see in particular R. Kekule, *Die Geburt der Helena aus dem Ei*; F. Chapouthier, *BCH* 66–7, 1942–3, 1–21; Beazley, *EVP*,

40–2, and *Attic Vase-paintings in the Museum of Fine Arts, Boston*, iii, 71–3; J. Moreau, *Das Trierer Kornmarktmosaik*, 15 ff.
To the list of South Italian vases illustrating this subject must now be added the neck-amphora recently found at Paestum and signed by Python (*Arch Reps* 16, 1969–70, 34, fig. 4; M.N apoli, *Il Museo di Paestum*, pl. 35, and *Paestum*, fig. 98) and an Apulian pelike in Kiel (B 501) by the Painter of Athens 1680.

IV, 27

Bari 8014.
Apulian bell-krater; second quarter of the fourth century B.C.

On a simple stage supported by posts are three phlyax actors. To left is a man (B) with a stick, then comes a woman (T) holding a fillet in her left hand and raising her right hand, perhaps in a gesture of farewell, to the other; to the right is another phlyax (Z) with goggling eyes, who holds a thyrsus in his left hand and a wreath in his right. The scene may well be associated with the *Dionysalexandros* of Cratinus, in which Dionysos enticed Helen away from Menelaus. This would explain the thyrsus held by the phlyax on the right and the gesture of the woman.

*PhV*², 28, no. 20, pl. 1a.

IV, 28

Matera 9579.
Apulian bell-krater; *c.* 370–350 B.C.

Two phlyakes with torches are escorting Helen of Troy to her wedding with Paris. The leader holds up his two flaming torches and appears to be singing, behind him another phlyax holds up a torch in his right hand, and embraces Helen with his left, looking up at her as if to give encouragement. She has put on a Phrygian cap for the occasion, doubtless in honour of Paris, over which is her bridal veil; her ugly mask (TT) is in striking contrast to her legendary beauty.

*PhV*², 38, no. 44, pl. 3c.

IV,28 (Matera). 'Helen of Troy' from a phlyax play

IV,29 (Berlin). 'The Death of Priam' from a phlyax play

IV, 29

Berlin F 3045.
Apulian bell-krater: Eton-Nika Group; *c.* 380–370 B.C.

The scene shown is a humorous version of an episode from the Sack of Troy, when Priam meets his death at the hand of Neoptolemos. To the left, seated upon an altar, beside which is a laurel-tree, is a phlyax actor dressed as Priam, wearing a Phrygian cap and raising his left hand as if to protect himself from Neoptolemos, who stands before him, drawn sword in hand. In the phlyax play Priam obviously delivered a long speech at this juncture to try to talk himself out of his impending doom; for a while, Neoptolemos hesitates, as if weighing the arguments Priam is putting forward, before he deals the fatal blow. The vase gives us a lively caricature of a theme popular in Attic vase-painting.

PhV², 29, no. 21; Gigante, *Teatro Greco*, 126 ff.

IV, 30

Rome, Villa Giulia 50279, from Buccino.
Paestan kalyx-krater, signed by Asteas; *c.* 350–340 B.C.

The subject of this vase is a comic reversal of the commonly-represented story of the rape of Cassandra at the sack of Troy. Here it is Ajax who has fled for refuge to the statue of Athena in her temple, where Cassandra (ΚΑ]ΣΣΑΝΔΡΗ) grasps his helmet, pushes her knee onto his back and is obviously about to deliver him a mighty blow, while the aged priestess (ΙΗΡΗΑ) runs off to the right with the temple-key, registering surprise and even horror with the gesture of her right hand and in the look on her wrinkled face (U). Even the Palladion raises its eyebrows at the unexpected turn of events. The fragment gives us one of the liveliest and wittiest of the phlyax scenes.

PhV², 54, no. 86; Mingazzini, *Greek Pottery Painting*, fig. 68 (colour).

IV,30 (Rome, Villa Giulia). 'Ajax and Cassandra' from a phlyax play

IV,31 (Salerno). 'Phrynis and Pyronides' from a phlyax play

IV, 31

Salerno, Museo Provinciale, from Pontecagnano.
Paestan bell-krater by Asteas; c. 350 B.C.

The scene shows a lyre-player inscribed Phrynis being dragged along by a white-haired phlyax named Pyronides. Phrynis was a celebrated musician of the fifth century B.C. (see *RE* xx, 925–8; Aristophanes, *Clouds*, 971; Pherecrates, *Cheiron* fr. 145 = Edmonds, *Attic Comedy*, i, p. 263) and is here shown wearing a mask (O) of Apolline type (cf. Leningrad 1660; *PhV²* no. 32), a laurel wreath, and the typical Paestan seamed tights, over which is a crimson padded jerkin. A cloak flaps out behind him, and in his left hand he holds by the strings a white lyre, in his right is the plectrum. He is resisting Pyronides, who tries to drag him off, and his whole body is braced against the attempt to do so. Pyronides wears the mask of an old man (M), and a costume similar to that of Phrynis, with the addition of a white tunic and a piece of drapery across the front of his body. The name was used as a nickname for the general Myronides (cf. Edmonds, *op. cit.*, p. 96, n. 5 and p. 360, n. 4). The scene may also refer to the quarrel between Phrynis and the Spartan ephor, who did not approve of his musical innovations (Plutarch, *Agis* x, 7).

PhV², 43, no. 58, pl. 3 b; Zschietzschmann, *Gr. Kunst*, pl. 162 b.

IV, 32

Naples, Ragusa coll. 13.
Apulian chous; second quarter of the fourth century B.C.

This vase gives us much the finest of the comic versions of the story of Oedipus and demonstrates the lively wit both of the writers of phlyax plays and of the painters who recorded

them. To the left is Oedipus, of whose name inscribed above his head; only the letters ΔI now remain. The swollen feet, from which he derived his name, are very clearly depicted, and he has been walking along the rocky road from the meeting of the three ways, where he unwittingly slew his father Laios in a chance encounter, towards the city of Thebes, now under the menace of the Sphinx, who propounds her riddle to all comers, slaying those who cannot give the correct solution. She is shown to the right, part woman, part animal, squatting on the top of a lofty rock-pile, with the inscription ΣΦΙΞ above her head. She wears a small crown on her rolled hair and her many-coloured wings (cf. Euripides, *Oedipus*, *Pap. Oxy.* xxvii, 2459) are spread out behind her. The comic effect is heightened by her hag-like features, pendulous breasts, sagging belly and, as a final touch, by her phallic tail. In front of her, on a smaller rock-pile, sits Kreon (ΚΡΕΩΝ), who turns his head back in animated conversation with Oedipus, with whom he seems to be haggling over the reward to be given should he succeed in solving the riddle. The Sphinx looks down upon them with an almost smug look, ready to propound her riddle and then pounce upon her victim, little realizing that on this occasion it is she herself who will play that rôle. The masks of all three characters (O, G, RR) are particularly expressive and contribute greatly to the liveliness of the scene as a whole.

Eubulus wrote a parody of the *Oedipus* of Euripides, and it may have provided the inspiration for this vase. There are several other comic versions of the story of Oedipus and the Sphinx (see p. 32), and II, 5 is a parody of it.

PhV², 62, no. 115, pl. 8b; Lo Porto, *BdA* 51, 1966, 9, figs. 27–8.

IV, 33

St. Agata dei Goti, former Rainone coll. 1.
Apulian bell-krater by the Rainone Painter; c. 380–370 B.C.

The scene depicts a travesty of the story of Antigone, who, contrary to the edict of Kreon, buried herbrot her Polynices. In the centre is an actor wearing the mask of a white-haired, balding old man (G), dressed as a woman in a peplos with a long overall, beneath which, however, his phallos is clearly visible, and holding in one hand a female mask with short, parted hair (S), while clutching a hydria to his bosom in the other. He is in the grip of the watchman, who wears a fur cap and carries two spears, and who has brought him before Kreon, who wears a similar white-haired mask, with a Phrygian cap, and carries a staff or sceptre in his right hand. Kreon has a look of surprise, clearly at the unexpected sight of the old man when he had expected to see Antigone. The hydria would contain either the ashes of Polynices for burial

IV,32 (Naples, Ragusa coll.). 'Oedipus and the Sphinx' from a phlyax play

IV,33 (S. Agata dei Goti). 'Kreon and Antigone' from a phlyax play

or perhaps earth to sprinkle on his corpse; the vase-painter wishes to convey to us that in the farce Antigone was impersonated by an old man, and as the actor cannot wear both masks at once, he is shown carrying that of Antigone in his hand.

PhV², 44, no. 59, pl. 4a.

IV,34 (Basel, Cahn coll.). 'Elektra' from a phlyax play

IV, 34

Basel, Cahn coll. 223.
Fragment of Apulian krater; mid-fourth century B.C.

This fragment shows the head of a woman beside a column; thanks to the inscription above her head (HΛEKT...), she can be identified as Elektra. The column will be part of the grave-monument of Agamemnon and the whole scene would probably have shown the meeting of Orestes and Elektra, a subject very popular with South Italian vase-painters (cf. III. 1, 3–6). Elektra, however, is clearly wearing a mask (type R) which from its appearance suggests that we have here a comic version, or parody, of the familiar story (as possibly referred to by Aristotle, *Poetics* 1453a 36).

PhV², 71, no. 145, pl. 9 f.

IV, 35

London British Museum F 151.
Apulian bell-krater: Group of the Painter of Perseus and Athena; *c.* 380–370 B.C.

The scene, in which the principal character is identified as Cheiron by the inscription above his head, provides an amusing skit on comedies dealing with healing-places, like the *Plutus* of Aristophanes or the *Asklepios* of Philetairos, and may have been directly inspired by one of those which dealt specifically with Cheiron (e.g. by Pherecrates or Nicochares). According to Pausanias (v. 5, 10) Cheiron, accidentally wounded by one of the poisoned arrows of Herakles, was cured by washing in the stream Anigrus, fed by a sulphureous spring close to a cave of the nymphs. Our vase perhaps reflects a comic version of this legend and shows us the aged Cheiron being assisted up a flight of steps to enter the porch-way of a sanctuary, where his travel-pack and *pilos* have already been deposited. The slave Xanthias ([ΞΑ]ΝΘΙΑΣ) grasps him by the head to pull him up the remaining steps, while another slave pushes him up from behind, merging in the process to some extent with his body to produce something like the form of a centaur. To the right, in a cave behind a rock, are two nymphs (ΝΥ[ΜΦ]ΑΙ) of the spring, in animated conversation; they are represented as old hags, and their hideous aspect contrasts sharply with the beauty that would normally be associated with them. In the bottom corner below, a draped youth placidly watches the proceedings; it may be the young Achilles, one of Cheiron's most distinguished pupils.

PhV², 35, no. 37; Richter, *Perspective*, 45, fig. 188.

IV, 36

Paris, Cabinet des Médailles 1046, from Capua.
Campanian squat lekythos: Foundling Group; third quarter fourth century B.C.

The unwanted child, abandoned with a few trinkets which may later serve to establish its true identity, is a very popular motive in New Comedy; various terracottas testify also to the use of this theme in Middle Comedy, but this is the only vase from that period which shows such a scene. On it is a phlyax, probably a reveller on his homeward way, since he is wearing the sort of wreath often used at banquets, who sees an abandoned girl wrapped in swaddling clothes, and makes a gesture of surprise at the sight. His discovery would doubtless have provided the mainspring of the plot, leading later to her recognition at a crucial moment in the story.

PhV², 67, no. 133, pl. 6d.

IV,35 (London). 'Cheiron' from a phlyax play

IV,36 (Paris, Cabinet des Médailles). 'The Foundling' from a phlyax play

IV,37 (Naples, Ragusa coll.). 'Warrior and Monster'

IV, 37

Naples, Ragusa coll. 8.
Apulian pelike; second quarter fourth century B.C.

The representation on this vase is one of the most remarkable in South Italian vase-painting and, so far, has no close parallel. It shows a young warrior, armed with a spear and carrying a sheathed sword on a baldric, attacking a curious hybrid monster, which has something of the air of a creature from another planet. It must be a stage monster, since it has the appearance of a human being, wearing close-fitting striped tights and a mask made up of various elements calculated to strike terror into the beholder – a semi-human mouth with bared teeth and lolling tongue, a large round eye, a tattooed dromedary on the cheek, a spotted brow with curious antennae, huge ears and a boar's crest on top of its head. To judge from the prominent breast the creature should be female – a veritable Empusa (cf. Aristophanes, *Frogs* 293). It does not, however, look to be marine, in which case the youth can hardly be Perseus, despite the ingenious suggestion of Lo Porto (*BdA* 51, 1966, 8) that he has the gorgon's head concealed beneath the drapery over his left arm. It looks more as if he is using his cloak as a sort of shield against the monster. The warrior cannot be Herakles, since none of his normal accoutrements are shown, nor does the scene correspond with the standard renderings of Cadmus and the dragon or Theseus and the sow. It seems safer to regard it simply as man versus monster in a comic representation of a legend not otherwise known to us.

*PhV*², 84, no. 192, pl. 12a; Lo Porto, *BdA* 51, 1966, 8–9, figs. 23–6.

V. NEW COMEDY

V, 1–2 (repr. opp. p. 8)

1. Naples, M.N. 9987.
Mosaic signed by Dioskourides of Samos from Pompeii, Villa of Cicero; 100 B.C.
2. Mytilene, House with Mosaics.
Mosaic, Menander's *Synaristosai*, Act 1; A.D. 300.

There is no doubt that the two mosaics represent the same scene. The Mytilene mosaic gives the title of the play 'First Act of *Synaristosai*' (women at breakfast) and the names of the characters; the old woman is Philainis, the woman in the centre Plangon, and the other young woman Pythias. The discovery of the Mytilene mosaic confirms an old conjecture that the Dioskourides mosaic represented the beginning of Menander's *Synaristosai* adapted by Plautus as the *Cistellaria*, in which Pythias (Gymnasium in Plautus) and her mother Philainis (*lena* in Plautus) visit Plangon (Selenium in Plautus) and the old woman complains of the quality of the wine.

The two mosaics illustrate different productions. The flanking figures have changed sides and the masks of both the young women are different. The production which the Mytilene mosaic illustrates (or rather its original, since it seems likely that the eleven Menander scenes so far discovered go back to an illustrated edition of Menander, not entirely different from the original of the illustrated Terence manuscripts) cannot have been earlier than the third century A.D., since costumes and masks find their nearest analogy on terracottas of that date from the Athenian agora. The original of the Dioskourides mosaic is dated in the third century B.C. by the shape of the silver cup in the old woman's hand and the repetition of two of the figures in the second mosaic (V, 3) in terracottas from Myrina (V, 9, 10). Pergamon with its known interest in drama and its very fine mosaic tradition is certainly a possible location.

The old woman wears the fat old woman's mask (no. 29 in Pollux' list, which seems to go back to a good Hellenistic source). The young woman in the centre wears on the Dioskourides mosaic a mask with a yellow band fastened by a silver clasp in the middle; this is the New Comedy successor of the Middle Comedy mask V (cf. IV, 9, Auge); in Pollux' list it is no. 35, the second Pseudokore, used for a girl who will turn out to be a free citizen but is at present living as a hetaira, exactly Selenium's position in the *Cistellaria*; Menander called her Plangon, a name elsewhere given by him to poor girls of free birth. On the Mytilene mosaic she wears the mask of a free-born girl: Pollux, no. 33. Pythias (Gymnasium), who is

a hetaira, on the Dioskourides mosaic wears a mask with a triple band of yellow and is probably Pollux' scarfed hetaira (no. 14). On the Mytilene mosaic she seems to have an ivy wreath and braided hair, which is common on female masks from the second century A.D.

(1) Webster, *MNC*, NM 1; *Hellenistic Art*, 129 f.; L. Kahil in *Ménandre* (Fondation Hardt, *Entretiens sur l'antiquité classique* 16, 1970), pl. 3.
(2) *MNC*, YM 2; S. Charitonides, *PAE* 1962 (1966), 138; id., R. Ginouvès and L. Kahil, *Les Mosaïques de la Maison du Ménandre* (*AntK*, Beiheft 6, 1970), pl. 5; L. Kahil, *op. cit.*, pl. 2.
Terence manuscripts: *MNC*, IP 2. Agora terracottas: *MNC*, AT 28–44.

V, 3–4 (repr. as Frontispiece)

3. Naples, M.N. 9985.
Mosaic signed by Dioskourides of Samos from Pompeii, Villa of Cicero; 100 B.C.
4. Mytilene.
House with Mosaic, Menander *Theophoroumene*, Act II; A.D. 300.

The connection between the two scenes is not so close as in the other pair. Common to both are the boy dancing with cymbals (Lysias on the Mytilene mosaic) and the flute-girl, represented small on the right in the Mytilene mosaic. But the slave Parmenon cannot, I think, be represented by the small unmasked figure on the left of the Dioskourides mosaic, and Kleinias, the other young man on the Mytilene mosaic, does not appear to have a tympanon. It is possible that the two scenes succeeded one another in the play and that the act opened with a scene between Parmenon and the two young men; Parmenon went off (the actor being needed for the girl when she came out); the two young men were left to serenade the girl in the house (this scene is partly preserved in a papyrus fragment) and this brought the girl out, singing a hymn to Kybele (partly preserved in a Florentine papyrus).

Parmenon wears a normal leading slave mask (Pollux no. 22). The young men's masks differ: Kleinias' face is broader and his hair rises higher over the forehead. On the Dioskourides mosaic the youth with the tambourine has raised brows (Pollux no. 10) and the youth with cymbals smooth brows (Pollux no. 13).

(3) *MNC*, NM 2; Havelock, *Hellenistic Art*, 256, colour-plate XIII.
(4) Bibliography as for V, 2; L. Kahil, *Mosaïques*, pl. 6, and *Ménandre* pl. 4.
Papyri: Loeb Classical Library, D. L. Page, *Greek Literary Papyri*, I, 256; E. W. Handley, *BICS* 19, 1969, 88.

V,5–10 (Athens, Agora; Heidelberg; Corinth; Lyons; Athens). Actors in New Comedy

V, 5–10

5. Athens, Agora Museum, T 942.
Attic terracotta mask; late fourth century B.C.

6. Athens, Agora Museum, T 213.
Attic terracotta mask; third century B.C.

7. Heidelberg, TK 98.
Attic terracotta mask. Late fourth century.

8. Corinth, 1904.
Terracotta statuette from Corinth; 250 B.C.

9. Lyons, E-272-43.
Terracotta statuette from Myrina; second century B.C.

10. Athens, N.M. 5060.
Terracotta statuette from Myrina; second century B.C.

No. 5 is an early, well-dated example of the slave with wavy-hair, Pollux no. 27, cf. the Middle Comedy mask K (IV, 9). No. 6 is an old man with a good beard and a certain amount of hair which is represented as curly: he is Pollux no. 7, the Lycomedian; he is said to be 'interfering' and would admirably suit Smikrines in Menander's *Epitrepontes*. No. 7 is a young man wearing an ivy-wreath; he has hooked nose raised brows, wavy-hair. This is Pollux no. 15, the braggart-soldier, and would be worn by Polemon in Menander's *Perikeiromene*. No. 8 is an actor carrying the long-haired girl's mask, Pollux no. 33, the successor of the Middle Comedy mask SS, cf. above IV, 8b. The two statuettes from Myrina, 9 and 10, repeat the postures and costumes of the two young men on the Dioskourides mosaic (V, 3). As in Athens in the mid-fourth century, terracotta statuettes of comic actors were extremely popular in the second century B.C., and many of them may have been copied from third-century paintings. In this pair the terracotta-maker has switched the heads: the youth with the tympanon has the younger mask with smooth brows (Pollux no. 13) and the youth with cymbals the older mask with raised brows (Pollux no. 10).

(5) *MNC²*, AT 5; *JdI*, 76, 1961, 101, fig. 1.
(6) *MNC²*, AT 2; Pickard-Cambridge, *Festivals*, fig. 111.
(7) *MNC²*, AT 12.
(8) *MNC²*, CT 1.
(9) Webster, *MNC²*, MT 1; *Hellenistic Art*, fig. 36; Pickard-Cambridge, *Festivals*, fig. 114; Bieber, *History²*, fig. 341 is another example of the same type.
(10) Webster, *MNC²*, MT 15; *Hellenistic Art*, fig. 35; Bieber, *History²*, fig. 342.

INDEX OF COLLECTIONS

The index which follows lists all the monuments illustrated in this book (in the order: vases, mosaics, terracottas, marble reliefs) under the museums or collections in which they are to be found.

GENERAL INDEX

References to the Introduction are by page numbers, otherwise to the numbers of the relevant monuments.

Acheloös III. 2, 11
Achilles III. 3, 47–49; III. 4, 2
Admetos III. 3, 5
Adrastos III. 4, 1
Aeschylus 4 ff.
   Agamemnon 8
   Choephoroi 5; III. 1, 1–6
   Diktyoulkoi 8; II, 3; II, 8
   Edonoi III. 1, 13–16
   Eumenides 5, 8; III. 1, 8–12
   Kares or Europa 8; III. 1, 17
   Myrmidons III. 1, 18–19
   Nereids III. 1, 18–19; IV, 5
   Niobe III. 1, 23
   Phineus 6; III. 1, 24–26
   Phryges 2; III. 1, 19–22
   Prometheus Lyomenos I, 10; III. 1, 27
   Prometheus Pyrkaeus II, 2; II, 4; III. 1, 24
   Sphinx II, 5
   Toxotides 5; III. 1, 28
   Xantriai 5; III. 1, 28
Agamemnon III. 3, 19; III. 3, 47–49
Agrios III. 3, 41
Aigeus III. 3, 1
Aiolos III. 3, 4
Aixone IV, 8a
Ajax IV, 30
Akamas III. 3, 20–21
Alkestis III. 3, 5
Alkmene III. 3, 6–8, III. 3, 21; IV, 19
Althaia III. 3, 40
Ammon IV, 20
Ampelis III. 6, 2
Amphiaraos III. 3, 25–26
Amphion III. 1, 23; III. 3, 14–15
Amphitryon III. 3, 6–8
Anakreon I, 8
Anavysos IV, 1
Antenor III. 3, 8
Antiope III. 3, 14–15
Aphrodite I, 4; III. 3, 12, 16–18, 23–24, 44, 50
Apollo III. 1, 8–12; III. 1, 15; III. 3, 5; III. 3, 24; III. 3, 28; III. 3, 36; III. 3, 47–49; III. 4, 1–2
Archemoros III. 3, 25–26
Ares III. 4, 1
Argiope III. 2, 9–10

Argonauts III. 1, 26; III. 5, 4
Ariadne II, 1; III. 3, 50–51
Aristophanes I, 9; I, 11; I, 17; III. 3, 22; IV, 2–4; IV, 7a; IV, 15; IV, 35
Aristotle 15; IV, 34
Artemis 7; III. 1, 28; III. 3, 27–31; III. 5, 6
Astyanassa III. 3, 44
Astydamas III. 4, 1
Atlanta III. 3, 37–39; III. 4, 1
Athena III. 1, 11; III. 1, 27; III. 3, 20; III. 3, 24; III. 3, 29; III. 3, 50–51; III. 4, 2; III. 5, 4; III. 5, 6; IV, 30
Athens 3 ff., 7 ff., 15; I, 18; III. 3, 20–21; IV, 6; IV, 7a; IV, 9; V, 5–6
Auge IV, 9; IV, 24
Aurai III. 3, 33

Bari IV, 26
Beazley, J. D. I, 8; I, 14; II, 12; IV, 13
Bellerophon III. 3, 43–46
Birds 15; I, 12; IV, 4
Briseis III. 1, 18–19
Buccino IV, 30

Canace III. 3, 4
Canosa III. 3, 11; III. 3, 39; III. 5, 4; III. 5, 6
Capaneus III. 3, 26
Capodarso III. 6, 1
Cassandra IV, 30
Ceglie del Campo III. 5, 5
Chaeremon III. 4, 2
Chimaira III. 3, 43
Choregic monument IV, 8a
Chrysippos III. 3, 16–18
Clouds III. 3, 8; III. 3, 33
Clytemnestra III. 1, 11; III. 3, 47–49
Comedy 10, 12, 15; IV–V, *passim*
Copreus III. 3, 20–21
Corinth 7; V, 8
Costume
   comic 9 f., 12 f., 15; IV–V, *passim*
   pre-dramatic 12, 15; I, 1, 3–16
   tragic and satyric 9 f; II, 1; II, 2; II, 5; III. 2, 7–8; III. 3, 1–2; III. 3, 8; III. 3, 10; III. 3, 19; III. 3, 20–21; III. 3, 27–30a; III. 3, 34–39; III. 3, 41; III. 3, 44;

Costume (*contd.*)
   III. 3, 49; III. 4, 1; III. 5, 4–7; III. 6, 1–3; III. 6, 5
Cratinus I, 10; IV, 27
Creusa III. 3, 35
Cyrene IV, 2

Dance steps 15; I, 1, 3–8, 16–20; II, 1, 2, 4, 7, 9, 11, 13, 14; III. 2, 9–10; IV, 4
Darius III. 5, 6
Deianira III. 2, 11; III. 3, 40
Delos 2; IV, 8c
Delphi 4; III. 1, 8–12; III. 2, 9; III. 3, 9
Demetrios II, 1
Demophon III. 3, 20–21
Diomedes III. 3, 41; III. 4, 2; III. 5, 7
Dionysios I, 3
Dionysos 2 f., 7, 12; I, 3–4, 15; II, 1; III. 1, 13–14; III. 3, 25–26; III. 3, 50; IV, 8 b and c; IV, 10–12
Dioskourides of Samos 2; V, 1 and 3
Dirce III. 3, 14–15
Dithyramb 2, 6, 15; I, 17–20
Dolphin-riders 15; I, 11, 14–15; III. 1, 18; IV, 5
Dryas III. 1, 13; III. 1, 15–16

Ekkyklema 8; II, 3, 7, 8; III. 1, 25; III. 2, 8; III. 3, 5; III. 3, 10; III. 3, 33
Elektra III. 1, 1–7; III. 2, 5; IV, 34
Eos III. 3, 8
Ephippus IV, 5–6
Epicharmus I, 6; IV, 21
Eriphyle III. 5, 1–3
Euaion 4; III. 1, 28; III. 2, 1; III. 2, 9
Eubulus IV, 8, 21, 24, 32
Euneos III. 3, 25–26
Euripides 11
   Aigeus III. 3, 1–3
   Aiolos III. 3, 4
   Alkestis III. 3, 5
   Alkmene III. 3, 6–8
   Andromache III. 3, 9
   Andromeda III. 2, 1; III. 3, 10–13
   Antiope III. 3, 14–15
   Auge IV, 9, 24
   Chrysippos III. 3, 16–18
   Cyclops 3, 11; II, 11; III. 6, 2

LIST OF ILLUSTRATIONS

I. PRE-DRAMATIC

I, 1 Balat; Geometric fragment from Miletos. Photo: P. Hommel

I, 2 Nauplion; terracotta mask from Tiryns. Photo: German Archaeological Institute, Athens

I, 3 Paris, Louvre S 1104; Corinthian alabastron. Photo: Louvre

I, 4 Athens, N.M. 664; Corinthian amphoriskos. Photo: National Museum

I, 5 Paris, Louvre CA 3004; Corinthian skyphos. Photo: Louvre

I, 6 Paris, Louvre E 632; Corinthian krater. Photo: Louvre

I, 7 Berlin 1966, 17; Attic black-figure krater. Photo: Staatliche Museen

I, 8 Amsterdam 3356; Attic black-figure cup. Photo: Allard Pierson Stichting

I, 9 Berlin F 1697; Attic black-figure amphora. Photo: Staatliche Museen

I, 10 Christchurch (N.Z.), University of Canterbury, Logie Collection 41/57; Attic black-figure amphora. Photo: courtesy Miss M. K. Steven

I, 11 Boston 20.18; Attic black-figure skyphos. Photo: Museum of Fine Arts, Boston

I, 12 London, B.M. B 509; Attic black-figure oinochoe. Photo: British Museum

I, 13 Thebes, B.E. 64.342; Attic black-figure cup. Photo: Mrs. Evi Touloupa

I, 14 Palermo, from Selinunte; Attic black-figure lekythos. Photo: Soprintendenza alle Antichità, Palermo (courtesy Prof. V. Tusa)

I, 15 Cambridge (Mass.), Norbert Schimmel coll.; Attic red-figure psykter. Photo: courtesy owner

I, 16 New York 25.78.66; Attic red-figure bell-krater. Photo: Metropolitan Museum (Funds from various donors, 1927)

I, 17 Copenhagen 13817; Attic red-figure bell-krater. Photo: National Museum

I, 18 Taranto, from Satyrion; Attic black-figure lekythos. Photo: Soprintendenza alle Antichità, Taranto

I, 19 New York 27.74; Attic red-figure kylix. Photo: Metropolitan Museum

I, 20 Oxford G263 (305); Attic red-figure kylix. Photo: Ashmolean Museum

II. SATYR PLAYS

II, 1 Naples 3240 (inv. 81673); Attic red-figure volute-krater. Photo: Hirmer

II 2 Sydney 47.05; Apulian red-figure bell-krater. Photo: Nicholson Museum, University of Sydney

II, 3 Princeton (N.J.), Chr. Clairmont coll.; Attic red-figure pyxis. Photo: Ernst Winizki (courtesy Prof. C. Clairmont)

II, 4 Oxford 1937.983; Attic red-figure kalyx-krater. Photo: Ashmolean Museum

II, 5 Naples 2846 (inv. 81417); Paestan red-figure bell-krater. Photo: Soprintendenza alle Antichità, Naples

II, 6 Boston 00.366; Early Lucanian red-figure oinochoe. Photo: Museum of Fine Arts, Boston

II, 7 Ferrara T.579; Attic red-figure column-krater. Photo: Soprintendenza alle Antichità, Bologna

II, 8 Oxford G.275 (525); Attic red-figure volute-krater. Photo: Ashmolean Museum

II, 9 Stockholm N.M.6; Attic red-figure bell-krater. Photo: National Museum, Stockholm

II, 10 Matera 9975; Early Lucanian red-figure bell-krater. Photo: German Archaeological Institute, Rome

II, 11 London, B.M. 1947, 7–14. 8; Early Lucanian red-figure kalyx-krater. Photo: British Museum (courtesy of the Trustees)

II, 12 Parma; Etruscan red-figure kalyx-figure. Photo: Museo Nazionale di Antichità

II, 13 Milan, Moretti coll.; Apulian red-figure bell-krater. Photo: courtesy Cav. A. Moretti

II, 14 Taranto 124007; fragment of Apulian red-figure bell-krater. Photo: Soprintendenza alle Antichità, Taranto

III. TRAGEDY

1. Aeschylus

III. 1, 1 Berlin, inv. terracottas 6803; Melian relief. Photo: Staatliche Museen

III. 1, 2 Copenhagen 597; Attic red-figure skyphos. Photo: National Museum

III. 1, 3 Syracuse 36334; Sicilian red-figure kalyx-krater. Photo: Soprintendenza alle Antichità, Syracuse

155

2. Sophocles

3. Euripides

V. NEW COMEDY